CLAIRE PETULENGRO

Love Stars
Health Signs
Diet Signs

LIFE SIGNS

*Let the power of the
stars guide you to success*

CLAIRE PETULENGRO

PAN BOOKS

First published 2009 by Pan Books
an imprint of Pan Macmillan Ltd
Pan Macmillan, 20 New Wharf Road, London N1 9RR
Basingstoke and Oxford
Associated companies throughout the world
www.panmacmillan.com

ISBN 978-0-330-46063-7

1 3 5 7 9 8 6 4 2

A CIP catalogue record for this book is available from
the British Library.

Typeset by SetSystems Ltd, Saffron Walden, Essex
Printed and bound in the UK by
CPI Mackays, Chatham ME5 8TD

*To Jonathan Nicholas Mark Ledgard, thank you
for being an amazing husband and daddy and for
remembering the colour of my eyes when my
back was to you in China! I love you.*

*For Paris, Carmen Valentine, Lucy Victoria May
and Honey, life is what you make it!
Make yours count, my babies. Mummy xxx*

ACKNOWLEDGEMENTS

Thank you to Ingrid Connell and my extended family at Pan Macmillan.

To my wonderful parents, especially my mother and mentor, Eva Petulengro, love and gratitude for teaching and nurturing me in astrology and everything else in life! Thanks also to my lovely uncle, Leo Petulengro, for his artwork.

Much love and respect goes to Vicki McIvor, for being the best literary agent I could ask for, while still being a great mum to the lovely Lara.

Gratitude to my agent, Sara Cameron, a brave woman to take on looking after someone like me and for all the adventures I know we will share along the way in the years to come. Thank you for what is sure to be a colourful journey.

It would be unthinkable not to say thank you as always to Melanie Cantor for a great beginning. I would not be where I am today if it were not for you and your Cancerian honesty.

And thanks to Gordon Wise, a great person and a wonderful friend, who first gave me my dream of writing books.

I am grateful to Elle and Mitchell Phillips from Studio 58, for their expert health and fitness advice. The best in their field!

And last but not least, this book would not have been possible if I didn't have a husband who does night feeds, school runs, nappies, washing-up and hoovering while still paying me compliments. Thank you, super daddy!

CONTENTS

Introduction

YOUR ELEMENTAL
LIFE PLAN

'As above so below.'

There are many self-help books available in this day and age. Indeed, most of us will have at least one, if not several, lurking somewhere in our homes or bags. Whether it's how to make a million, how to retire early or how to find true love, there's a subject covered that touches each and every one of our hearts. However, no other book has joined together the obvious link between our star sign and the pattern by which we live our lives. *Life Signs* is tailor-made with *your* sign in mind to help you find success where before you may have failed.

Working with clients from all walks of life and understanding the way that different star signs approach the hurdles of life has taught me a lot. I've seen that Pisceans are drawn openly to experiences that they know are going to hurt them, that Geminis always think the grass is greener on the other side of the fence and that Librans allow themselves to be emotionally manipulated time and time again. Over the years I have felt my role change from client to client. Sometimes I am like a priest, hearing confessions that the person I am seeing needs to get off their chest – that affair, that lie, that guilt. Sometimes I am like a best friend, someone who gives the client the support they need to take an important step forward in life. The roles vary but the problems are often the same: people are living life in the way they think others want them to do, rather than believing in themselves and valuing what they really want and what will make them happy.

My family are Romanies and have studied the human race for generations. Our Romany upbringing and heritage is all about people – their lives, their loves, their fears and their problems. In the past Romanies, being travellers, never went to school and weren't taught limitations. Quite the opposite – Romanies are taught to say what they feel. Giving readings is second nature to us, and as a child I would sit with my mother and grandmother when they were reading their clients' palms. I would be asked, 'Claire, what do you feel about this lady?' and I would say what I felt without hesitation, whether it was sadness at a recent loss, pain due to an illness or joy concerning a pregnancy. Children from a different background would have been more likely to answer what they knew they were supposed to be thinking and feeling rather than trusting their gut instinct.

My great-grandmother kept the secrets of the rich and famous. My grandmother knew whose children had fathers they would never meet and which wealthy faces didn't have a penny to their name. Sitting with my mother when she gave readings exposed me to a multitude of experiences before I was even twenty-one. By her side, I saw clients grow and change before my eyes. I also saw beliefs that had previously been set in stone melt away, like a snowflake in the sun. Illegitimate children were no longer a sin, unmarried couples were the norm, and sleeping together for fun was as acceptable as sharing condiments. While social values may have changed, human emotions have stayed the same; only now the influence of the internet, television, chat and reality shows and our increasing openness to analysis have made us more self-critical and aware than ever before.

So what will you find in these pages that can change and inspire you? We will analyze your love life, your needs and desires, your weaknesses and the rules you should follow to find success. Each sign has different weaknesses in relationships. Libra is far too easily emotionally manipulated, and Aries jumps in feet first before thinking of the consequences. It is usually only when baby number two comes along that Aries realizes that this should have been just a fling. Learn to recognize when you are being untrue to yourself and you can prevent these problems. I don't think that the divorce rate is higher because we've become more open-minded; I think we've become more narrow-minded as we increasingly judge ourselves on what our next-door neighbours are doing and what the glamorous magazines and A-list celebs are able to achieve. We set impossible dreams as targets instead of allowing ourselves to get what *we* want and need.

We will look at careers and what working environment best suits each sign, making sure your job can be something you enjoy and look forward to each day. If you feel sluggish in the morning (especially Aries, Cancerians and Pisceans), I'm going to give you back your energy and glow, and teach you the right foods for your sign to fuel your body.

Money can attract us to someone, but it can also tear us apart from the one we love. How many of you have lied to a partner or family member about what an item cost to avoid embarrassment? Geminis, Aquarians and Scorpios most certainly have, and Sagittarians and Leos don't do a bad job of fibbing over prices either. Let's tackle finances head on. There is no reason for you to feel you can't cope. I'm here to show you the most up-to-date ways to deal with money worries and to work on getting your bank balance out of the red and into the black. I've done it before for clients, and I can do it for you.

Are you living in the wrong surroundings to bring out

your true potential? I have tips on everything from where you should be holidaying to how you should style your home and what kind of parties you will like best.

It's hard to know the right thing to do in life at the best of times. We get over one obstacle only to discover another. Sometimes it can seem as if life is one big challenge with no breaks in sight. Working as an astrologer has enabled me to meet a range of people, from royalty to pop stars, politicians, doctors, lawyers, teachers, policemen, clergymen, shopworkers, showgirls and ladies of the night. An astrologer's job is not an easy one. We're supposed to have all of the answers. However, a good astrologer doesn't tell you what to do but helps you find the answers in your own heart, because when your crisis is over and you continue on your journey in life, you need to have the confidence to face the next hurdle on your own. We can't always have someone with us twenty-four seven. If we did, life would be pretty boring. I want to teach you how to have confidence in yourself and trust your instincts. By getting to know yourself better, you can learn your strengths.

You would be surprised how many people try to conform because they think that they will get laughed at if they trust in what they feel or if they have the confidence to take control of their destiny. We often say what we think other people want to hear because we don't want to seem different. I've been laughed at, believe me, but not since I left the playground. In fact I got an email only recently from one of my bullies who apologized for the hard time they had given me at school. It sort of came full circle for me, especially as she had been a non-believer in all things psychic and was asking for advice on the doctorate she was now taking ... on astrology and its relationship with modern medicine.

By reading *Life Signs* you will learn that we all have hurdles to overcome. You will learn how to be *you* – how to respect yourself, love yourself and learn to love your faults. Many of us are living out our parents' dreams or paying the price for their mistakes. It's time to break free from those restraints and I'm going to show you how. Let the new you begin and let a better life commence.

WORKING OUT
YOUR STAR SIGN

Here's a quick guide for those of you who don't already know
your sign:

 ARIES: The Ram
21 March to 20 April

Ruling planet: Mars, the Roman god of war
Triplicity or element: fire
Keywords: headstrong, opinionated, initiator, leader, loyal to
a cause, egotistical, passionate
Lucky day: Tuesday

 TAURUS: The Bull
21 April to 21 May

Ruling planet: Venus, the planet of love
Triplicity or element: earth
Keywords: stubborn, sensual, loyal, affectionate, materialistic,
craves stability and security
Lucky day: Friday

GEMINI: The Twins
22 May to 21 June

Ruling planet: Mercury, the planet of communication
Triplicity or element: air
Keywords: generous, restless, adaptable, excitable, fickle, two-sided
Lucky day: Wednesday

 CANCER: The Crab
22 June to 23 July

Ruling planet: the Moon
Triplicity or element: water
Keywords: changeable, protective, loving, shrewd, caring
Lucky day: Monday

 LEO: The Lion
24 July to 23 August

Ruling planet: the Sun
Triplicity or element: fire
Keywords: generous, warm-hearted, proud, fun-loving, dignified
Lucky day: Sunday

 VIRGO: The Virgin
24 August to 23 September

Ruling planet: Mercury, the planet of communication
Triplicity or element: earth
Keywords: modest, shy, practical, intelligent, over-critical, perfectionist
Lucky day: Wednesday

LIBRA: The Scales
24 September to 23 October

Ruling planet: Venus, the planet of love
Triplicity or element: air
Keywords: balance, justice, harmony, partnership, sociability, refinement
Lucky day: Friday

SCORPIO: The Scorpion
24 October to 22 November

Ruling planet: Mars, the Roman god of war, and Pluto, the god of the underworld
Triplicity or element: water
Keywords: intensity, depth, determination, jealousy
Lucky day: Tuesday

SAGITTARIUS: The Archer
23 November to 21 December

Ruling planet: Jupiter, the planet of self-expansion
Triplicity or element: fire
Keywords: optimistic, freedom-loving, philosophical, expansive, honest
Lucky day: Thursday

CAPRICORN: The Goat
22 December to 20 January

Ruling planet: Saturn, the planet of structure
Triplicity or element: earth
Keywords: cautious, reserved, prudent, ambitious, constructive, disciplined
Lucky day: Saturday

AQUARIUS: The Water-Bearer
21 January to 19 February

Ruling planet: Saturn, the planet of structure, and Uranus, the planet of disruption
Triplicity or element: air
Keywords: independent, intellectual, distant, idealistic
Lucky day: Saturday

PISCES: The Fishes
20 February to 20 March

Ruling planet: Jupiter, the planet of self-expansion, and Neptune, the planet of confusion
Triplicity or element: water
Keywords: emotional, sensitive, moody, imaginative, impressionable, changeable
Lucky day: Thursday

IF YOU ARE BORN ON THE CUSP

I can't begin to count the number of times I have had people tell me that they are not sure if they are a Gemini or a Cancerian, a Scorpio or a Sagittarian, because they were born on what is called 'the cusp'.

To me, this is unthinkable and I will often go out of my way to find out which sign the sun was in at the precise time that they were born. In different years the sun comes into the signs at slightly different times. Because it would take a newspaper or magazine too many pages to list all of the crossover dates for each sign over the last hundred years, they only print a general guide. There are many of you sneaky signs out there who just enjoy reading two horoscopes for the day and picking the one you prefer.

9

If you are one of those people who have spent the last seventeen or seventy years not knowing your sign, then find out today. It could make the difference between success and failure, and it will certainly explain some of your idiosyncrasies. If you are on or near a crossover date, then look it up on one of the many free astrological websites or log on to my website, www.claireshoroscope.com.

Part 1

LOVE

Chapter 1

LOVE OR LUST?

Most of us have been there. You're living your life as best you can when suddenly – *bang* – out of nowhere your eyes lock and you realize that someone has hit you like a bullet. You want to be with them and spend your time with them. You want to know everything about them; you want to inhale them and be them; you are in love. Or are you? How do you know if the person you fancy or the person you are with is the one for you?

Compatibility is a big part of any successful relationship, be it marriage, work, children or friendship. If you have any doubts about your compatibility, ask yourself if the other person is making you happy more than they are making you sad. If the bad times outweigh the good, then you know you have to make some changes. There is always a choice and always another route you can take. Dead ends do not exist, no matter how bleak the view.

We have all been guilty of following our hearts, and various other parts of our bodies, rather than our heads, but a real partner should be a best friend and lover rolled into one. It is no good *saying* you love someone. You have to *feel* it with your heart and soul. Some of us have even been guilty of going out with someone who looks good but isn't quite as shiny under the surface. Sex is an important part of a relationship but, as many of my older clients will tell you, it is certainly not the be-all and end-all. You need to be able to talk to the person you are with after your two minutes, two hours, two days or even two years of passion are over. So to find out if you are truly compatible, you have to answer the following questions honestly:

1. Do you love the person you are with – or even just fancy them if you are not going out with them – because they are popular or because they make you happy?
2. Have the good times when you have seen them or been with them outweighed the bad?
3. Would you trust this person to make the right choices with your best interests at heart?
4. Do they treat you in a manner that leads you to feel you are special and that you have something to offer to the world?

If you can answer 'Yes' to these questions, then you are already on to a winner. Now let's take a look at the different sign combinations.

If you fancy a fire sign

If you fancy a fire sign, Aries, Leo or Sagittarius, then you will probably initially have been attracted by their sense of humour and the way that they can make a joke out of any situation. They will have raised a smile, but can they keep that smile on your face? If you are a fellow fire sign, then you shouldn't have trouble understanding the way that they operate and you will in fact fall in step over the years so that eventually you walk to the same beat. If you are an air sign, Gemini, Libra or Aquarius, the more you get to know them the better you will be able to understand them. Your flirtation will continue to improve with age.

If you are an earth sign, Taurus, Virgo and Capricorn, or a water sign, Cancer, Scorpio and Pisces, the relationship will still function well, but you may have to work a little harder to understand why you both act the way you do. You will know if it is lust rather than love if their sense of humour starts to go. Fire signs can always laugh in a crisis, and if they no longer seem able to have fun, you would be better to let them go.

If you fancy an earth sign

Earth signs, Taurus, Virgo and Capricorn, are very sexy people indeed and you probably first noticed them by the way they walked and the way that they wore their clothes with just the right bit of flesh showing to turn you on. If you are an earth sign yourself or a water sign, Cancer, Scorpio or Pisces, then the sex will just get better and better and you will have the best of both worlds – love and lust. If you are a fire or air sign, then you need to make sure you don't change too much for the earth sign that you fancy. It is one thing to adapt but quite another to submit completely.

If you fancy an air sign

Air signs, Gemini, Libra and Aquarius, need someone with whom they can talk about anything and everything. They love fellow air signs and adore fire signs, Aries, Leo and Sagittarius. Nothing is too much trouble for them when they are together and within a few months of meeting they are usually hopping on a flight to somewhere different and exciting. Earth signs, Taurus, Virgo and Capricorn, can tend to play things a little too safe for air, but water signs Cancer and Scorpio and Pisceans actually walk too far on the wild side and have to work hard to find a happy medium.

If you fancy a water sign

Water signs, Cancer, Scorpio and Pisces, want love and lust together and can find it with their own element. They can find it with earth signs also, Taurus, Virgo and Capricorn; but air signs, Gemini, Libra and Aquarius, and fire signs, Aries, Leo and Sagittarius, can tend to be a little too independent for watery souls, who like to be in control in all manner of ways! I think the trick here would be letting these signs think they are in control – a skill that if learnt can make for a happy and fulfilled life for both parties. In fact I'm sure it's been the secret to many a happy marriage over the years.

Meeting someone who is compatible with us is one of the most wonderful experiences we can have. It affects us in so many ways. Some of us lose our appetite, especially the Scorpios and Virgos of the zodiac, while the Aries and Pisceans can't seem to stop scoffing once they're in love. There is rarely a better time than when Cupid first fires his arrow your way. Let's take a look at the different signs and how they act. You may just be able to uncover the tell-tale signs as to what your friends are really up to when they say they're working overtime! You can also learn how to recognize when you're in step or out of sync with a partner. This is a valuable key to reducing stress and to making sure that you're with the right partner and not the wrong one!

Aries

Should I stay or should I go?
The Ram is a sign that is passionate by nature and so when they embark on a new relationship, they tend to act like a love-struck teenager. No one else in the world will exist for them, and work falls by the wayside. They shouldn't try to lie to their boss by saying they're ill, though, for the truth will be obvious from the expressions on their face. They also seem to think more about what they're wearing when in the first throes of love. (Although I'm afraid to say that this does tend

to go out of the window three months down the line – sorry to disappoint you!)

They will want to know everything about you, even going so far as buying your family presents in order to soften them up for the exciting first meeting. Being ruled by Mars, the planet of unpredictability, you may want to check what they're wearing before you take them round to meet the family. They're likely to have gone overboard and you may have to tone down the very colourful display they've put on in your honour.

Before you know it, they'll be planning your life together. You'll catch them writing their name with yours on napkins, and I've even known a woman of this sign who was discussing with her brand-new partner how he would have to take her maiden name as his just didn't suit her Christian name. (In spite of this, they went on to get married and he did take her name!) My point is that they are a little tactless but in the nicest way, and what they are thinking while in this giddy, loved-up phase often tumbles out of their mouths. The good news is that they do slow their pace after about six weeks and so the drawer at your house that they claimed pretty much immediately will start to become less full and life will gradually become more manageable. In fact one of the complaints I often get from partners and ex-partners of this sign is that the Ram goes all out over the first few months and then backs off. As long as you know this early on, you will be less inclined to take it personally.

Money is not the most important thing to this sign, so you won't need to take them out to expensive restaurants. You may have to order takeaway, though, as when they first fall in love, they're not going to want to leave the bedroom for days if not weeks to come.

Signs that an Aries is not happy

A clue that the Ram is not happy is when they don't make up after an argument but simply sweep any issues that were being discussed under the carpet. Watch out – they haven't forgotten, they are simply simmering, and there is a cork that is about to burst in your direction if you don't tackle the contentious subject head on.

If you're an Aries who thinks they're having problems with their eyes but never did before, then take a love check not an eye test, as Aries rules the head and this sign often gets major headaches when under stress and pressure. You need to retain some independence and keep your own life ticking over. When you make major changes quickly, it can all too often lead to disaster. I know you don't want, to but you have to make changes a little more slowly if you are to achieve longevity with a partner.

I once had an Aries client who spent the first six months of a new relationship travelling around the world and staying at different top hotels with their partner. Luckily they could afford to do so, but I could have saved them a lot of hotel bills. Once the couple returned home and normality kicked in, they couldn't stand each other. The Aries began showing sides to their character that the Taurean involved couldn't live with. The unpredictability and excitement were all very well when in exotic places with new experiences, but back on home ground the rubbish wasn't getting put out and the food wasn't being put on the table, something the Taurean couldn't stand.

Learn to be yourself. Aries are known for being impulsive and you should explain to all new partners that you are an unpredictable and spontaneous sign. Don't try to pretend that underneath that almost shy and reserved air you are not a born leader who wants to decide at a moment's notice to change plans, and that for anyone to try to rein in your sense of adventure would be like asking you not to breathe.

Best place for a first date: comedy club, to find out if your date has as alternative a sense of humour as you do!
Key lesson for an Aries: slow down – if they love you, they're not going anywhere.

Taurus

Should I stay or should I go?

Now this is a sign that was born to love. Taureans are natural and instinctive lovers who will go out of their way to make a new partner feel cared for and appreciated. A somewhat alternative view of sex can produce a few raised eyebrows among the more conservative of signs, but don't worry – Taureans won't go too far.

It's hard for many people to see immediately that this sign finds them attractive, as they are deep thinkers who take time to come round and find the courage to put their heart on the line. Once you get them talking, you're sure to discover a sensual, loyal and affectionate person who will show you unparalleled sincerity.

The funny thing about Taureans is that they tend to become childlike when they are in love. I'm sure that this is something their loved ones find very funny indeed, for people of this sign are usually leaders and dominant. Even their voices can take on a childlike air, but this is simply their way of giving up the natural power of their sign to show that they like you and are making space for you to have a say in their life.

Be careful if you're a sociable sign, though, as you're not technically allowed to have any other friends in your life.

Now that you've found a Taurean, you have a best friend and a lover rolled into one. You've heard people say that some men want a woman who's a lady in public and something quite the opposite in the bedroom. Well, now you've found out who it is they were talking about. A Taurean will help you to take stock of your life, and you will probably find that you've never been better looked after and that your abode has never looked more like a home. The problem is that your Taurean will have neglected their own life in the process. If they say you can't come back to theirs, it's probably because they've spent all their time and energy on your place and so are embarrassed by the mess in their own home. It's unlikely any housework has been done since they met you! I once had a client who pretended to his partner that he was still going to work when really he was going down to the Job Centre as he had been sacked for not turning up at work during the first two weeks of their relationship.

Signs that a Taurean is not happy

A clue that a Taurean is unhappy is when they start to let themselves go and stop taking care of the things they usually take pride in. One of the good aspects of this sign is that they're not backward in coming forward. You won't need to ask twice if you've upset them. If their pet name for you is replaced by a less kindly one, then you know you've started on the downward spiral. This earth sign can be as bad as its polar opposite, Scorpio, when it comes to sticking the knife in, and indeed sometimes their words can cut to the bone.

The problem is that it's hard to talk them back round again once they've started falling out of love. It's taken them a long time to feel this way, you see; so if you really do love them, you're going to have to pull out all the stops to make it up to them.

Trust is the main issue for a Taurean, and if they can't trust you, then do them and yourself a favour and cut each other loose. If not, you may be like one of my clients who only discovered after his beloved wife had died that his severe upset stomachs were in fact down to the eye drops his long-suffering spouse regularly used to place in his evening meal. Ouch!

When in love, Taureans will turn their whole world upside down for you, so when they start to put friends before you, then you know that they're not truly happy. They do find it hard to talk about their problems, though, so at the first sign of strange behaviour make the effort to go for a walk and talk to them about life and how they're feeling. The trick with this sign is to catch them before things go too far. As long as you're still talking, then there is every reason to believe you can work things out.

Over- or under-eating is also a tell-tale sign that something isn't right in the relationship – unless the Taurean is in the first throes of love – so watch out for this confusing but revelatory signal.

Bless them – all they want is to be loved and to love you in return, so give them a break.

Best place for a first date: the nicest restaurant you know.
Key lesson for a Taurean: fear of failure will bring on failure. Let go and have faith.

Gemini

Should I stay or should I go?
After I've given a Gemini a reading, their friends often try to find out what's been said and tell me that their friend can't possibly be happy, because they've gone from being a carefree spirit to one who is penned in and is no longer seeing the lighter side of life. I just smile to myself and explain that the Gemini they know wasn't carefree at all but was in fact

restless and unhappy, and has been waiting for someone to come along and help them stop playing games and simply settle down. What the Gemini's new love needs to understand is that no matter how much a Gemini wants to settle, and intends to do so, there will always be a gypsy in them who wants to explore life and live new adventures. The only difference now is that once the honeymoon phase is over, they've got a pal by their side to share their antics – if you can keep up, that is!

They won't like the characters in your life who tell you what to do, so beware and hide away anyone in your family who has strong opinions. Gemini won't hold back from telling them what they think and feel.

This is a sign that longs to have someone to take care of them. They are like a superstar who has finally come off-stage and can kick off their shoes and not worry about being seen without their make-up. This is because life really is like a performance to them. So if they've let you in, then you must be very special indeed. You may have a problem putting up with the vast array of characters they have in their life, but this is all part and parcel of what makes them such a magnetic sign. They have a charitable side to them, which I'm sure you will grow to love over the years you're with them.

Geminis can do more than one thing at once – this sign is the ultimate multitasker – so don't think they're being rude if they email or make phone calls while talking to you or even while in the throes of passion (yes, I mean it). They won't be neglecting you; this is what they're good at and they are quite capable of sealing a multi-million-pound deal while bringing their partner to a high-pitched squeal of delight!

Signs that a Gemini is not happy

It's a sure-fire thing that a Gemini is not happy when they are physically tired all the time. This is one of the signs whose health really is a mirror image of their emotional state. They also tend to become loners when in the midst of getting out of a relationship, which is an obvious clue that they're not being themselves. This is one of the most individual signs you will ever meet. Fun is the key to this their happiness. They were born to laugh and to socialize, and the minute they stop laughing, you know you've got trouble.

A Gemini's nightmare would be watching one of those couples you see who have been married for a long time and sit opposite each other in a bar or a restaurant with nothing to say. The couple may claim they don't need to talk, but a Gemini would beg to differ.

Make sure that you keep yourself looking good for this sign. Many people believe that once you're in love you don't need to keep trying, but you do with a Gemini. If they're no longer thinking about how they look, then they've stopped caring, and it's vital to their happiness that the attraction is kept up and that the excitement remains. It's when the excitement is over that this sign tends to stray. Yes, I know it can be exhausting trying to think up ways to keep a relationship alive and the spark strong, but many couples do it and a Gemini will accept no less from you.

If you can lead the conversation with a Gemini for more than five minutes, then you know that their mind is elsewhere. By that same token talking is this sign's saving grace. Ask what's wrong and they should tell you; they're far more upfront than Aries and Taurus in that way. Nerves often get the better of them, though, so becoming ill is often a sign for this usually bubbly personality that life is not as they like it.

Best place for a first date: an airport, and don't forget your passport!
Key lesson for a Gemini: it doesn't hurt to stop and take in the views of others once in a while.

Cancer

Should I stay or should I go?

This sign is so changeable in nature that it is hard at times for even the most astute of people to work them out! They are born carers who know how to make someone feel loved but whose feelings are often not reciprocated in the manner they should be.

Be honest with this sign and they will love you until the end of time. They are more than capable of taking on your troubles for you, but lie to them and they will never forgive you. They can't comprehend why, when they're willing to accept your past, you won't open up to them and tell them everything. Some people would say they are a little cold, but that's not true; they just want the facts and they want them now.

It's true they don't forgive, but as far as they're concerned, they can't and shouldn't have to tolerate a lie. They are faithful and supportive and have been the support system for many a successful man and woman who has risen to the top.

Don't expect them to fit in with your friends. It is impossible to expect that they get along with everyone you know. You can also guarantee that you'll have at least one friend who will ask you what on earth you're doing with such a sign, as some would label them as nutty as a fruitcake. The way you've got to look at it is that fruitcakes are delicious and delectable even if they need careful handling. And what fun! Just don't give them too much to drink. This sign is not known for taking alcohol well and will be liable to say things they don't mean.

You certainly won't find a more original sign when it comes to Christmas or birthdays. In fact they go overboard. Don't try to second-guess what they want from their relationship with you. They'll constantly surprise you and will always make life interesting. Respect is a key ingredient for getting along with this sign and is what will help keep you together too. Their friends mean a lot to them, so if you want to impress them, then be nice to their nearest and dearest. It could end up being a vote-off between you both if you insult a loved one or put them down, and if they've known their friends longer, you may well end up with the short straw!

Signs that a Cancerian is not happy

You can tell a Cancerian is feeling the strain when they start to attack. Just like a crab, when they decide to fight they go all out. Whoever said attack is the best form of defence must have been talking about a Cancerian. They don't cope very well with long-term problems, and if something doesn't get fixed quickly, they can fall into a depression from which they can take weeks if not months to recover.

Their stubbornness is their own worst enemy and, like their polar opposite, Capricorn, can often be an unnecessary reason for the breakdown of a relationship. If you love them and want to keep them, then back down because they're certainly not going to!

This is probably the sign that is most obviously affected by the moon and tides. When there is a full moon, you'd better run for cover, and if a Cancerian looks at their diary, then they're likely to see it was during a full moon that they broke up with an ex or gave in their notice at work.

Health-wise, when this sign gets down it's hard to lift them up again, and they need constant care, love and attention to make sure they stay on the right track in life. Relationship problems affect them more than most. They are not as good as other signs at forgetting things that have been said or at sweeping wrongdoings under the carpet.

The other problem is that they often talk to their nearest and dearest about their problems before you. If Auntie Jane or Uncle Mick is giving you funny looks, it's probably because they know you're going to be chucked! If you've made a Cancerian feel inadequate or hurt, then they will try to cover things over with a smile, but look into their eyes and you'll see whether the smile is hiding heartache.

In some ways they're like a child – full of innocence and hope for the future. What's wrong with this, though? Surely to have a sign that is so full of genuine and lovable traits should be an asset. The time you spend placating and reassuring them will be returned tenfold, so make the effort. Words of comfort and reassurance can work miracles.

Best place for a first date: at their home, so they can see if and how you fit into their surroundings. (If they even let you in the front door, you know you're off to a good start!)

Key lesson for a Cancerian: don't expect. Allow a blank canvas with no preconceptions.

Leo

Should I stay or should I go?

They don't mean to, but this is a sign that really can't help acting on impulse. They are not frightened of the kind of experiences that the rest of the zodiac would run a mile to escape. Born initiators and leaders, they take partners to new heights and push the boundaries, making life fun and fresh for all around them. However, their intense attitude can make a relationship with a Leo a little scary. After all, who wants to talk about wedding plans when you don't even know if their favourite drink is tea, coffee or wine? Such minor details don't put off a Leo. What you must know is that after the first six months they back off and they probably won't even remember asking you what song you wanted to be played on your wedding day. They will, however, remember how to make you laugh. In fact it's their humour that will keep the rest of the signs coming back into their life year after year.

The problems begin when a Leo falls for a partner who is as impulsive as they are. That's when you need to take care that you don't end up at a drive-through wedding chapel!

With their magnetic personalities and ardent natures, they are usually very attractive both physically and mentally. They also have a tremendous affinity with the younger generation, for this is truly a sign that is young at heart. Watch out, though, for it is a determined sign and I've witnessed many a client unsuccessfully try to fight off a Leo's attentions. It's their sheer determination that often sees a partner capitulating. That teamed with the charm that this sign naturally possesses is a sure-fire recipe for a dramatic and memorable relationship.

Keep a sense of humour at all times – you'll need it. You'll probably never have as much fun with anyone as with this sign. And don't worry about their flirting, by the way; they can't help it, and if they love you, they're probably telling those they're flirting with how much they care for you.

They love to tease, which is why they're so irresistible. This really is a case of the chase being every bit as sweet as your wildest dreams could imagine!

Signs that a Leo is not happy

When this larger-than-life character no longer has a smile on their face, you know that trouble is coming. Depression in a sign such as this often affects them physically. The calm before the storm is an uneasy time and you'd best run for cover to ensure damage limitation.

Money problems can affect a Leo's personal life more than most signs. Because Leos are such proud characters and like to be able to treat those around them, they find it hard when they can't afford to do so. Any gathering or party appears to be theirs even if it's not. They command a room without effort and want all eyes to be on them. This is why it has such a catastrophic effect when things aren't working out. Feeling humiliated because something isn't working is devastating for this sign, and they have been known to go to extreme lengths in order to try and cover up problems.

If you ever find out that a Leo has been cheating, then be glad that is the only fallout you've experienced, as Leos wouldn't cheat unless they weren't happy. They would rather show their dissatisfaction through actions than words. It's part of their animal make-up that they don't see the need for trivial talks and discussions. They will force both your hand and theirs by making a situation impossible to ignore.

This sign can't bear to be controlled, so be wary of telling them what they can and cannot do or of giving them too many limitations in life. Remember that a Leo is a born explorer and to be told they can't do something is like giving them permission to be bad!

If you stop taking care of yourself, then they will lose interest and stop taking care of you, because they think that the people they love should always make the effort for them. If you see things starting to go wrong between you, don't wait to sort them out. Leave it a night and it could be a lifetime before you get the chance to win them back. Deal with problems as soon as they happen and talk things through. They respect honesty but can't tolerate a liar. Having said that, they're allowed to tell white lies when required. To them, a white lie is simply adding colour to a story, and who'd dare to argue with this delectable and very colourful sign?

Best place for a first date: somewhere loud and colourful, so you can let them know you're not afraid of a bit of drama.

Key lesson for a Leo: let others take the lead; it's sure to prove more interesting.

Virgo

Should I stay or should I go?

Once you have a Virgo in your life, you won't have need for a personal secretary, a best friend or a parent, for you have all three rolled into one. Some may say they're boring, but others find it a turn-on to get a text or an email telling them when and how they're next going to have sex. While some signs are flirting with the idea of seduction, Virgo will have it planned right down to the colour of bed linen you'll be lying on afterwards!

The beauty of this sign is that they will take your life, dissect it, work out where you are going wrong and instantly make improvements. OK, so you may not have planned on having a life make-over, but you won't be able to deny that your life is better for having this sign in it.

With their competence, quick thinking and compassion, Virgo can make you feel loved as never before. They enjoy life and are able to adapt to situations that many other signs in the zodiac could not.

Some would say that this sign is boring, but I disagree emphatically. Flirting with wild ideas is exciting enough, but here you actually have a sign who is willing to carry them out. Talk about pushing the boundaries!

Virgo spends a lot of time counselling friends and family, so you are going to have to be prepared to share this loving sign. It isn't unheard of for a Virgo to take phone calls while in the throes of passion as their role of listener is of para-mount importance, even in the most intimate of moments. This sign probably celebrated when earpieces came out for phones as it made them immediately available to the many friends who can't live without their advice – or so Virgo seems to think.

Don't take it personally if they dissect your performance in the bedroom. They're only trying to help and will probably be able to improve your skills. They're not necessarily experienced, but they've talked to so many people that their tips are probably worth picking up!

Don't make the mistake of thinking they are unhappy with you if they are moody or acting strangely. They find it hard to compartmentalize so it could just be down to a bad day at the office – it isn't necessarily anything to do with you.

Signs that a Virgo is not happy

A Virgo is clearly unhappy when they go off into a dream world and pretend that a situation is diversely different from the way it really is. I once had a client who became so embarrassed when he separated from his wife that he lied to his family and told them there was nothing wrong. He went so far as to leave things of his wife's about when his family came round and told them that she'd just popped out to the shops. He simply couldn't admit that his marriage had failed. Of course his family found out in the end and he is now happily married to a real person again. They should have guessed when he said she'd popped out shopping, for Virgo would never let anyone go shopping without them in case they bought the wrong thing!

Although exciting, Virgo is a very draining sign to be with. Don't think that they don't know exactly what they're doing, as they will have planned their seduction of you, from how many children you'll have to looking up your family tree on the Internet to make sure the breeding line is up to the standards they require. If they don't want you, then it won't take a scholar to work out that they're not interested any more. This is a sign whose emotions are written on their face, and they will drop you faster than a hot brick if you're no longer showing your affection for them.

Best place for a first date: let's be honest here – let them decide. They've probably already got a table booked somewhere anyway!
Key lesson for a Virgo: don't judge others on who they were before they met you.

Libra

Should I stay or should I go?
Life with this sign is a mixture of highs and lows. You may be scared off at first, but think about it – what's more fun than living with such an extreme array of emotions? It depends on your own sign and how seriously you take this fun-loving character.

Librans are natural flirts. They just can't help it. The flirting is not about trying to win hearts; it's about having fun. They don't even flirt to get people to like them. They just love life and the fun that comes with simply being here on earth.

When it's time for the serious stuff such as paying bills and day-to-day living, they can be somewhat unpredictable. They have an eye for beautiful things and so may be prone to spoiling you with gifts. All very well until you find out a month later that your present has been charged to you own credit card!

It's not part of their make-up to want to hurt you; in fact they'd go out of their way to make sure they didn't. They just can't seem to help acting on their emotions rather than with their brains, which means that inevitably they don't always make the best choices. They feel their way through life and love, and wouldn't be with you if they didn't utterly adore you.

They know, thanks to their ruling planet, Venus, how to get what they want, and even though they themselves often suffer from emotional blackmail, they also know how to use it to their advantage.

So what, you may ask, do they want from you? Your complete attention and devotion is the answer, even though they probably won't be able to give you theirs. They are attracted to age differences, usually going for someone older as they want to be with someone who can teach them things. Ever the explorer and researcher, life is for learning and making more beautiful. Not only will this sign build a life with you, they will decorate it too!

Signs that a Libran is not happy

It's not easy to spot when this sign is unhappy as the Libran character is made up of so many layers that it can take a while to find out what they are really thinking and feeling. When they fall for the wrong type of person, they can go a long way down the wrong path before they find the strength, courage or fortitude to do something about it.

Those Librans who have been severely hurt in love take on physical problems as well as emotional ones; it really is as if they have had their heart broken and it's a very sorry sight to see. They are not the easiest sign to help, so once you see the tell-tale signs and the puppy-dog eyes, help them to help themselves. This loving sign thrives when in love and is an extremist. Then again, being ruled by Venus, the planet of love, would you expect anything less?

There are often hidden meanings to their words. They inadvertently give clues. If a Libran's prepared something different for dinner when you sit down to eat together, then start asking questions. Their emotions are revealed in their actions and this could well be their way of telling you they want something from you.

If a Libran starts to insult your family, then you really know it's over. After all, this sign loves the unity and closeness that family ties bring. I have seen even the worst family legal scenarios be worked out thanks to the support of a Libran. So when they no longer support your difficult parent and start knocking down your familiar walls of support, then you know that the gloves are well and truly off.

Oh, and if you already have your suspicions that your Libran love has strayed, then watch and see if they're still flirting with the person concerned. If they are, then you know you're safe. The chase is the best bit to them, so if they're still flirting with someone, they haven't conquered them.

Best place for a first date: somewhere they can appreciate true beauty and art. A work of art or a city by night, the choice is yours.

Key lesson for a Libran: be yourself; don't act the way an ex would have wanted you to.

Scorpio

Should I stay or should I go?

I don't know why people ask me if they should stay with a Scorpio or leave them. You see, you don't actually get a choice. A Scorpio does the deciding, not their partner. They are great at being in charge but letting you think that you are. This intense, determined and at times very jealous sign will keep you interested throughout your life. I have even known clients who had a teenage relationship with a Scorpio being unable to resist checking up on their ex year after year in order to find out what this dramatic sign has been up to.

Friends are important to them, but unlike some of the signs, family has always and will always come first to the Scorpio. Blood is most certainly thicker than water, and when they are feeling happy and confident, they can make really major changes in their lives. I have had Scorpio clients over the years who have altered their lives beyond recognition, and this is because they don't see the same limitations that many of the other signs do.

The right partner is not just important to them, it is essential. Love is what helps them to breathe. You may think from your experience with them that they are thoughtful and intense, but I call it wise. They watch, wait and learn, and that's why their moves seem so dramatic when they make them. They've planned everything down to what outfit and shoes they're going to wear for the showdown.

Love and hate can come very close together for this sign. They do everything in their life with such intensity that it can often be hard to tell the two emotions apart. Love Scorpio and they will go to the ends of the earth for you. They'll even up sticks and move wherever you want. Making dramatic changes is the norm for them, but don't think they'd do this for anybody or just for the excitement. They have to be in love with you even to take a step in your direction.

You see, Scorpio doesn't suffer fools gladly and is likely to have a small, select group of friends rather than a crowd. They may not talk about the past but that's not a conscious choice. To Scorpio, life probably didn't exist before you came along, not in their mind anyway.

Signs that a Scorpio is not happy
A Scorpio is not happy when, like their sign of the Scorpion, they sting and ruin lives and say things that hurt. Why? Because when a Scorpion stings it is the last resort, so they really will have been pushed too far.

Whatever you do, don't cheat on this sign and expect to get away with it. You may be sitting pretty thinking dumb old Scorpio never found out about the fling you had, but you'll soon realize that they do know and probably followed and photographed every moment of your indiscretion, which they'll post on the Internet for your friends and family to see. They actually knew you were thinking of straying even before you did. Look again at the fine food you are being served and ask yourself why you've not felt right of late. Look deeper still and you'll find the detergent that's been put in your food drop by drop every day. Revenge is a dish best served cold to this unforgettable sign.

A friend of mine who is a Scorpio used to say to her children, 'Don't even think about it!' The horrified children would gather in their room to ask how on earth she'd guessed what they were up to before they'd even finalized their naughty plans. Scorpio just knows!

Although a very sexual sign, they cannot give love freely if their heart is not in it, or at least their libido. That's why if a Scorpio is no longer accepting your amorous advances, you know that they no longer feel the same way about you. They have to be in love with you or very much in lust, and be able to trust you if they are to give themselves to you. It's all in the eyes with this sign too. They may not show it in the way they stand or the things they say, but the eyes really are the windows to this sign's soul. If they can no longer make you eye contact when they look at you, then you know there is something bubbling under that cool, calm exterior.

Talking is important to them and if you stop talking and communicating, then they will shut down on you too. They need to know what you're thinking and feeling every step of the way. They want to share the experience with you, and to shut them out of your life is like shutting off their life-support system.

Such a powerful entity is the Scorpio that when they enter your life, you'll feel as if you didn't know what it was to live before; but if their feelings wane, then you'll never have known such pain. Be true to them and avoid lies and they'll respect you. This is certainly not a union to be entered into lightly, but it is one that will change your perspective on life for ever.

Best place for a first date: your home, so Scorpio can investigate, save themselves time and find out *everything* about you.

Key lesson for a Scorpio: you don't have to reveal your whole life story on the first date.

Sagittarius

Should I stay or should I go?
When things are good, you will probably never have been happier, but when they are bad, you will wonder how you got into the very flamboyant world of the Archer.

Part of the problem is that while some of the other signs may want to consume you and be with you twenty-four seven, Sagittarians can find it hard to give themselves to you completely and so part of you is always going to be wondering what your union really means. There is no real reason for this; it's just part of their make-up. They have one foot out of every situation in case they need to make a quick getaway. This isn't always due to a past experience with an ex; it's just in the nature of a fire sign to have an escape route ready and waiting in case the alarm goes off.

It's not unusual for this sign to have boxes in the attic that they haven't unpacked even though they moved years ago. They're so busy hurrying on to the next thing that they sometimes fail to finish what they've already started. That said, this really is a highly successful sign who can excel at whatever they put their mind to, if in fact they can put their mind to any one thing.

Their saving grace is their common sense, which tends to kick in just in the nick of time. They can take a normally diffident sign of the zodiac and help them to excel and make their mark in life. They don't tire as easily as many other signs, so while some of us are packing our bags and giving up on a relationship or a dream, a Sagittarian is getting their second wind.

Their way with words is another fantastic quality. I have watched friends being talked back from the brink of ending a relationship and start planning their wedding the very next day. You have to admit that is a talent worth its weight in gold. This strong sign can draw you into their world and make life such a special place that nothing else and no one else matters. The Archer has a charisma likened to celebrity. It's no wonder so many of their partners feel lucky to be with them; they believe they've landed a saint!

Signs that a Sagittarian is not happy
When they tell you so! This is an honest sign who doesn't have time to play guessing games. They'll sit you down and get straight to the point, and could save the rest of the zodiac a lot of time with their tips on speaking frankly.

When predictability and routine become the norm, then you can start counting down the days to their exit. Surprise them with loving gestures and thoughtful actions and you'll keep this sign by your side until the end of time. Don't expect to retire where you live now, though; Sagittarians rarely stay in one town for too long!

Life with a Sagittarian can be heaven and hell combined. One minute you've planned a future and the next they're telling you that you're not part of it. Their impulsive nature can deter others from telling the truth as they serve their opinion as cold as ice and straight to the heart.

You will notice that this sign is naturally quite healthy, so clues that problems are coming can be spotted when they start to catch everything that is going. Believe me, a Sagittarian doesn't make a good patient. So rare is it for them to get ill that they act as if the common cold is the plague.

If you love this sign and want to keep them, then be as straight with them as they are with you. It can be all too easy to tell this sign what you think they want to hear for fear of letting them down. However, not all of us operate at the same velocity as the Archer, so slow your pace and make them follow your lead every now and then. It can do them the world of good to take in the view instead of acting as if everything in life is a competition.

They would rather be broke than live with a liar, so tell it like it is to keep this sign. They can forgive even the worst of sins if told straight, something that often shocks the more conventional signs in the zodiac.

Best place for a first date: their work; it's sure to give you an insight into the mad empire they run!
Key lesson for a Sagittarian: don't pretend to like things you don't just to impress others. Be your own person.

Capricorn

Should I stay or should I go?
It is not easy for a Capricorn to commit themselves in love, so if you have managed to attract this very sensual sign into your life, then you have done very well indeed. They are cautious by nature and it can take an eternity for them to commit to the most trivial of things, let alone something as major as a relationship.

When I'm in a queue and the person in front of me is taking their time, I often joke that they must be a Capricorn and I'm usually right. It's for a good reason, though, and they can save their friends and family a fortune by informing them how much they could have saved by buying two of such and such, or by getting a larger size of an item.

This sensible approach doesn't follow through in the bedroom, though, for this is one earth sign who knows how to make their partner feel at home. In fact it's probably the home many of us have been looking for, as a Capricorn can make you feel as if they've known you for your whole life and bring a uniqueness to many unions.

Their sense of humour deserves a mention, as they can say something with a straight face but on the inside they know that they're joking with you and it can take hours if not days for outsiders to get the real joke.

The more in love a Capricorn is, the younger they seem to appear. It's as if love is a wonder drug. I have a Capricorn friend who regularly has Botox and also has many men friends. When I see her looking well, I have to check whether it's because she has a new man or has simply had a shot of Botox! A truly happy Capricorn won't need any help from a needle, though; an injection of romance is all they need to make everything else in their life slot into place. They may have said they were happy as a singleton, but when you see this sign as part of a couple, it's a truly amazing sight. They do need to stop treating their partners as if they were a prize or a trophy, though. They can't help it; they're proud and probably in shock that anyone could find their very specific ways work well for someone else too!

Signs that a Capricorn is not happy
There are no half-measures with this sign. Home is where the heart is, and if their heart is no longer with you, then their time and energy will no longer be where you are either. With the strong likes and dislikes this sign has, your phone number will be deleted within the week, and if you've done something

to hurt or upset them, then they will probably have already arranged for your number to be barred too.

They don't want a humdrum existence; they have standards to keep, and if you can't keep up with what they want, then they see no reason to waste any more of their precious time. This is where their very individual sense of humour comes into play again and their ex is sure to be the butt of all their best jokes. If you are placed outside their circle, then you can expect to find yourself on their list of funniest things to say.

It's not that Capricorn is lazy. It's just that they very often start new relationships before old ones are properly tied up and put out to pasture. If there is a nearly ex still on the scene, it's probably not actually Capricorn's fault. They're just a little slow in getting to the point when trying to finalize things.

A word of warning if you think there's something going wrong in your relationship with Capricorn: check your bank balance! Earth signs value their money and their possessions, and I once had a Capricorn client who suspected his relationship wasn't going to work out. Before he even attempted to fix the problems between himself and his partner, he drained all their joint bank accounts as back-up in case things didn't work out. This was more important to him than talking things through. So check your joint account as you may be in for a shock. Your balance may tell you whether you can expect to find your Capricorn partner there when you get home.

Best place for a first date: an impressive place with impressive service. With the right service, ambience and decoration, they'll be putty in your hands.

Key lesson for a Capricorn: don't be afraid to be yourself. Avoid saying you don't know.

Aquarius

Should I stay or should I go?
If you manage to get a word in edgeways with this excitable sign, then you will soon discover that they already know more about you than you think. You see, an Aquarian will not enter into a union without having done their homework first. To them, it's essential to make the round of phone calls to find out where you've been, what you're doing and where people think you're headed in life.

You have to forgive the Aquarian, though, as they can't see they're doing anything wrong. Great at social networking, they are able to get the kind of information out of people that others can only dream of.

The good news is that if you're with an Aquarian, you can be sure it's because they *want* to be with you. This is not an easy sign to hold on to, as their flirtatious nature means they often find a relationship is hard work. If they are with the wrong person, it can make them feel tied down. That's why they don't commit unless they think you could be 'the one'.

They are good judges of character, which is another reason why embarking on a romantic relationship means they really do believe you can make it work. Just try not to dredge up too much about their past. They believe that life is about the future and not about going over old ground. They grow bored talking about what has been and would much rather work on what could be. This forward-thinking, ambitious and very fun sign can make any situation enjoyable.

If they make plans that don't involve you, then don't get paranoid and think it's over. This is a sign who can have a life and a lover. They don't need to be handcuffed to you to love you. They have a wide social circle, and if you want them to want you, then let them be free. They go where the wind takes them, which is where there is choice and laughter. They have a point: life should be fun, and if trust is present in the relationship, then there is no reason not to give them the benefit of the doubt.

They will change their plans and even move towns and countries for you if they think it would make you happy, which many of the other signs would not. All you have to do is keep the fun and sparkle in their life, as this is the very air that they breathe!

Signs that an Aquarian is not happy

When the laughter stops. It won't stop for long, though, as they need to be able to smile. They are naturally happy people who don't enjoy looking at life's negatives. They won't run out on you when the chips are down; they'll help you move onwards and upwards, but they expect you to remember that the glass is always half full, never half empty.

Many problems occur for this sign when the partner they are with becomes lacking in self-confidence and thinks that they are not good enough for popular old Aquarius. The truth is that an Aquarian will never pick the type of partner that others would choose. They go for the outsider, someone they believe to be out of their league. They see the potential in people and can turn an average character into a superstar by the time they've built up their confidence.

Don't forget that although this is a forward-thinking sign, it is also a fixed sign and so has some very traditional values. Stick to the promises and plans you've made or you could find yourself exiting the next phase of your union, rather than entering it.

Others may say that Aquarians are easygoing, but those who live with this lovable character will know that's not true. You've heard of people who moan about partners who squeeze the toothpaste tube in the middle or can't stand it when their loved ones don't close the lid on the washing-up bottle. Well, they were talking about Aquarians!

If you stop taking care of your physical appearance, then your Aquarian will lose interest. It's not that they are shallow; it's the opposite in fact, as this is one sign for whom a mental and physical attraction really does go hand in hand. You have to seduce this sign's mind as well as their body, as they go for the whole package. Hard work, you're absolutely right, but worth the effort, I can assure you.

Variety is the spice of life to this sign, and if they're stuck in a rut, then you will be too. Arrange a night out or book some train or plane tickets; the rewards are sure to be worth every penny!

Best place for a first date: an eclectic music mix while cooking in the kitchen. (Remember to put the lids back on the ingredients as you go!)

Key lesson for an Aquarian: don't make promises you can't keep. Enjoy today without wishing for tomorrow.

Pisces

Should I stay or should I go?

Never enter into a union with a Piscean lightly, for your life will never be the same again. I mean this in the most fabulous way you can imagine, and I mean in a way that you will never, ever forget. This emotional, impressionable and sensitive sign will add colour to your life and ignite your interest in completely new areas and subjects. Even the way you look at yourself, your family and your future will take on new meaning.

They will love you unconditionally and take on your faults

as if they were their own. They don't mind baggage; they handle it better than most when in the mood, and worse than most when feeling out of control.

Pisceans work well as a team, for they throw themselves into a situation with more strength and gusto than many of us have seen in a lifetime. They have an instinctive knowledge and know what to do to make things right.

They are unselfish to a fault and won't think twice about taking on things that other signs would run a mile from. Here's where the catch comes in, though, as they will expect you to love them back in return and they will notice the minute, the second that your feelings begin to wane. It's a hard union for anyone because it's so mentally and physically exhausting, but for those of us who enjoy the highs and lows of life, it also offers a buzz that proves truly addictive.

It could take you ten lifetimes to work out what makes a Piscean tick and even then you wouldn't have every question answered. Don't expect them to tell you everything that's gone on in their lives, though. It is rare to meet a Piscean who doesn't have some sort of secret hidden in their past. Because they are such dramatic characters, their secrets can range from a past marriage to simply lying about the price of a piece of clothing they own.

You can be married to this sign for sixty years and still not understand them, but that's often why their marriages last so long. With the trust issue out of the way, there's room for mystery and excitement, something that helps many of the signs feel truly alive. To come home and find out you're off on holiday for the weekend instead of to the supermarket would not be uncommon when living with this sign, but with their ambition and drive they'll support you and can help you realize your wildest dreams and desires.

If you stay with them and work things out, then you will be unbreakable, but if you do decide to part ways, then you can be sure that your dalliance with them will go on to shape every single relationship you will have. They place as much importance on little things as they do on big things. This is where problems can begin, as it can be as important to them that you commit to the holiday of their choice this year as the marriage contract.

I had a client who made his marriage with a Piscean last years longer than anybody had ever expected. When I asked him the secret to his happiness, he simply smiled and revealed, 'I let her think she's in control.' This is a really interesting concept and could, I believe, be a major key in making a union with this larger-than-life character go the distance.

Signs that a Piscean is not happy

If you go to hold their hand and they pull away, you know you've got problems. This sign needs to have lots of genuine affection if they are to give themselves fully sexually. Otherwise they can be all talk. I have known two people of this sign who planned weddings to other signs of the zodiac and didn't go through with them on the day. Even though they'd put all that work and expense into their big day, they weren't prepared to go through with something they weren't 100 per cent sure about. Luckily one of the weddings went ahead a month later, but only when the Piscean had the answers and reassurance she needed. It cost an absolute fortune for the couple, but she didn't care. She had her man the way she wanted him and walked down the aisle with a positive mind. A Virgo would not have dared plan a wedding unless they were sure, and they certainly wouldn't have cancelled it at such short notice, but be prepared to have your cheque book ready when making up with a Piscean; you're probably going to need it!

Be true to this sign and give them your heart and your

commitment. That's all they want — to know you won't embarrass them and that you will support them and be by their side. Their life takes such unexpected turns that they can't afford to have their co-pilot hit the ejector button when they don't expect it.

Best place for a first date: delving through your old photo albums. They want to know where you've been and what they're getting.
Key lesson for a Piscean: don't get to know them through what others think of them.

Meeting

Where are you most likely to find each sign of the zodiac, though? Want to mix with your own, or just learn where the sign of your dreams can be found? Read on to discover where the confident ones of your sign hang out.

Aries

Jump on a course for inventors, go to a seminar for setting up your own business or find out who else is patenting a new design. Expect to see Aries composer Andrew Lloyd Webber or fashion designer Vivienne Westwood, and maybe even an Aries soulmate too.

Taurus

Any good restaurant, or perhaps eating the starter in one, the main in another and dessert somewhere else. Bump into

Taureans Jack Nicholson, George Clooney and chef Gary Rhodes for a sight and night to remember.

Gemini

Working in a social place or just hanging out, even during the week, as they can't stand to be alone for long. Expect to get served by Gemini types such as ad man Charles Saatchi and Gemini singer Kylie Minogue.

Cancer

Campaigning for some great charity. Expect to find Cancerian Richard Branson there too and turn an ordinary night into an incredible one. Life will never be the same for you again once you've mixed with this magical sign.

Leo

Wherever is the showiest, most over-the-top, extravagant place to be, with an outfit to match of course, and looking great. Think Leos Geri Halliwell and Madonna. Spice up your life and you'll soon be getting into the groove.

Virgo

While sorting out the glass and paper at your local recycling centre, expect to bump into a Virgo, who'll be taking care of the environment and making sure everyone else is all right. Virgo Sir Richard Attenborough did this for people and animals alike.

Libra

Poetry readings and places of inspiration and gorgeousness. Libran T. S. Eliot won hearts with his words, and Librans will do the same for you.

Scorpio

Simply stand outside a stage door or hang out where the actors go and you'll expect to see Scorpios such as Whoopi Goldberg, Danny DeVito and Goldie Hawn. Bring the curtains down in spectacular style with a Scorpio.

Sagittarius

At the local sports centre but hanging out as much as working out. They're known for their great figures, especially the legs, such as Sagittarian Tina Turner, though they don't need a lot of work to stay looking on top form. Fly high and reach for the stars.

Capricorn

Out walking the dog. The irresistible Capricorn has even been known to look like their pet. I bet Capricorn Nicholas Cage has no shortage of offers from dog walkers when he's out and about.

Aquarius

Down at a comedy club or anywhere that has humour on offer, the drier the better. You're likely to find a 'friend' like Aquarian Jennifer Aniston hanging out there. Take things a step further and discover the magic that is an Aquarian.

Pisces

The latest art showing. Beauty and architecture are irresistible to this sign. Michelangelo was a perfect Piscean as his work in the Sistine Chapel testifies. Create beautiful art and music with this beguiling sign.

Secret Hangouts

Let's take a look at where the twelve signs would go but wouldn't want to be found. By understanding that we're all allowed a little room for mistakes, we can forgive each other's foibles.

Aries

The racetrack, where they just know their horse will come in this time.

Taurus

The takeaway, before they go home for their dinner.

Gemini

One more pub or coffee shop on the way home, for a final social.

Cancer

Shopping with the credit card they swore they'd cut up.

Leo

Out with the friend they hate and swore they'd never be seen with again.

Virgo

Sidling up to an ex, agreeing how they've both moved on.

Libra

Buying tickets, which they'll claim they've been given by a friend for free.

Scorpio

Buying more of what they've already got.

Sagittarius

At the place they said, but not for the very important business meeting they insisted was taking place.

Capricorn

Flirting with that new face at work to see how far they'll be allowed to go.

Aquarius

Writing cheeky texts and emails too good not to send.

Pisces

Going to places they know they can goad an ex or even just the new competition.

Chapter 2

LET'S STAY TOGETHER

Understanding how your sign tends to behave when in a relationship can boost your confidence when you are faced with the kinds of problems life inevitably throws your way. It's OK to feel nervous about a relationship and to question what you want, but it's also good to trust and to move forward.

Aries

All too often you have rushed into unions and have been left feeling as if you have taken on more than you wanted. When these nerves kick in, you tend to blame those closest to you for tricking you into a situation you didn't ask for. The only problem is, you did ask for it – insisted on it, in fact! The key to confidence in relationships for your sign is to take things more slowly. You may say that it's others who are rushing you, but stop and take stock and you'll soon realize it was *you* who initiated every change.

Believe in the power of patience. Have faith in your loved ones and listen to them. You frequently tell them what they're thinking and feeling before they've had a chance so much as to open their mouths. You're very good at finding humour in situations and you must use this ability in order to laugh at things that go wrong. I had an Aries client who called off her wedding the night before because she was frightened she had rushed into things. She was so good at finding humour that she even talked her husband-to-be into having a 'not-married' party at the venue, which had already been paid for. Luckily the groom in question was a Gemini and had no intention of turning down a social opportunity such as this.

Key word to learn: patience.

Taurus

Many clients I have had of this sign have stayed and stayed and stayed in a negative relationship, for the children, the dog, the house, the material things . . . the list really is endless. What is clear when talking to these clients is that something else is always given as a reason to stay. The truth is that 50 per cent of the time Taureans can be too lazy to leave. You see, emotionally they've put so much of themselves into a relationship that they're not entirely sure they've got the strength to go through what it would take to get out!

Talking is the key for you, Taurus. You all too often bury emotions, which in turn makes you physically ill. One doctor friend of mine actually asks his patients what sign they are when faced with a mystery illness. If he's dealing with a Taurean, then 70 per cent of the time he believes that it's emotional stress causing the physical problem.

You have to learn to accept the fact that not everyone will do things your way and agree to have some 'me' time so that you don't get driven crazy by not having things done exactly the way you want them. If you've got a more dominant partner, this can often be the case. Communication counts for everything.

Key word to learn: talk

Gemini

We all know by now that you are a social animal and like to flirt when you get the chance, but if we look at the other side of the coin, we see that you are also a very private creature when you choose to be. Close ones may think they know what's going on in your mind, but you still manage to surprise them. I actually had a married Gemini client who managed to form another relationship, put a deposit down on a house and get engaged before her husband even had a clue what was going on.

The popularity of your sign is the reason for the very dramatic life you lead. You get opportunities that many of us can only dream of and you have a charismatic quality, which means you will have supporters and admirers waiting in the wings should current faces let you down. However, with your sign it's always a case of believing that the grass is greener and that you have to keep up with the Joneses. You must learn to appreciate what you do have before you start complaining about what you lack. You also need to stop looking for compliments and start giving them out to your loved ones. No one would choose to be with your sign if they didn't love you, so appreciation and a bit of commitment are what you need to learn if you are to achieve a permanent, and not just temporary, buzz in life.

Key word to learn: value.

Cancer

It's hard for you Cancerians to believe what you're told by your loved ones as you're emotionally scarred from birth – you can't quite believe your mother put you through such a traumatic journey! There is a small part of you that believes the world owes you. This is not quite as harsh as others may think. From early on in life you give your heart and soul to all you meet, so of course you're going to be crushed and hurt by those who don't do the same in return. While other signs have flirtations, every contact that you have is a relationship that has touched you to the very core of your being.

The only problem is that you often miss out on the fun that normal, day-to-day experiences can bring, as you're far too busy looking for those highs and lows. You don't really understand normality and have been known to make a change just for the sake of it. I've had clients of your sign who have left their partners because they were bored. When I asked why, it was because he or she just sat there and watched TV or because all they did together was the school run and cooking dinner. To you, this is not the norm. It's only when you experience a divorce or a major break-up that you go looking for the very qualities you threw away!

Key word to learn: faith.

Leo

You very attractive Leos have spent your life being told how great you are and if one person happens to tell you that you aren't so great, then you go on to believe this for years to come, no matter how hard new faces try to repair the damage. People will look at you and see someone who is confident, but they need to know that any arrogance you exhibit is purely there to conceal the fact that inside you are terrified that someone won't like you any more, or that they'll discover you're not as intelligent as they thought you were. You are clever and very lovable; it's just that you constantly raise the stakes for both yourself and those close to you. You're like an athlete who's run a huge distance but won't believe you're great until you've beaten your personal best.

You need to learn that it's OK to let others take the lead and that allowing someone else to choose the restaurant or arrange a night out doesn't have to be a recipe for disaster. You also need to know that you don't have to be held accountable for your family's mistakes. Being born under this sign, you think that you have to take on the world's problems, whereas all loved ones want is to see you relax, something that's not easy for any fire sign.

Key word to learn: acceptance.

Virgo

If you didn't set up the meeting, make the first approach or decide to take things to the next level, then there are likely to be problems. You don't want to be in control – in fact you'd love nothing more than to leave others to do all the work – it's just that you don't trust anyone! One of the main problems you experience in life is that you can't stand not knowing what's going to happen next. If you could know what your close ones were going to say in advance, you'd be as happy as Larry.

You are often attracted to the type of person friends and family would never choose for you. You see, you like people for what goes on in their mind and not just the superficial face that they present to the world. You expect others to be loyal to you, but you also want them to put you before anyone else. You're not used to being second best, and the real reason for this is because you lack the confidence to believe you're worthy of them. Poor thing, you don't believe you're an asset to anyone. You need to have faith in yourself, and others need to learn to bend a little more. It's like asking someone to take a rollercoaster ride for the first time – you're petrified and need talking to, along with support and love. Fear of the unknown can cause you to leave a relationship, but trust and courage can make incredible things happen.

Key word to learn: flexibility.

Libra

Yours is a sign that often falls in love far too quickly because the idea of love appeals to you more than the reality of the situation. Close ones should not worry if they hear you talking about an ex with love. It's not the ex you're remembering; it's the picture of them you built up in your mind. If you have found the right partner, there's no way you'd willingly let them go. Your loyalty is fierce and your love undying. If you do get out, it really is because it isn't working. You expect relationships to shape up immediately and don't let partners know what is wrong.

How can someone fix something if they don't know what's wrong, though? Emotional blackmail is something that you are all too often subjected to. You want to please your loved ones, but find it hard to know how far is too far and so you end up doing things that you wouldn't otherwise have done. I had a Libran client who was unhappy with the pet name her partner had called her for forty years. It took a visit from me for her to resolve this bone of contention, which she was about to leave him over. You Librans must learn to feel with both your head and your heart, and never with your libido. It is only by doing this that you will find your world to be a fair and just place.

Key word to learn: patience.

Scorpio

Yours is a sign of such extremes that it would be hard *not* to know when you are feeling happy or sad. The problems begin when you start going into self-destruct and hurting yourself because you have been hurt. This destructive behaviour can range from giving up on your career to under-eating and over-eating. Loved ones know when you are happy, though, for you will have an inner confidence that others won't be able to help but comment on. By that same token, if you are with the wrong person, others will be able to tell. They wouldn't dare tell you, though, as they know you'd bite their head off.

Having said that, you Scorpios can do a very good job of pretending to be happy when you're not, because you can't stand the thought of ridicule or of the world finding out that you made the wrong decision. If you could stop living your life as if it were a soap opera and start to enjoy day-to-day things, then you would soon relax. You are always looking for the next drama, but the problem is that not all dramas are constructive. You should try to get this sort of excitement from other areas, such as your career, so that your loved ones don't have to continually check to see if they're in or out of the doghouse.

Key word to learn: enjoy.

Sagittarius

Because your career is often so very important to you, it's hard for your loved ones not to feel as if they've been placed second. Even if you are in a career that doesn't pay a lot of money, it's still your vocation and you expect your nearest and dearest to respect that. If you don't have a career, then you'll definitely have a hobby that one day may be a career, and once again your loved ones have to bow down to this and accept that they come second.

When you want to, you can make your close ones feel incredibly loved and wanted. Yours is a sign that holds the power to make others feel safe. You were born wise and know more than most because you understand that the world is a tough place. Because of this, you set out in life ready to tackle anything that might come your way. Your heart is not so strong, though, and it's only by giving time to love affairs that you learn to trust, no matter how loyal a sign you have chosen to be with. People can never quite work your sign out and that's because life is a continual learning process for you and so you're never ready to let anyone settle on a firm summation of you – not for a long time anyhow!

Key word to learn: mellow.

Capricorn

You Capricorns love your friends and families, and if your partners can't get on with your loved ones, then they may as well head for the door now. If there's a best friend they can't abide or an auntie who rubs them up the wrong way, then they should call a truce as they're going to need them in their corner at some point in their relationship with you turbulent Capricorns.

For some reason yours is a sign who is always looking over your shoulder. You feel like you're on the run even though you probably haven't done anything wrong (most of the time). There is something smouldering about your sign (think Kate Moss) that cries out to be cared for, but you won't let others too near. You know when you meet someone famous who has a presence about them? Well, this is the normal

Capricorn. You have something about you that others just can't put their finger on but which is irresistible. The danger comes when you feel that close ones' loyalty has strayed and so you look elsewhere. With the number of friends you have, you won't find it hard to keep yourself busy somewhere else. The problem for you, Capricorn, is that you're like a kid in a sweetshop, but who needs a bar of cheap chocolate when you could have one quality square? Prioritize and enjoy life should be your new motto.

Key word to learn: relax.

Aquarius

It's all too easy for you to believe that you've done exactly what close ones wanted when in fact you've done precisely what *you* wanted. You speak but don't always listen, and it can be hard for you to see things from others' point of view. That said, you are a great visionary, but it's usually your dreams and ambitions that you've shaped so perfectly. You ignore advice and do things your way. You are a great leader, though, and by understanding the mood of a nation or the feel of an era you can bring much pleasure into the world. Think songwriter and singer Aquarian Robbie Williams: he tuned in to the nation's changing mood to have hit after hit, but in his love life he has never been able to understand what works for him. All too often relationships end up like oil and water. The answer is to keep both feet in your relationship and stop having one foot out. It can do neither party any good if there is only one of you in a relationship most of the time.

Key word to learn: listen.

Pisces

You have this fear about life, as if you're going to fail in what you do no matter how hard you work. You see, you have always lived through hardship in some form. It's not surprising because you live life at such a fast and dramatic speed. You have people whom you have known and loved and admired, and you also have people whom you have hated but still admire. You are a complicated and fascinating sign who is sure to heavily influence the life of everyone you touch. Once someone falls in love with you, they will never again experience life in the same way. You change the way others perceive the world because you see things through such an alternative view.

Your need to live life to excess and overdo things must be addressed. If you can focus this energy positively, then you can have a successful career and a happy family, and what's more you'll do it with style. Your problems come when you lose respect for your mate, which happens when you're let down. Learning to address a problem before it escalates is a core ingredient to success.

Key word to learn: breathe.

Jealousy

I'm going to end this chapter with a short section on jealousy, a very human emotion but one that can easily threaten a relationship. Some signs are more jealous than others. Water signs, Cancer, Scorpio or Pisces, feel that the people in their life belong to them and them alone. Sometimes they don't even like to think about their close ones having a best friend apart from them, let alone anything more. Earth signs, Taurus, Virgo and Capricorn, are actually real home bodies and don't like to have their personal lives invaded unless it is by invitation. Sometimes even if you give them a month's notice that you will be going out without them or having people round, they can become jealous and lose control.

Whatever sign we are, in this day and age we often spend more time with the people we work with than with those at home. This can lead loved ones to feel as if they're second choice, even if they're not. That's why communication is important, so that we feel secure enough to have it all: a good job, a happy family, the right circle of friends. There will be times when we can't be at home as much as we want, and it's important we have a secure base for when we can be there. Trust is essential.

Air signs, Gemini, Libra and Aquarius, are a little more laid back than the rest of the zodiac. This is because they are more open to social aspects than the other signs, not to mention the fact that they enjoy flirting! They tend to know more often than not that if someone close is talking to another, it does not necessarily mean that they fancy them.

I have to say that a little bit of jealousy every now and then never did anyone any harm. What about that friend who has bought the very outfit that you had your eye on last week but weren't able to get your hands on? Half of you is hoping that they don't look as good in it as you would, aren't you? Well, that kind of jealousy really is at the bottom of the scale and isn't anything to worry about. It's when you begin throwing darts at pictures of your partner's new workmate that you need to start questioning if your emotions are a little out of line.

The first step to finding out how jealous you are is to ask yourself if the real reason you don't like a person is because they are taking a close one's attention away from you. The next question has to be, is what they want to do any real danger to what you have together? Is the life and the relationship you built up changing? If it is, then you may need to sit down and work out a strategy so that you approach your partner in the right tone and manner. If you're not careful, your insecurities can be the factor that breaks you up.

If your partner is a fire sign, Aries, Leo or Sagittarius, then they do tend to go through phases when they want to explore new areas or faces. It means they're bored, so you would be best to lead their attention away from what they are doing by keeping your spirits up and talking about new things you can do together. Don't accuse them outwardly as it was probably a fire sign who invented the saying that the best form of defence is attack, and you'll only find yourself worse off.

If your partner is an earth sign, Taurus, Virgo or Capricorn, then you first need to question what may be wrong in the home. A move or even a more orderly home may be required. Your partner may well be seeking security elsewhere. I am not saying that this is a fact, just a possibility and a way for you to test things out.

If your partner is an air sign – that's Gemini, Libra or Aquarius – and is making you rage with jealousy, then whatever you do don't try to put a stop to their socializing. This sign loves people and hates their own company. Your first stop has to be, if you can't beat 'em, join 'em. Get your glad rags on and show them that you too can mix and mingle should you so desire. They'll soon be dragging you back home for some of your undivided attention.

And last but not least water signs do, I'm afraid, get a kick out of making people jealous. If a Cancerian, Scorpio or Piscean doesn't have at least one person who is jealous of them, then they don't feel alive. This is usually because underneath they are slightly jealous of the face concerned.

Don't indulge in games with these water signs, though, or you'll end up in a stalemate. They are a determined bunch, but wouldn't be with a partner if they didn't really love them. Sit them down and talk to them face to face; you will be able to read their thoughts in their eyes.

If a relationship is meant to work, then it will. If your fate is sealed in the stars, then so it shall be, but whatever sign you are born under don't be frightened to talk about how you feel. If you don't do this, then you will never be able to feel happy and be yourself. If something is so fragile that it is easily broken, then it was never working properly in the first place. Be strong and move on to better times.

Chapter 3

WHEN THINGS GO WRONG

Some of us will admit a relationship is not going to work within five minutes of meeting, but others will need to experience every level of joy and pain before we consider parting ways. Admitting that things aren't working is all about being honest with yourself about what and who makes you happy. It's no use pretending you can live a life that is not you just because it looks good from where others are standing. No one is perfect, but each of us deserves to acknowledge what we need. The first step is the hardest, but knowing that there is always a tomorrow can help you to find the honesty and humour to leave the past behind and embark on a new future.

Cheating

It is never easy when we find out that someone has cheated on us. It can leave us in a mess. Often we are too quick, whatever our sign, to blame ourselves. The reasons behind infidelity are numerous. Geminis often think the grass is greener on the other side of the fence and want to know what they are missing. Scorpios and Pisceans cannot resist their emotions or their physical needs, while Aries, Leos and Sagittarians all too often just act on pure impulse.

Although earth signs, Taurus, Virgo and Capricorn, are the least likely signs in the zodiac to cheat, they can do if circumstances push them in this direction. However, these three signs hate to break up a home, as their base is one of the most important things to them, the one constant that makes the rest of their life work.

Whether or not you forgive an affair is up to you, and different star signs handle betrayal differently. Water signs, which are Cancer, Scorpio and Pisces, find it hard, if not almost impossible to forgive. You see, they wear their heart on their sleeve and you might as well hit them as betray them. It hurts them both physically and mentally. Earth signs, which are Taurus, Virgo and Capricorn, worry more about other people than themselves in any time of crisis and do tend to find themselves dealing with an issue later rather than sooner. Of course, a delayed reaction can cause numerous other problems and they need to try being as honest with themselves as they would like others to be with them. Air signs, which are Gemini, Libra and Aquarius, just have to talk about what has happened, and counselling or a good friend who is willing to listen is essential to their road to recovery.

Just remember that whatever sign you are, only you can decide what you can or cannot live with. Every sign has its good points, and every sign has its bad points. You know what you can forgive and what you can't. Always remember that honesty may be dearly bought but can never be a penny badly spent. Don't pretend something isn't happening. You'll only make it worse for yourself in the long run. Bring anything that is bothering you out into the open or you will never find the tomorrow you are searching for.

I know many clients who have forgiven affairs and continued on to have a good life with the man or woman they share it with. I also know many others who could not forgive and who split up. Life is what you make it, and sometimes Taureans, Virgos and Capricorns tend to stay in a situation for the sake of their family, all the while making themselves more and more unhappy. There is always another sunrise, and there is always another choice, so sit down and work out what you want and not what suits others. If friends don't support you in your decisions, then they are not your true friends. Go on and find some friends who will let you live your own life and help rather than hinder you.

I Love You Darling, But . . .

OK, so you now realize that the relationship isn't working, but what should you do about getting out of it? Many water signs, Pisces, Cancer and Scorpio, will probably reach for the bottle and aim to get drunk in order to gain the confidence to announce their imminent departure, while Virgos and Librans will have a far more concise plan that has been written down with diagrams and time schedules (along with a 'who owns what' section of course). Here are a few tips for the most painless way to get out of a relationship that just isn't working any more.

Aries

Write down how you feel before saying it. Show it to a friend you know and trust and ask them to write a better version of what they know you are trying to say. A sense of humour is not appreciated at this point, so resist making that all-too-easy joke on exit, please.

Taurus

Don't start telling the person concerned how well they've done out of you because you've spent x, y and z over the last month and they have spent nothing. You're ruled by Venus, so put their feelings first and tell them how much you care for them before giving them a bill for their half of the meals you've eaten together over the last ten years!

Gemini

Many exes of Geminis find out they've become an ex when they meet or catch their beloved in the arms of their new love. Resist the temptation to start new relationships until you've finished the old. And remember, if you become friends with an ex, it doesn't mean you can go on sleeping with them!

Cancer

It takes you a long time to come to the point where you admit something is not working, and then you can be as cold as ice. Try to show some compassion and bear in mind that an ex doesn't have to be an enemy. Remember the good times and promise to part with a smile. It will mean a lot to you later.

Leo

If they've stopped treating you well, then you don't want to be anywhere near them. Lack of respect is the number-one reason for this sign to leave someone. Your partner should be able to tell by the power-dressing you do that you're there to break up with them. Learn to talk and not shout. I know you want to hear their side of the story before you leave.

Virgo

You've been planning this right down to the perfume you'll wear when you walk out of the door. Just remember that no one is perfect and a person's foibles are all part of their make-up. Too many Virgos want to get back together with their ex the next day, so make sure you're doing what feels right to you and not what looks right to others.

Libra

If they don't show you love, then you can't show them respect. Pride is important to you and it takes you a long time to get over a break-up. Relationships become a part of who you are, so you can all too often lose sight of yourself as an individual. Talk to the person concerned in the same way you talk to their friends, who can't fill in the missing blanks with the same honesty and clarity.

Scorpio

You'll be all out for the person who has upset you and they'd be well advised to cross the road if they see you coming. Calm down and count to ten. The truth is, you're better off without them if it's not working. You'd only end up slowly torturing them if you stayed.

Sagittarius

You may not even bother to tell them personally that you're leaving. Your sign has been known to do so by fax or email. Have the heart to at least make a phone call. You'll feel more at peace with yourself if you do.

Capricorn

You'll talk about what went wrong until the end of time, as you want to be sure there was no way you could have worked things out. You'll also be tempted to go back and give it another go if the person concerned is any good at emotional blackmail. Writing down pros and cons is perfect for your sign.

Aquarius

You'll have told all of their friends before you get round to telling them, and you're actually very good at humiliating an ex too. Leave with pride and tell them to their face; you'll feel far more like a grown-up if you do.

Pisces

You may have had professional counselling to decide this. You may have spent days confiding in friends, or – like one client of mine – you may, have drained the joint bank accounts before you informed them. Either way, it's like being hit by a train when you leave. Word of advice: play fair. Your reputation precedes you, my friend.

Getting over a broken heart

Whether you were the one who was dumped or whether breaking up was your idea, the end of a relationship can still be very painful. If you're finding it hard to move on, try these top tips for your sign.

Aries

Embark on something you've always wanted to do but have never done because of your ex-partner, whether it's a trip somewhere they wouldn't visit or a hobby or interest you placed to one side since being with them.

Taurus

Dress for yourself again, and start to enjoy the personal pleasures of music and entertainment that make you happy, rather than what fitted in with your ex's tastes.

Gemini

Call up the friends you dumped for your partner. With your effervescence and passion for life, they'll be glad to have your company again.

Cancer

Spend time with family and talk about the past and your loved ones without fear you're boring anyone. A perfect partner for you will not mind if you talk about things that they have not been a part of; they will encourage it.

Leo

You can have a career and ambitions again without worrying that you are threatening your relationship. Make this the time when you go for the career you had put to the back of your mind. With your insatiable appetite for success, you're sure to pip others to the post.

Virgo

Say what you want to without fear of being judged harshly for your opinions. Move on to a better future by being you again. You all too often shape your opinions based on what you think a loved one wants to hear.

Libra

Enjoy some time on your own and take any lessons you have learnt as something constructive. You have to be able to acknowledge and let go in order to move on. Talk to someone, a friend or a professional, and you'll find you become a better person and partner for it.

Scorpio

Write down your feelings and experiences, but don't go back to a bad relationship. All too often your sign returns to give things 'one last try'. You would not think about leaving if you were happy. Make new plans that are bigger and better than ever before. With your luck you'll pull them off if you focus.

Sagittarius

Don't feel you have to prove what a good time you're having as a single by staying out late at all the popular hotspots. This is an obvious and bad choice for you. Instead enjoy the normality that comes from not having to try so hard. The natural and relaxed you will instantly attract a better life and a better partner.

Capricorn

Further education and picking up on something you enjoyed but left behind for a partner will give you joy. Your sign never stops learning and loves travel. Mix the two together and put the spark back in your life and eventually it will be in your heart too.

Aquarius

Talk about what you want and don't spend ages blaming yourself for all that went wrong in the relationship. You're great at focusing on the future, so use this talent to put a bad experience behind you by knowing and accepting what and who didn't work. Do this and what you need for the future will become clear.

Pisces

Don't drag yourself down further by way of punishment. Wallowing will only make you feel worse. Turn a bad experience into a great one by proving that you now know what you don't need. Don't be tempted to punish yourself; instead reward yourself for getting out of a situation that was not working by making better choices and putting yourself first, which all too often you have failed to do when in a relationship.

Ex-Directory

Ever heard your partner say or do the following? This is why you should be pleased you're not with your ex any more!

Aries

MAN: Always knows a short cut even though it takes you miles out of your way.
WOMAN: Can't wait to tell you a secret.
BOTH: Act first, think later.

Taurus

MAN: Is always right. His is the only way.
WOMAN: Has no sense of time.
BOTH: Are hopeless at repeating jokes or messages.

Gemini

MAN: A little backward in coming forward. You can lead him but never drive him.
WOMAN: Happier with a safety pin than a needle and thread.
BOTH: Need a gun to get them up in the morning, or to go to bed at night.

Cancer

MAN: Over-considerate, like when you're halfway across a crowded restaurant and he calls out to tell you where the loo is.

WOMAN: Won't leave the house unless every hair and eyelash is in place.
BOTH: Take too long over every detail.

Leo

MAN: Thinks nothing of telling your friend how much you paid for your new coat.
WOMAN: Excessively house-proud and over-protective.
BOTH: Must have the last word.

Virgo

MAN: Is very punctual, but can't understand others aren't the same.
WOMAN: Waits until you're miles from home before she remembers she's left the cat in the oven.
BOTH: Can't help doodling.

Libra

MAN: Always tells you what a mess you look, after you've left the house.
WOMAN: Just can't help flirting.
BOTH: Are great critics.

Scorpio

MAN: Can't keep his hands off his tie.
WOMAN: Asks what you'd like for tea and then serves something completely different.
BOTH: Are clumsy and erratic.

Sagittarius

MAN: Thinks nothing of bringing friends home when you're not prepared.
WOMAN: Spends all the housekeeping money on things she didn't want.
BOTH: Are manic finger-tappers.

Capricorn

MAN: Can make popping out for a minute last two hours.
WOMAN: Is always wise after the event.
BOTH: Are back-seat drivers.

Aquarius

MAN: Tells white lies as often as he takes a breath.
WOMAN: Always takes a suggestion as a promise.
BOTH: Talk too much.

Pisces

MAN: Can't help the nervous action of pulling or scratching his nose.
WOMAN: Uses chairs and floor as a wardrobe.
BOTH: Never bother with a coaster when there's a clean surface waiting to be ruined.

Part 2

FAMILY

Chapter 4

STAR BABIES

Is your Katie or Kim destined to be the next Kylie? Are you giving Liam football lessons when he should be getting singing lessons? Let's find out what life plan the stars have in store for your offspring while you've still got time to guide them in the right direction.

Aries

Imagine having a child such as Elton John or Diana Ross running around your home. You're sure to have realized the very day that you brought your baby back from the hospital that this little bundle of joy was different, and you'd be right, as those babies born under the sign of the Ram are all ruled by Mars, the planet of change and unpredictability, and they will do what they want when they want, so get ready for a life that, with these folks in it, is sure to be interesting, to say the least. Princess Eugenie is an Aries, and Fergie and Andrew are certain to have found their royal offspring coming out with some very dry humour indeed. Her sign is hot and explosive, and has great physical courage. Eugenie may have her mother's red hair, but she'd still be the fiery type even if she didn't. They want to make a difference in the world, and I'm sure Eugenie will in years to come.

The Aries baby

Most Aries babies like to have noise around them, so if you've been creeping around your Aries angel, then stop and put on some loud music instead; you're sure to see them tapping on the side of the cot in no time. They don't like their own company and will scream the house down if you dare to put them in a room on their own. In fact they will sleep far better if you set up their cot in the front room, where they can be sure they're not missing anything. These babies look more delicate than most, but believe me, as you'll soon discover for yourself, they're not!

The five-year-old Aries

This child will have perfected more than a few bad habits by this age and they have a tendency to rebel more than most against cleanliness and good manners. Don't worry, though, as this is a stage and is unlikely to last for long. It is a test to see how far they can go. You would be best to ignore these antics; anything that they know gets attention can become a device that they pull out as and when they need. Tantrums come and go, but don't usually last too long and this really is a vital time for them, so set the ground rules now and not later.

The eleven-year-old Aries

The more artistic side of their nature is coming out at this time, as is their sensitivity. Many Aries children join theatre groups or beg their parents to send them to stage school. They learn much now by becoming an agony aunt to friends and are sure to know all of the latest gossip. This is a role that will continue with them for the rest of their lives. They are quick to learn at this age and, if put in contact with the right teachers, their brain can see them at the top of their class.

The sixteen-year-old Aries

At this age they are really being pulled into artistic professions and many teen stars are born under the sign of the Ram, such as Victoria Beckham, who joined the Spice Girls to train for fame when most girls her age were thinking about getting a Saturday job. Those who do pursue the arts do well, but they need to make sure that they keep their feet on the ground. Too much energy and early success can fire off the rocket but doesn't make for an easy landing! If you want to support them, then just remember to be persistent. This sign doesn't always listen first time round.

Taurus

Watch out, Mums and Dads, for you could well have a William Shakespeare under your roof if you have a child born under the sign of Taurus! On the downside you might also have a forty-year-old living with you in years to come, as this is a sign who loves their family and their home and will probably be one of the last signs in the zodiac to want to set up home on their own. If they do, then they will probably still bring back their washing for you or pop round for food every week, even if they are married. They need their kin to feel happy and loved, and for some reason bringing home their dirty laundry makes them think you feel cared for!

The Taurean baby

Taurean babies can be demanding and have irregular sleep patterns. They seem to want a lot more attention than other star signs, but this is only because they want to be sure that you love them. They want and need lots of cuddles. Amazingly enough, though, by three months old this is a child who literally overnight turns into a little angel. Once they learn the art of walking, which can take longer than most, they will get their noses into anything and everything, particularly the kitchen cupboards and anywhere with food!

The five-year-old Taurean

This is a child who is impulsive, inquisitive and full of initiative. They are also really stubborn and if they decide that they don't want to go somewhere or do something, then you will have to enlist the help of at least a couple of family members to pry their fingers away from the door frame. You will be surprised at the way they develop and their achievements at school. They are not afraid to put their time and energy into their projects, even at this tender age!

The eleven-year-old Taurean

The biggest problem encountered in their education at this age is if they don't like their teacher. So if you have noticed that they excel in any area, make sure that they are happy with the way that their teacher is developing it. Pushing little Bobby's love of computers could well see him becoming the next Bill Gates if you play your cards right! Their personality begins to develop around this time and their independent nature becomes much more evident. They love music and should be encouraged in their fantasies, as these stand a stronger chance of becoming reality than you may think of.

The sixteen-year-old Taurean

They now have magnetic sex appeal. They won't really have a very high opinion of the opposite sex, though, and can be callous in the extreme, but they will attract admirers like moths to a flame. By now you will have realized that this is a teenager who knows they command respect, even if they do have their own somewhat strange ways. You can be sure that leaders in life such as Taureans Eva Peron and even ex-prime minister Tony Blair knew that it wasn't a run-of-the-mill life that was in the stars for them. Taureans make the best singers in the zodiac, so don't mock them when they start telling you they are going to be the next winner on *Pop Idol*. Just look at famous Taurean singers such as Barbra Streisand, Engelbert Humperdinck, Bono, Bobby Darin and Janet Jackson. Get your cash out and buy them the train ticket; it's sure to be an investment that will keep you in clover for many years to come, especially as the Bull will always take care of their own!

Gemini

You'll need to be ready for anything with a child like this in the house, but you can also be sure that life will be entertaining. Don't be surprised if this child is an early talker. They have plenty to say and won't mind joining in with adult conversations. Not that they always make sense, though; in fact some would say the older they get, the more rubbish they talk, but it still keeps partners and loved ones coming back for more, time after time after time.

The Gemini baby
This is a most individual baby. Some mothers of these children do tend to worry that Gemini Georgie prefers playing with cars rather than dolls or that Gemini George wants to trade his train set for his sister's Barbie, but don't fret. They are just covering all bases and need to make sure that the grass is not greener on the other side.

The five-year-old Gemini
They enjoy ripping up paper and books, so don't leave your favourite novel lying around or you'll never get to find out the ending. These kids are daydreamers, and their eyes are usually a really distinctive feature. Even without talking they will be able to relay their feelings with those eyes. You will be

able to take them to most adult functions without worrying that they will misbehave, and they tend to get on better with older children. Don't expect their educational reports to be fantastic. There is some way to go yet before teachers realize just what an individual they are dealing with.

The eleven-year-old Gemini
This is a child who should start to show a love of the arts, and this is probably the time when Gemini star Kylie Minogue took aim with her ambitions. They are starting to learn more and more from people now instead of from things. They love new experiences and will learn and pick up new skills quicker than most. They are not liars at this age, but they certainly know how to stretch the truth. You can hear them coming a mile off, as I'm sure Gemini Paul McCartney's mum can remember about her famous Beatle son!

The sixteen-year-old Gemini
You will be amazed at how much energy your child exerts at this age, as they can work two jobs, do their schoolwork and still find time to sneak into the local disco. By now they are more independent than ever and won't like being told what time to come home. They will not necessarily show great interest in the opposite sex, but they are attracted to characters and personalities. Friends are likely to be really varied as they try to take elements from each person to help them along their path in life.

Cancer

You have a really caring child here, but do bear in mind that you also have a very emotional one, as their ruling planet is the moon. When the moon is full, you may want to run for cover, because quite honestly anything can and quite often will happen. Most children of this sign have round faces and can turn on the waterworks and make you feel like the worst parent in the world. However, this is a child who learns the fine art of emotional blackmail surprisingly early and is very good at it too. This sign has an affinity with water and will probably even end up living near it. If they don't, they should, as it will keep them sane in times of trouble.

The Cancerian baby

This is a beautiful but rather fussy child, although well behaved with it – until the age of three, when they gain a bit more confidence and adopt a somewhat cheeky and pushy attitude. Do not turn your back on this child for long; here is a baby who could escape the clutches of an armed guard. Don't waste your money on expensive toys either: this is one infant who will have more fun playing with a tin of soup than a toy.

The five-year-old Cancerian

This child cannot be conned. You would think they have been on this planet before, they are so wise and clever. In fact at the age of five they may be a little too wily for their own good. From time to time they will go off into a world of their own, but they have a lot to think about, so give them space when they need it. Their shrewd business sense has already kicked in by now and they will want to know the pros and cons of everything. The 'why?' phase will be particularly trying with this child.

The eleven-year-old Cancerian

They are sure to shock and please you at this age, as they are surprisingly self-sufficient. Even if they get stuck with their schoolwork, they will endeavour first of all to find a solution on their own before seeking your advice. It is the deep and very thoughtful nature of this sign that makes them so worthy of the label 'wise', and is also why they can often appear much older than their age.

The sixteen-year-old Cancerian

I think I can safely say you now have the kind of teenager any parent would love to have. By now they have more often than not experienced a broken heart as they treat everything and everyone really seriously. They exude a kind of sexiness, which will probably cause quite a bit of stress for you. Just imagine how Cancerian Pamela Anderson's parents must have felt letting their sixteen-year-old *Baywatch* babe out with her mates! But all in all you have a character that is sure to be an asset to any parent's life.

Leo

Dylan Michael Douglas, son of Catherine Zeta-Jones and Michael Douglas, won't have any problems growing up with famous parents. Leos are born show-offs and leaders, although they are unlikely to want to go into their parents' professions. They are pioneers, just like Leo Louise Brown, the world's first test-tube baby! What you will find with this fire sign is that they are a little erratic with their behaviour and energy levels. One minute they can be talking ten to the dozen, and the next they can be as quiet as a mouse. This is due to the fact that they put their all into everything and so often have to take time out to refuel, as friends and family are sure to discover for themselves.

The Leo baby

This is a baby any mother would be proud of. They very quickly show off all of the skills and qualities that their loved ones could hope for. Alertness and intelligence often reveal themselves within weeks of birth. They are willing to amuse themselves for longer than most babies. They love attention too, though, and once they start talking, they find it hard to stop.

The five-year-old Leo

Your child will by now be full of energy and raring to go. Don't be surprised if they creep into your bed at 1 a.m. with an array of books for you to read to them. Don't even think about force-feeding them; they will let you know what they want, and as long as you can wait out this somewhat difficult phase, then you will have a loving child who will while away their time singing songs they have made up.

The eleven-year-old Leo

Poor old Madonna's dad must have had his hands full with this eleven-year-old living under his roof. When your child tells you that they want singing lessons or football lessons, or whatever their passion may be, you should get your wallet out, for they're certain to repay you ten times over when they turn it into a vocation. They will also remember your support or lack of it, so bear this in mind when the half-an-hour journey to a football match is becoming a chore! It won't be a hardship in ten years' time when you're making longer journeys by private jet while drinking champagne!

The sixteen-year-old Leo

It's hard to stop this child from talking, and they won't always say the right thing. They are not afraid of hard work or of working for a low wage if they know it will lead to the job of their dreams.

Virgo

This is the perfectionist of the zodiac who wants things their way or not at all. I mean, just imagine poor old Liam Gallagher's mum trying to force-feed him brown bread instead of white and think of his reaction! Children of this sign also have a tendency to be hypochondriacs. They are really good at listening to friends' problems, but will want their home run as they like it from nine years old, if not younger. They will decide what you do and when you do it, and no matter how much you swear that you are the boss, I'm afraid you're fighting a losing battle. The advantage is that this child will actually enhance your life, as if they don't like that new face you have introduced them to, there is usually a very valid reason, so back them up. They deserve it.

The Virgo baby

This is a baby who usually starts out in life looking more like their father and taking on their mother's temperament and personality. Virgos are actually not the most patient of babies, and even a minor job such as heating up their milk will take seconds too long for their liking. After the first four months any tantrums and crying should stop and you will be left with a baby that is weighing up your every move. Keep them occupied or they will catnap during the day and keep you up most of the night.

The five-year-old Virgo

You should now start to see the determination that is associated with this sign. If you don't start to get their number, they will have you over a barrel for the next twenty years, so make sure you put plenty of time and energy into this phase. Virgo Prince Harry is sure to have kicked up a right royal stink if he wasn't watched closely. In fact you can tell even now just from the twinkle in his eye!

The eleven-year-old Virgo

This child will make it clear that they don't mind not being the leader and are more than happy to take on the role of second in command. They can be a bit of a teacher's pet around this time and are more mature than most children of their age. They won't like going to school in dirty clothes or with loose buttons, so make sure you play the role of parent well or they may end up reporting you to social services!

The sixteen-year-old Virgo

They are still the golden child and give off a very sensible air, but what Mum and Dad don't know can't hurt them as far as they're concerned. They won't mind doing things themselves that they would be quick to reproach others for. Vanity and self-indulgence are their main downfall, but are also easily avoided. This is one teenager who's not afraid to take their education further.

Libra

Libran babies really do look as if butter wouldn't melt in their mouths. Just look at Leo Madonna's daughter, Lourdes, the image of innocence but with a strong will. Libran babies love to play devil's advocate, and if you say black, then they will say white. Don't think that Guy Ritchie has developed those frown lines on his forehead for nothing. If you have a Libran child, then just make sure you say 'no' and mean it when embroiled in a heated discussion with them. If not, you'll have them reasoning with you until dawn, and you'll probably end up losing, if they are typical of their sign.

The Libran baby

The Libran baby will coo and sing to you like the perfect child and you'll have visitors galore to admire your seemingly cute baby. Not so cute when you want to go to bed, though, for this sociable baby is not the best sleeper, I'm afraid, preferring to catch up on their sleep when the rest of us need to start our day! They don't mind playing on their own, but their downfall is their lack of confidence, which only their parents will be able to help them overcome. It is important that you encourage them as much as possible.

The five-year-old Libran

At five years of age this child becomes strong-willed and moody, and they have an opinion on everything. Don't even think about force-feeding them; you'll be wasting your time and theirs. It is easy for them to single out a member of the family to make their special friend. They do this with the intention of having influence on their side should Dad or Granny be thinking about not letting them have that new Barbie or football kit they've seen.

The eleven-year-old Libran

These are alert kids with quick wit and are musical by nature, so don't be surprised if they join the school choir. This child is sure to excel in one special subject at this age and more often than not it is art. They don't like to be told what to do, though, so their school report is bound to tell you that they frequently go off on a tangent. They are the class clowns and have plenty of friends, but they also tend to notice the opposite sex a little earlier than most.

The sixteen-year-old Libran

The teenage Libran usually adores their mum, and with their gift of the gab you are sure to feel as if you are talking to a friend and not a child. They don't mind hard work and are attracted to figures, both on and off paper! Music is a passion and this is probably when famous Librans such as Bob Geldof and Danni Minogue started singing into their hairbrush. They're definitely not all innocence and light, though. In fact you're sure to catch them behind the bike sheds sooner than most of the zodiac. This kid is a natural flirt, as I'm afraid you will discover for yourself. Don't knock it – this is a talent that will open many important doors for them in the future!

Scorpio

This child will have a sixth sense from birth. You'll feel as if you are looking at the past, present and future all rolled into one. The timeless and penetrating gaze of this child can also lead you to believe that they can read your every thought. They probably can. This is the second most psychic sign in the zodiac, with Pisces being the first. They tend to mix with other water signs as friends and love the drama that life offers. Good job too, with acting stars such as Brittany Murphy, Matthew McConaughey, Katharine Hepburn, Burt Lancaster, Sally Field, Joaquin Phoenix and Richard Burton among the famous line-up of Scorpio stars.

The Scorpio baby
This is an endearing yet restless child who will not really be able to understand the word 'no'. They love to feel in charge and show dominance from an early age. This bossy attitude can shock new parents, especially if this is their first child. Whether they have siblings older or younger than them, they will have them eating out of their hand and you'll just know there's something special about this bundle of joy.

The five-year-old Scorpio

By now they will have moved on to driving their teachers crazy as well as their parents, and their mysterious behaviour will really keep people on their toes. They enjoy a bit of mischief and know just how to create a drama. Those tales that they tell about what happened at school are unlikely to be as dramatic as they sound, so check your facts before you go complaining to the head.

The eleven-year-old Scorpio

By now this child will be showing a real skill for writing and storytelling. They have the whole class under a spell and are probably capable of leading a revolution. They usually take a dislike to one teacher in particular and if they choose to can make their life hell. They do nothing by halves and excel at some subjects while bombing at others. They usually hate the opposite sex at this stage, because they despise all that they do not understand.

The sixteen-year-old Scorpio

They have a flair for acting by now, and if they decide not to use it in their professional life, they are sure to do so in their personal one. If they have a problem, they are not upset, they are devastated, and their strong sexual drive can turn out to be a parent's worst nightmare. They are extremists who when they are good are very very good, and when they are bad, you can only imagine what they may be getting up to. It has to be said that this sign is tempted by experimenting with drugs and the like, so keep them well informed and maintain the strong bond they will have established with you.

Sagittarius

Sagittarians are great at the things they focus on, but when they don't have ambitions, they can become very lazy, so it's imperative that their parents encourage them to find their niche in life. I wonder if Steven Spielberg or Beethoven's mother knew they had a producer or composer in their arms? If they looked at their stars, then they would have seen that no dream was too big and no mountain too tall for their boys. If you believe in your Sagittarian child and help them to keep going and stay focused, then who knows what you could add to the list of famous Archers' achievements!

The Sagittarian baby
This is a baby who will do what they want when they want, but they do it with such determination that they get *you* into a routine. Don't knock it – this is a formula that works for some strange reason and you'll soon end up napping when they've taught you to. Their sense of spirit is formidable and will have friends and family commenting on how they have obviously been here before.

The five-year-old Sagittarian
Young Sagittarians are like clockwork toys – they rush about like mad things, then collapse in a heap. You might want to supervise playtime carefully to avoid tears before bedtime. Watch out for a ferociously sweet tooth too and ration the chocolate. They speak their mind when they should be quiet, and at this age, when they are prone to repeating what they hear, you could lose quite a few friends if you've talked about them behind their backs.

The eleven-year-old Sagittarian

By this age Sagittarians should already have a firm set of ambitions in their sights. Woe betide the parent who doesn't share them, as they will set out to prove to both their elders and their equals that they are a force to be reckoned with. It's when they don't know what they want to do that they become a worry and grow vague and lazy. Support them, for with vision and direction they will excel and make a fortune, though that is not to say they won't still be a handful, albeit a rich one.

The sixteen-year-old Sagittarian

By this age all that energy will ensure that Sagittarians reign supreme on the sports field. They'll be captain of this and champion of that, and the first in the class to have a boyfriend or girlfriend. Flirting is second nature to Sagittarians. Here's a surprise: many teenage Sagittarians will spurn the romantic opportunities that come their way for the sake of study and brilliant exam results. The dedication that made them school sports champions will give them a flying start in their careers too.

Capricorn

Nicholas Cage and Jude Law may well be Hollywood heart-throbs, but I bet they are still mummy's boys. You see, earth signs love their home and their roots, and no matter how famous they get, they will always want to keep that family bond. But just how easy was life bringing up Capricorn stars such as Mel C. and David Bowie? These children don't take well to being moved about a lot when they are young. In fact they find it hard to move out of home when the time comes, and if the stars of this sign have to stay in a hotel, then they are sure to have the urge to take a favourite pillow with them to ensure they have sweet dreams.

The Capricorn baby

This baby is very little trouble and is in fact extremely perceptive. They even seem to know when their parents need a little peace and quiet – when they are in a happy frame of mind, that is. They do suffer from teething problems more than most, but fit family life very well. Sleep is not usually a problem for them. They are a delight to have around. In fact you may find yourself having to wake them up.

The five-year-old Capricorn

The placid Capricorn child is easily taken advantage of by their brothers and sisters. They are obedient and like to do as they are told. They wouldn't dare risk a telling-off for anything trivial; it would have to be something worthwhile. They are observers and like to watch what everyone else is doing. These clever little souls are learning by others' mistakes, and they will make their move when they are good and ready.

The eleven-year-old Capricorn

They finally come into their own around this time and develop a flair for various things. They can actually surprise their close ones, who have witnessed a slow start. They do what their parents tell them, but more slowly than most. They want to make sure it's just right. This can come across as laziness, but they are simply making sure, so don't be too hard on them. Conflict with fathers can occur at this age, but you'll be pleased to hear it's only a phase.

The sixteen-year-old Capricorn

They are now keen students of life, but will listen and learn rather than push themselves forward. The boys like football, and the girls analyze the opposite sex as a full-time occupation. A shy streak can stand in the way of having a relationship, but if they do find a partner at this age, they may well stick with them for life. They like to build on things and people, and this is the attitude that sets them up for the rest of their very successful lives.

Aquarius

You're going to find it hard to get this child to shut up, as they have much to say about life, love and anything else. Don't knock them for it, though, for it's the very trait that can set them and you up for life. Aquarians include Robbie Williams, Emma Bunton and Justin Timberlake – just imagine what the world would have missed out on had their mums told them to pipe down when they were singing at inopportune moments. People may think that Elvis's daughter Lisa Marie is quiet, but believe me, behind closed doors she's certain to have displayed a most colourful and vocal side indeed, which is probably the reason Capricorn Nicholas Cage felt so 'shook up' after their divorce.

The Aquarian baby
This is a baby who is destructive by nature and is sure to reject cuddly toys in favour of an old slipper or a blanket. Nonetheless this is a happy baby who is sure to bring joy into the life of any parent. Don't leave them on their own for long, though – they like company and would far rather you have a party around them than go out and leave them on their own with a babysitter.

The five-year-old Aquarian
These are the kids who put on shows in the front room, but the difference is that the forward-thinking Aquarian will actually have the brains to charge the audience and to put the other performers on wages depending on skill and age,

reserving a large percentage for themselves of course. Some people say that they have an old head on young shoulders, and I have to say that I agree.

The eleven-year-old Aquarian

This child is popular with friends of all ages, and although they probably have a best friend, they will also participate in numerous clubs and after-school activities. A natural on computers, they can probably work out your technology at home far better than you or your family can. They are only bad at subjects that they find dull. They don't like routine, but want to be able to act on their instincts and ideas.

The sixteen-year-old Aquarian

They have a keen business sense and a capacity for hard work. They can work for really long hours without feeling tired or fatigued. They are not very good at attending to detail, though, so if you ask them to take the teacups out of their room for the tenth time, they will probably tell you off for interrupting the new computer program they are designing to aid travel and communication across the world, and they're probably not lying!

Pisces

Brooklyn Joseph Beckham may have been born with a silver spoon in his mouth, but being born under the water sign of Pisces, he is sure to have given his famous parents a few sleepless nights. You see, Pisceans come alive at night and so if it's not his crying as a baby that kept them awake, then it will certainly be his key in the door at 3 a.m. when he's a teenager. You just know that there's something special about the Piscean baby, and they know you know. They can guess things about you that will astound you and are naturally gifted and psychic, as you're sure to know if you have one in the family.

The Piscean baby

This is a baby who will show their true self as soon as they emerge from the womb. That is the only time in fact when you will see the Pisceans without all the dramatics that they soon start to display. They will constantly surprise and please you with their exploits and joyful expressions. I would be astonished to hear of any parents who got a whole night's sleep during the first very entertaining yet endearing year. When they don't go to someone or don't like someone, then trust them; they have a hunch about people from day one!

The five-year-old Piscean

A selfish streak can develop here if you are not careful and it's important to suppress it early on. Sharing toys will be practically unheard of, and they are sure to have an array of imaginary friends whose names and likes you are supposed to remember. This is when you will start to see their very vivid imagination emerge.

The eleven-year-old Piscean

It's a bookworm you have in your home now. Your child wants to read every bit of information that they can about life so that they can decide which very dramatic path they are going to follow. Don't tell them no, though, or they will set out to prove you wrong. They also have a habit of changing their room at about this time, so if you can't find Piscean Penelope in her bed, then look in the kitchen cupboard, where she's sure to be camped out for her latest adventure!

The sixteen-year-old Piscean

When this sign does something, they go all the way. Barings Bank trader Nick Leeson obviously went too far, but Piscean Albert Einstein goes to prove what a dramatic effect this sign can have on the world. So whether you've got an inventor or an actor in your Piscean child, then back them to the hilt. Just don't let them handle your bank accounts!

Chapter 5

SCHOOL DAZE

In this chapter you'll find out what your children are really getting up to behind the bike sheds these days. And what about you? Did you tell them what an angel you were at school? You can even read about your own sign and admit if those after-school clubs were really a cover for the many detentions you got. Do names from your past search for you on Facebook? Are you first on the list at your school reunion, or are your schooldays something you'd rather forget? I wonder how many of us remember what we were really like in our schooldays. Maybe you gloat that you were the school prefect or teacher's pet. Read on and relive your schooldays.

Aries

This is the schoolchild who leads the way in the art of class disruption, although after they have started the class humming to annoy their teacher, they will be sitting with such an innocent face that even the wisest of teachers will not suspect them. They really do look as if butter wouldn't melt in their mouths. They are both artistic and sensitive souls who will excel in music, and more often than not are to be seen with an impressive music collection in their schoolbag. They are quick to learn and are not bothered about staying up all night before an exam to revise. They will have a quick read on the bus on the way home from school and another one in the morning, yet often these jammy little dodgers can pass with top marks.

They like to be the leader of the pack and are quite often class captain or organizer of discussions. They need to be able to have freedom of expression, so even if there is a strict uniform code, you can be sure that when you look closely, there is some symbol of rebellion lurking, such as red socks or the wrong-length skirt. They can't help but show the world that no matter how much they are made to conform, they are and always will be an individual in their exciting lives!

Taurus

This child has a really strong personality and is hard to miss in a classroom, no matter how many other children there are. They tend to have a voice that is not easy to forget. In fact they can often be found in the school choir, where they will of course expect to be picked to sing lead every time. They love their food too, so woe betide you if you try to push in front of them in the school dinner queue. This is a child who will have both a packed lunch and a school meal if they can get away with it. Their worst subjects are usually sport and mathematics – they are not lazy, but the only way you would get them to take part in a sports day is if you dangled a chocolate bar on the finishing line. They really do have a natural ear for music, though, and if possible should be encouraged to take after-school music lessons. You could have the next Cher, Janet Jackson, Joe Cocker or Bing Crosby on your hands, who were all Taureans! They are not afraid to strut their stuff around the classroom, and their parents may well find that this is one child whose uniform bill is above and beyond the average.

I'm afraid they can become bullies and this must be nipped in the bud. As they can be a little bigger than other children of their age, they learn early how to throw their weight around; but if they can resist this temptation, then they should find themselves one of the most popular signs, for their love of life really is contagious. Just remember to keep an eye on their extra-curricular activities. This is one school-child who knows just how to find their way to the back of the bike sheds, and I'm not talking about smoking behind them!

Gemini

This child will probably be the head of the drama club and will most definitely be prepared to do dastardly deeds to become the editor of the school paper. You see, Gemini children were born to be in the media and they can't help but be fascinated with such areas. Marketing and selling come naturally to them, so when they ask to look after the tuck shop, you'd better check the price list; those crisps are likely to have gone up fifty pence when they're in charge. They love new experiences and have plenty of friends around them – people can't help but find them fun to be with, and they mix well with any age, so you are just as likely to see them hanging around with sixteen-year-olds as with ten-year-olds. I wouldn't call them liars, but they certainly bend the truth when the mood takes them.

Geminis show an interest in the opposite sex from an early age, and the majority of these air signs tend to have a crush on one of their teachers, going to great lengths to make their feelings known. Oh yes, this sign will bring the teacher of their dreams an apple a day and they can sometimes take things a tad too far. So if you hear of their decision to run off with Mr Jones, it's probably more of an obsessive fantasy than reality. They are dreamers and excel at staring into space, yet their gift of the gab can make them front runners in any class discussions. So as long as a test requires spoken as well as written skills, they may just pass with flying colours.

Cancer

This child is really self-sufficient and can manage to get themselves up, dressed and off to school without a parent yelling their name ten times or physically dragging them out of bed. They usually have younger friends as they like to be cast in the role of teacher themselves, so if they are able to pass on any knowledge to those younger, all the better for them. They stick up for their friends and are not generally seen as the bullying type, although they get an A for emotional blackmail and that's a trait that they take with them to adulthood. They are able to give the impression that they are good at things they know nothing about, and French is likely to appeal to them. Parents must make sure they send this child on any school trips, as experience is essential to their growth. They will probably spend much of their time in the school sick bay, not because they are ill but because they have a fascination with playing doctors and nurses. Not so bad, as long as they don't take their experiments with young Joe or Joanna too far or you could have the headmaster on the phone.

They will look up to their teachers as role models and can do extremely well in their school years owing to the support that those with power feel obliged to give. Teachers don't mind explaining things properly to a Cancerian as they feel that their help and advice are really being taken in. Relationships too young can be their downfall, though, so when

Tommy tells you he's going to Russell's for after-school studying, just check he doesn't mean Rosie's house for a whole different kind of studying!

Leo

The Leo schoolchild will have a pencil case or a schoolbag with a picture of their favourite celebrity on, and they will tell everyone that they too will be as famous as their idol. Don't laugh – they probably will. They tend to develop a little too quickly, so when the aftershave or eye shadow starts to become part of their morning routine, you know it's time to rein them in before you have a horde of screaming admirers camped outside your front door every evening. They are not silly, though. They have a great deal of self-control and won't be forced to do anything that they don't want to.

They will want to wear something to school that breaks the rules and that makes them different, but if they start complaining that all of the other schoolchildren have got Gucci pencil cases, just turn a deaf ear. When they have their own money, I am sure they will be able to indulge their designer tendencies, but until then just take them down to the local shops like all their friends, or you may have to move town and schools when your next bank statement comes in.

Virgo

Don't be angry when this child comes home from school with their best friend and proceeds to get them a sandwich from the kitchen, make them their favourite drink and watch their favourite cartoons. Virgo, you see, likes to please and is one of nature's reliable second in commands. Don't underestimate them, though, as this child knows just what they want out of life and they prefer to learn from other people's mistakes. So when their best friend is trying out the latest fashions, they will be quietly watching from the sidelines to make sure that their classmates are not laughing at them. They are the sort of child whom the teacher likes to make their pet, but don't be fooled when they are asked to get the basketballs out for the sports coach, they will still make sure they do it in their own time. They are born organizers and are extremely intelligent. Once centred, they can excel in any subject that they turn their hand to.

They are more mature than most kids their age, and will usually have their eye firmly on one person whom they will admire from afar, rather than having tons of sweethearts. Their problem can often be that they make their feelings in love known too late and so by the time they speak out, the person concerned has become interested and intrigued, followed by confused and bewildered. On the other hand, you will find them in the playground counselling all their friends on their problems. Believe me, their advice is spot on, so seek them out – they could just help you turn your life round. Adults will have found they can confide in them, so their advice is worldly, even if it is second-hand.

Libra

The Libran child has a way of doing things that is highly artistic – even the way they wear their school uniform will make them appear different from other children. They are not afraid to be different in their musical tastes either, and a love of the arts could see this child asking their parents for tickets to the ballet or the opera rather than the local disco.

They are not the best eaters, so if you give them a packed lunch, make sure you don't find it stuffed down the back of the car seat after you've dropped them off. They will have plenty of admirers, but I'm afraid they tend to go for a bit of an age difference, so just make sure that the birthday party they go to when they are eleven is not full of seventeen-year-olds. Many Librans pick up their first musical instrument during their school years and don't put it down again until they are well into their eighties. Teachers will love this child but will also have to watch them like a hawk, as they tend to grow up just a little too quickly for their own good. However, once you see the sparkle in their eyes, even you will forgive them for putting that frog in your desk.

Scorpio

This schoolchild will bring home their new best friend on Monday and by Friday will have declared that they don't even know their name, as new and improved offers will have come their way from more intriguing characters. It is quite likely that they will be head of the drama club, but if they're not, then their theatrics in the classroom will be enough to keep both pupils and teachers amused through the most boring of lessons. They have the ability to make you think that they excel in subjects that they know nothing about, so when Scorpio Sophie or Simon offers you tutoring in French, then they are more than likely winging it. Bypass their offer and learn the hard way – it will save you a lot of bother in the long run.

The lucky thing is that they don't usually have much of an interest in sex during their school years. They are more interested in themselves and how they can best explore the intriguing world they find themselves living in. It's the later years when you have to worry about sex with this sign!

They do nothing by halves, and if they decide to study something, then you can be sure they will excel in it. They may even have a habit of changing their name or nicknames at various points, but don't worry – their experimental nature nearly always leads them to a life that most of us could only ever dream of, so let them be themselves. Don't try to change them; have faith.

Sagittarius

The Sagittarian child will be one of the most popular characters in the class. The children around him or her will just know that this is a person who is destined for success, and as the years ahead will prove, they are right. Sagittarians are one step ahead of their classmates in their clothes, fashions and in loving a band you have never heard of but will be the latest thing next month, so don't mock them; they remember who their friends and enemies are.

If they are not interested in a subject, then there is nothing you can do to force them to learn, but once they take aim and focus, then, like their sign of the Archer, anything is possible. They are good at sports, so don't be surprised to find them captain of the hockey or basketball team. They are competitive by nature and, luckily for their parents, are clean and neat by nature too. You should find them an asset to any class, except when they are not in the mood. Then they're the child you will see standing outside the classroom or the headmaster's office. They will talk their way out of trouble, but not as well as a water sign. This is a child who will make your school years both memorable and fun.

Capricorn

At first glance you may think that this is a lazy child, but they are anything but. They are just slow and meticulous in their work and will go to great lengths to make sure that they can be proud of their projects. They do their homework slowly. You may think that they have been playing on the computer, but check and you will soon see that they have been making sure that they can be happy with their efforts. To the Capricorn child, if a thing is worth doing, then it is worth doing well. They will have long-term plans from an early age and it is not unusual for a nine-year-old Capricorn to talk in great detail about which universities they intend applying to. As far as sports and games are concerned, they may not be first on your list to pick for your team, as by the time the teams are lining up, Capricorn is still tying his or her shoelaces.

They have quite a deep and dark sense of humour and so will be able to come out with a one-liner just when the teacher has had enough, but their sensible appearance can usually win the day and the heart of the teacher, because this sign usually knows how far is too far. Friends they make they tend to keep through their life and for good reason – this is a mate who will not let you down, even if they do take twice as long returning any favours.

Aquarius

Talk about the chatterbox of the class – this is one sign who is sure to get into trouble time and time again for speaking when they should be studying. Class discussions see them at their best and they are actually extremely bright and intelligent souls who will surprise their parents by passing exams with pretty impressive marks. They should excel in computers as this is a sign that is forward-thinking and quick to pick up anything that helps the world to move forward and communicate at a quicker pace. You might think that they aren't taking in what their teacher is saying, but how wrong you would be. They retain information like a sponge, which is a good job, given the speed with which their life moves along.

They are popular with people of all ages, and although they probably have a best friend, they will be members of numerous clubs and participate in many after-school activities. The relationships that they build up with their best friends last through thick and thin. They will not try hard in the subjects they find dull, and no amount of coaxing can talk them into studying something they don't want to follow. They don't take authority all that well and have been known to laugh at their teachers. However, get to know them and you will see there is no malice to their character, only fun. After all, to them, that is what life is about!

Pisces

Although the Piscean child is unlikely to share their games with you, they will share their packed lunch. This is a child who tends to have a selfish streak in some areas and an over-generous streak in others. They are born leaders who won't think twice about nominating themselves for prefect or class captain. They love their books too and probably frequent the library, but behind the rows of educational books they will be listening to friends' deep, dark secrets. They expect friends to remain loyal to the end, but woe betide you to ask anyone else home for tea before inviting them.

They are popular characters, but in rare instances they can be idle and arrogant, which must be nipped in the bud. They can bully too, but usually on behalf of someone else whom they feel is being picked on. They are more than aware of the opposite sex and know just how to wind them up. They are born dramatists, but don't be fooled, as that book on Shakespeare that they have under their arm is probably hiding the latest steamy novel. They are clever and business-minded, and if they can motivate themselves in business studies, they can earn the money they dream of. The key word for this water sign is dream, as they are capable of losing a whole afternoon thinking about their fantasies; but then again, some of the biggest success stories in the world chased merely a dream in the beginning, didn't they?

Chapter 6

MUMS AND DADS

Who is the person who brought us into the world, and who do we most commonly turn to when we have a problem? Our mum, of course. However, the relationship between mother and child is often a difficult one. The path is fraught with tensions and differences, which can eventually become a reversed relationship in which the mother becomes the child and the child becomes the mother. So here's your guide to getting the best from your mum through understanding her star sign.

We'll also take a look at Dad to see if you can find the man behind the boy. Just like mothers, fathers shape who we grow up to be, but the importance of Dad often doesn't hit home until our later years. While Mum teaches us the basics in life, a father's job can be more complex. Although many men raise their children and do just the same things that a mother does, for many of us it's not until we start getting involved in relationships that we look back to see what our own father did and didn't do. If our father treated our mother with respect, it can give us a sense of pride about who we are, while if a father was absent or a negative influence, it can leave us lost. By understanding how each sign deals with the role of being a dad, you can learn to appreciate why they did and didn't do certain things when you were growing up. It will hopefully allow you to form a better relationship with them.

Aries

Mum

Your Aries mother is quite a character. She has a strong and somewhat diverse personality and probably won't be averse to the odd tipple every now and then, although this is a fact she will not admit willingly to her children! Being ruled by Mars, the planet of change and unpredictability, she will constantly manage to surprise you. Red is her colour and one she will wear when she is going into battle. You'll know if she has this colour on that she means business. Let's just hope it's not you she's ordered a face-to-face with or you're likely to be in for a real tongue-lashing or dressing-down. You have to be aware that this is a mother who is expected to and is allowed to go over the top every now and then. You'll never be able to say that life with this woman is boring. Just be sure to let her know that you love her. She may not be able to admit it as readily as you would like, but she will expect loyalty from her children. What you may not have realized in the beginning, but will learn as life teaches you its lessons, is that this is one mother who would go to war for you. The world had better watch out, as she's likely to win too! Her advice will never be typical of the average mother, but she'll allow you to live your own life. She doesn't want to know all the finer details, though, so you'd be better off telling her the advice you want is for a friend. She'll know it's for you, but it's the only way she won't pull her punches. She is an asset to any child's life, even if the road is at times somewhat bumpy and unpredictable!

And what about Dad?

The Aries father is not like having a dad but is more like having a best friend. You see, he never grows up. This is all very well when you are young, but as you get older, it could become something of an embarrassment. He may think it's cool to join you on the dance floor; you, I think, will not. Be kind to him, as he really is only a child at heart. His life has never gone to plan but will always have been fun, and if he has raised his children, then he is sure to have made a lot of sacrifices in his personal freedom along the way. You are sure to hear him talking about the grand plans he had but never carried out. Whatever you want to do, he's sure to have done in his adventure days. The more time you spend with him, the more you will get to understand him. He doesn't mean to let you down, but his mouth runs away with him and he makes promises because he knows they make you happy. He is not always able to do what he wants to, as life and the adventures he is always finding seem to interfere. The best way to keep a positive relationship with him is to remember that he is really the child and you will always be the adult!

Taurus

Mum

Although your Taurean mother is more likely to give you beans on toast than cordon bleu cooking, you will never be able to say that you were not fed well. She knows how to make a home a home. Unlike some of the more fanatically clean signs, such as Virgo, the Taurean mum is only intent on making the abode a place you can relax in. She will put love and care into your life and is likely to favour pastel shades in her home, such as pale blues, greens and pinks, which all fall under her rulership's colours. She won't approve of the bright clothing you wear and will want you to promise to be honest with her about what is going on in your life. She wants you to feel comfortable and considers her belongings, pets and children her responsibility, especially when things go wrong. This is the kind of mother you will run home to for chicken soup and ice cream after a break-up, as she'll have the remedies to make you feel safe and secure again. You may want to tuck a bottle of wine under your arm if you're returning home, though, as mother Bulls like a drop or two of the old vino and that wine collection for cooking is likely to have seen the inside of more glasses than it will have cooking pans. She'll know that red wine goes with red meat and white wine with fish and white meat, so be sure to advise any suitors who may be coming round to pick the right colour – it's sure to be noted by Mum.

No matter how old you get, you will always be her child. Allow her this pleasure and indulge her; it's likely to have been her life's dream to raise a family, and being ruled by Venus she's sure to have had a few personal struggles on the way, so appreciate this gem of a woman. She really is an amazing asset to your life.

And what about Dad?

We've all seen those fathers who run for cover as soon as their kids' friends enter the house. That can't have been a Taurean dad, though, for he will go out of his way to show visitors how warm and welcoming his home is. Even if friends have eaten before they've come round, they'd better be prepared for seconds, as Taurus will be setting an extra place before they've managed to get their coats off. He is, however, very old-fashioned as far as values are concerned, so even though he may dance around with you to your favourite tunes, you can forget wearing the latest clothes if he deems them too short, too flashy or too garish. Others can dress like that, but not a child of his. Often red-faced from a little too much vino with his dinner, he's not averse to falling asleep in his favourite armchair. He will want to play sports with you, but would rather watch them and will flirt with friends without thinking. There's no harm in it, even if it can prove a little embarrassing; he just has a playful nature. Fantastic as a grandfather too and probably better, as he's had the chance to learn from mistakes he made the first time round!

Gemini

Mum

The Gemini mother is very individual to say the least, and you must not take offence if at some point she has given you the impression that you are standing in the way of her career, her love life or her dreams. You see, this is the woman who wants it all and is capable of having it all too. She is a clever soul who is able, when in the right state of mind, to juggle kids, career and numerous other responsibilities. Many women of this sign work from home and are able to do so very well. Buy her some daffodils – yellow is her colour and is sure to make her smile. She loves to travel, so expect to find yourself with more house moves than the average family if Mum has her way. She loves excitement and may even get excited about the prospect of a drama in your life, which she will try with the best of intentions to take over for you so that she can sort out what has gone wrong. She will by no means be your usual mother, but will have given you an alternative view of life that will equip you very well for life's unpredictabilities. Children of a Gemini mother are often only too happy to marry young and quickly, just to get a bit of peace and quiet and predictability, but what you don't realize is that she will instil in even the most staid of signs a thirst for excitement that will prove almost impossible not to chase every now and then.

And what about Dad?

I can't promise that you will like the way your Gemini dad dresses. In fact it's common for embarrassed children and partners of this sign to buy them clothes for birthdays, Christmas and in fact any occasion they can think of. This is a father who has really lived life, and what you know about him when you reach your thirties will shed a new light on him. He's not just a sign who has talked about travel and change but has most likely done it too. He made money and lost it, and he may even have had two marriages. When he's strict, he's a nightmare and to stand up against his wishes would be a foolish move indeed. When he's feeling liberal, then you can get away with more than any other sign of the zodiac would dream possible. Race him for the phone too – if he picks it up when your friends call, you're likely to get cramp holding out your arm waiting for him to stop talking and pass it to you. Word of warning: you may think that you can tell him everything and that he has an open mind, and he has, apart from when his children are taking unnecessary risks!

Cancer

Mum

The Cancerian mother may as well have been taken straight from *Little House on the Prairie*. She is a born carer and knows just how to speak to children and how to raise them with love and understanding. What better way to show her this than to buy her some of her favourite flowers? Acanthus, carnations, lilies, water lilies, geraniums, white roses and white flowers in general are all perfect for this mum. Her lucky colours are smoky grey and silvery blue, which will often form part of her make-up and clothing. She doesn't always dress like the average mum, though, and sometimes her choice in clothing can leave a little to be desired. Some of your friends may even whisper behind her back that she is mutton dressed up as lamb, but to me and to you she should just be called funky and very loving with it too. Cry and she will cry with you; be naughty and she will emotionally blackmail you, leaving you with a sense of guilt that you will take with you to future relationships and may well lead you to choose signs who are colder than the norm just to give yourself a break from the heavy-duty emotions that form part of life with a Cancerian mum. She will try to cook, but look in the bin and you're likely to see some ready-meal packages hidden there. Get used to pasta – it's probably a firm favourite if you are under her roof! Oh, and run for cover on full moons, as she's likely to say and do things that aren't pretty.

And what about Dad?

This is a father who doesn't need to raise a hand to make you see right from wrong. He uses emotional blackmail like a professional and can make you feel bad about things you haven't even done yet. His clothing can be a little old-fashioned, although he is sure to swear that what he dons has come back round. It has, but it's been and gone again too. He doesn't like getting older and will probably prefer for you to call him by his first name. When he was young, he wished his life away, and as he embarked on adulthood and parenthood he realized he had not taken the time to relish the joys of youth. He will love to hear what you've been up to and will take great joy in trying to make your dreams become a reality. He will invest his own savings and the family's finances into giving you the best start, even if it means going behind your mother's back! He expects his family to be a family and can't stand rifts or problems, even though there will be at least a dozen faces in his circle whom he can't stand due to one drama or another. Show him respect and he'll do anything for you, but don't laugh at him it's taken him a lot of self-confidence to get where he is, even though he pretends otherwise.

Leo

Mum

Being ruled by the sun, this is a woman who will know how to bring sunshine into her children's lives. Want to go and stay at your friend's house? Forget it – all your friends will want to come round to yours once they have met your mother. Reds, yellows and oranges are all colours that she will be attracted to, so you can bet her kitchen is a burst of colour and activity. Red walls are a favourite in this her most lived-in room. She is not, however, as confident as she makes out, so be sure to give her plenty of praise. She has struggled to get where she is, and no matter how well she has done, she will never feel that she has lived up to what she deems to be a perfect mother. Many women of this sign have problems with their relationship with their own mother and spend years comparing and questioning where they went wrong. Be careful they don't spend your childhood trying to correct your grandparents' failings. Let her know she's doing fine and work as a team. Family to her is a unit, and by working together you'll be able to take on the world. With her by your side there is no vision that is not attainable. She will also often talk about how she wanted one more baby – you see, Leos always feel that their family should be large, and no matter whether there's one child or several, her mind will be turning over what one more would have meant to her brood!

And what about Dad?

You're lucky enough to have a father who won't mind doing the things that a mum should do. In fact many Leo fathers are better housewives than their partners. They are perfection-ists in many respects and firmly believe that if you want a job done well, then you should do it yourself. He has worked hard and will expect his children to do the same. You will be given jobs and responsibilities from an early age, though your pocket money will be among the lowest in your class. He will know where his own upbringing went wrong, and he is more open to talking about it than most fathers, as he probably spent so long trying to come to terms with it when he was your age. He wants to be fit and healthy, but it is not uncommon for men of this sign to have a sports injury that stops them from indulging in all they desire with their children. Although he will allow you to have friends, he will want to have a hand in choosing which ones you hang out with. You can tell who he approves and disapproves of as some friends are kept waiting on the doorstep and others are sitting watch-ing TV with him when you are called down. Strict but caring are the key words for this father. You'll certainly always re-member that he was there for you, but you may not like the way he did things. Nevertheless you'll have to agree that he got the family where they needed to be in the end!

Virgo

Mum

Your Virgo mother is incredibly picky, and no matter who your friends are and what their parents do, they are never going to be good enough for your mum. If something gets broken when your parents are away for the weekend and you confess it was you, then Mum will still decide it was one of your friends and ban them. You are expected to do brilliantly in life, and if she can afford private education, then she will. If you can have links with the medical profession, then even better. She loves her home and her family, and will have proud pictures dotted around showing your achievements. Greens and dark browns are what she favours in furniture – nothing bright and garish. She will expect you to behave well when she takes you out and to have manners. If you don't want to have the life that she has planned for you, then be prepared for confrontation. The key is to let her know what makes you happy rather than doing things to please her. By doing this, you can save years of arguments. You've got to love her, though; she'd sell her most prized possession to make you happy and has spent her whole life wanting you, so communication is the key to getting the best from this very special and individual union.

And what about Dad?
The poor old Virgo dad thinks he knows his children so well and will go out of his way to make sure their lives are successful. Due to the fact that children learn from an early age not to tell Dad everything, the Virgo dad never of course really knows what his children are up to. The crafty kids of this parent will have managed to blame friends for the things they got up to over the years, and if they are clever will have learnt to twist him round their little finger. You are expected to do well because he wants you to succeed where he failed. If he sends you for extra homework lessons, then dig out his old school report from the attic and you'll see your tuition is in the very subjects he failed at when he was a child. Communication is essential or you will end up making choices that he has bullied or emotionally manipulated you into making.

Family holidays are likely to become a little boring as he'll make you all stick to the places that he liked ten years ago. This can be embarrassing if you invite your boyfriend or girlfriend along on a family trip later in life, only to realize that the karaoke machine in the hotel bar already has your family's favourite song up and ready for you all to sing, just as other families are making for the door. He doesn't have to know everything; he only has to know you are happy. You just have to learn to let him think he's in control.

Libra

Mum

The lovely Libran mum makes one of the best parents in the zodiac and you can bet that every problem you have had in your life she has taken on as her own, even when you didn't want her to! Shades of blue, pale green and pink are the colours that come under her rulership, and one of these is more than likely to be the colour she chooses to paint her most important room in the house, which is more often than not the bedroom. Librans have style and class, so try to treat her with respect. Bad language doesn't impress her, nor does impulsive spending. You may think it's OK to spend all your money on an item you've only seen a few minutes ago in a shop window, but tell her you've been thinking about it for months and she'll be highly impressed. She is one of the few mums in the zodiac who likes to listen to music around the home more than she does the telly. She's also pretty good with plants, and roses in particular should be something she will be able to cultivate with expertise. There is always the exception to the rule of course, but it's part of her make-up to have a natural tendency to green fingers. Washing and ironing are not a problem for her. However, her personal life sees emotions running very deep indeed. Help her to find the comedic value of problems and life and you'll find a mum who becomes your best friend, who will always listen and never judge you but always support you.

And what about Dad?

There is no other dad like a Libran dad; in fact they don't come much better. Here is a man who will take on the role of mother, father and best friend. He will make sure that whatever problem you have in life he is there with the right words to get you through. No matter what comes your way in life, with a Libran dad to guide you through you will find the confidence to make a success of things. The only trouble comes when you find out as you get older that he didn't really know everything. This can be devastating for many children, until you decide to take him off his pedestal and allow him to become a human being in your eyes. If you want something from the Libran dad, all you need to do is hit an emotional chord. He will spend his life giving you what he never had and telling you about his adventures. They may sound like fun, but underneath there will always be a word of warning attached to these stories, as he finds it hard to get straight to the point about any really delicate issues. Don't be angry with him when you find out that he couldn't give you all he wanted to. He'd give his Lucy or Lenny the world on a silver platter if he had the power to, as I'm sure you'll realize by the time you have children of your own!

Scorpio

Mum

Scorpio mothers are like no other; in fact they really are one in a million. You will find her both your best friend and a major headache. Her colours are deep reds and maroons, and these are usually the colours of lipstick she will choose when she's feeling confident in the world. Her drawers at home are sure to be crammed full. Above all this is a woman who likes mystery, and even if she tells you she doesn't expect you to tell her what is going on in your life, she will do everything in her power to work out what makes you tick. Don't forget her birthday, and don't make alternative plans for Christmas. This is her time and she will pull out all the stops to make sure you have fun. She would rather you bring your friends round than not see you during these important dates. Think *Ab Fab* and you will conjure up a vision of your Scorpio mum. When she wants to make an effort, she can look like a movie star, but that odd combination of clothing she wears at the school gates, with designer handbag, flip-flops and a heavy coat, means she has left in a hurry as she was busy planning a surprise in your honour. Love has no boundaries for her; she will go to the ends of the earth for you, even if you are the one who is in the wrong. You may, if she is particularly eccentric, have to get her to wait round the corner for you to save embarrassment, but when you get there, expect to find your mates deep in conversation with her. They'll love her and wish she was their mum, and you'll be glad she's yours, as you'll have no doubt her heart is in the right place.

And what about Dad?

The Scorpio father is heaven and hell at the same time as he makes you feel proud yet embarrassed, free yet restricted. He gives with one hand and takes away with the other because he always stretches himself slightly further than he can afford. If he can send you to private school, he will. He will try to educate you in the matters he has managed to blag his way through all of his life. He understands that his children, unless they are of the same sign, are not as blessed with intuitive skills as he is. He can strike a bargain and will make sure the home is a home, albeit an unusual one. Holidays will be fun and to unexpected places, and arguments will not be uncommon, but the making-up will prove to you that he is never too embarrassed to say he was wrong. He's a good judge of character and will be able to predict accurately which of your friends will let you down. He will also be able to spot the perfect suitor for you. Don't be afraid to listen to his advice; many people would pay for such words of wisdom!

Sagittarius

Mum

The Archer of the zodiac is a very ambitious sign, so to have had children would have been a sacrifice in her life no matter how maternal she is. Appreciate this fact by letting her know how able she is not just as a mother but as a person too. Strong colours such as rich purples and dark blues suit her. She won't be a stay-at-home mum and will like to get out for at least one night a week if she has her way. Don't chastise her for it: she'll be a better mum for being able to go out and let off some steam.

She is not predictable, so don't expect to be able to second-guess what she will say or do, but she will make sure she finds out the right school and the right clubs for you to belong to, and with the contacts that she makes in life she will ensure you jump any waiting lists. You represent her and so it is imperative that you do well. The funny thing with the Sagittarian mum is that she's very protective of you up until your teenage years but then she seems to see you as more of an individual and will often allow you free rein to make choices that other mothers in the zodiac wouldn't dare give to their children. She may not spend twenty-four seven with you, but they do say quality is better than quantity and that's just what you'll get with this very beautiful and able sign who will talk to you as an equal from the minute you take your first breath.

And what about Dad?

The Sagittarian dad wants to spend more time with his family, but also knows that his career is essential to the financial stability of his loved ones. That is why he finds it so hard not to put work before his children, something that takes many children years to come to terms with. His reasoning is quite simple: he makes the money; the family do well. It is not until later in life, when he has realized that success doesn't taste as sweet as he had hoped, that he learns to value the simple things in life. He is not predictable and you can expect to move house more than the average family, but you're sure to learn a lot from this impulsive and very fun sign.

This is also one dad who is willing to play sports with his children, at any age. He is naturally fit and will probably go on to beat your friends and his grandchildren. Don't ask too many questions about his past, though – he tends to make up what hasn't happened as he wants his children to believe only the very best about him.

Capricorn

Mum

A Capricorn mother may have been hard going at times, but I bet that you appreciate it now, don't you? She likes a routine and will have set a bedtime that your other friends will have laughed at, but just look at where you are in your career now compared with them. The colours she usually likes around her are dark green, grey, brown and black. You may think this sounds boring, but the most unusual combination of clothing works for her. She's not great at talking and so if you've had a problem, you're more likely to find a note in your bedroom asking for a truce than you are to have a debate round the kitchen table. She loves her family so much that it's sometimes too much and she can't deal with the bigger issues. This is where a third family member usually comes in handy to be her go-between and pass messages back and forth. Don't expect always to get to school on time, as she can be a little slow at gathering herself together, although she does of course embrace a routine once it is established. She likes younger children, and the older you get, the harder it will be for her to let you go. The dummy in the five-year-old's mouth is probably there because the Capricorn mother allowed it to be, but show her that you'll still be home for the Sunday roast even when you've left home and she'll let you go. She just can't bear the thought of not seeing her nearest and dearest on a regular basis; they're what makes her whole.

And what about Dad?

This is a father who can be testing, as he speaks before he listens and tries too hard to be a dad before being a friend. This is all very well, but unless he knows who his child is as an individual, he is going to have a hard time working out what is right and what is wrong for them in life. It is not unusual for this sign to want to live in the town they were brought up in, and I have in fact known several clients who have raised their children in the same house where they grew up.

He loves his family deeply and wants you all to work as a unit. This can often mean giving up or changing arrangements to fit in with what he deems to be 'family time'. He's not great at playing the dual role if he is a single parent, as he needs a mother to balance out and play the parts he can't. This is a time when things can really break down and he should enlist the help of family or friends. Trying to do it all is a recipe for disaster for this loving and somewhat old-fashioned sign.

He will probably have hated the way his parents raised him and yet he will fall into the trap of following the same rules;

it's inbuilt in him. As you grow up, you're unlikely to be given freedom as early as your friends, but this is only because he knows from his youth what dangerous ground romance and relationships can lead you to. He was probably the worst culprit of the lot. Learn to love his dry humour; it's seen him and will see you through many a crisis in life!

Aquarius

Mum

Air-sign mothers talk too much and you may even have been embarrassed as a kid when she spent more time talking to your mates than you did. I bet you appreciate it now, though, as this is a woman who will be a mother and a friend all rolled into one. Her colours are electric blue and turquoise, and she can often have really piercing blue eyes. Spare some time to sit down and talk to your Aquarian mum. She tells the whole world how proud she is of you and probably even carries something in her handbag from your childhood. She lives her own life, but what you don't realize is that the base for her whole existence was and still is you. She was probably a little wild in her younger days and you were the saving grace that helped her to become a better person.

She will talk about the past as if she were talking about a third party and is sure to have embarked on some travels that even the most courageous of men would never have under-taken. She's also likely to be far fitter than the other mums around you, as she can't bear the thought of not feeling the air in her lungs and living life to the full.

And what about Dad?

He can walk the walk, but can he talk the talk? is a question many children end up asking themselves about the Aquarian dad. He loves you with all of his heart, but he has a hard time showing it. He's too busy trying to make the perfect life for his family, who mean the whole world to him. Part of his problem is that he tries to spread himself too thinly. He thinks of work when he's at home and he just wants to get home to his family when he's stuck in the office. He can't do a normal job and neither can he work regular hours. When he's at home, you'll be sick of him, and when he's away, you'll miss him.

As you grow up, the Aquarian dad can turn out to be one of the best friends you'll have in life. After all, he knows more about you than anybody else and he's shared some of your most important experiences too. He's always young at heart and will probably know more of the latest tunes than you do. Just don't lie to him: he can't stand a liar, and once you break the trust with the Aquarian father, it can take years to regain that closeness.

Pisces

Mum

This is the most intriguing of all the signs in the zodiac and is even more dramatic than Scorpio (if that's possible). This is one mother whom your schoolfriends will still be talking about years on – agony aunt, best friend, sparring partner, the lot. Soft shades of green are her colours, and may even be the colour of her favourite sofa. She hates not being acknowledged, so if you have friends round, make sure they knock on her door to say 'hi' or they will be out of favour and out of your life within the week. She has a heart of gold and will turn heads wherever she goes, even now. You admire her and are embarrassed by her but wouldn't change her for the world.

If you go shopping together, she will barter as if she is in a market, and that's just in Marks & Spencer. Tell her something doesn't fit and she'll have it bagged and in front of the manager within the hour. She expects quality and enjoys sitting round a dining-room table with family, but not necessarily to eat her home-cooked food. She won't mind ordering in – it's the social aspect that appeals to her. Arguments will be colourful and loud, but the good times will be the best of your life. Just get some earplugs; she's likely to have the TV volume up louder than any teenager you know, even when she's sleeping. She needs the distraction to stop her imagination working overtime and interfering with her sleep. Boring never, unpredictable always, loving guaranteed!

And what about Dad?

There will be times when you want to push your Piscean father into the room first to represent you, and there will be times when you want to run for cover and deny any family link whatsoever. He likes things the way he likes them and has an imagination that could win him a prize for storytelling. You will have to accept, though, that he has a life outside his family too, usually a career or a hobby. He has to, for this is a man with so much energy that he has to put some of it elsewhere or you'd all go stir-crazy. If he did well at school, it was through sheer cheek and through sticking at things, and he is likely to have excelled in subjects that surprise your friends. He's not afraid to argue in public, and if you find a friend no longer calls you, it's likely to be due to the fact that your father has let them know what he really thinks of them! You will love him and hate him throughout your life, but you will know deep down that he will always be there for you when it really counts.

Chapter 7

PERFECT PRESENTS

Just what should you be buying your partner this festive season, or at any time of the year for that matter? Well, find out how to stay in the good books of your loved ones and to receive praise and attention from your family or even those you fancy with my indispensable guide to gifts for the signs of the zodiac.

Aries

For him

This is a man who craves excitement and really loves the unexpected, so don't go for the predictable. The look on his face will let you know if he doesn't approve of what you've bought him. Words will not be necessary, believe me; in fact he will never say he doesn't like a gift – it's not in his kind nature – but his expression will reveal all.

He would probably prefer a night out to remember rather than a new pair of socks. Many musicians are born under this sign, so why not think about music lessons? You could well uncover a talent he never knew he had! If you want to go for an aftershave, then choose something slightly different; he will hate it if everyone can guess the scent he is wearing, as he likes to keep a certain air of mystique. His ruling planet, Mars, is the planet of change and unpredictability, so why not give him a ticket to a mystery destination? The guessing will drive him wild and he is such an easygoing character that it doesn't have to cost you the earth; it is simply the fun of not knowing that will impress him. Tank-driving or flying lessons or a day at Brands Hatch will also win you favour, so get thinking and planning, and remember, make it different – that's what counts!

For her

This woman will want you to do something that will prove to her how much she means to you and how she is differ-ent from the rest. To buy her something that a friend owns just because she said she liked it would simply be insult-ing. Instead you are going to have to come up with a gift that she wants but hasn't mentioned. An unusual piece of art by someone she admires would be good, but if you are thinking of jewellery, then I have a word of warning for you: don't even think about buying costume jewellery, as she'll be getting it valued within the week and will not take kindly to a gesture that makes her feel cheap. You would be far better off spending your hard-earned money on a dozen red roses rather than a cheap ring. She can't help but sneak a look at the price tag; it's part of her inquisitive nature.

Flowers are a success with this woman, but you may want to think long term and invest in a nice plant. Again, though, it would have to be something different, so that she can talk to friends about it and impress them when they come round for one of the many social occasions that this woman likes to hold. Don't go for anything too boring. If she needs a new set of knives or saucepans, then believe me, she will buy them herself, so don't even bother looking in the kitchen shops.

Taurus

For him

He may not be aware of it, but he has a thing for leather. The perfect present for him could be a leather belt, leather gloves, leather wallet or even a leather jacket. I must stress, however, that it should be real leather and nothing fake; this man will know the difference and will think you are showing your true feelings for him if you put anything fake his way. Arguments could follow. He is a very sexy soul and so a nice piece of underwear would be successful, but I am afraid that being an earth sign, it is going to have to be practical. If he says he won't wear boxers, then don't try to change him. Chances are that he will never be forced into them and he is sure to have some very logical reason as to why they are not for him. A nice address book would also be good to help organize his life, but choose a hard cover, not a soft one – he will plan on keeping it for years if he has taken the time to write all of his important numbers into it. Oh, and if you want to go for an aftershave, then choose something musky. It's the only smell he'll put on; any others will just be worn to please you.

For her

The Taurean woman is passionate, with a discerning eye for both the elegant and the beautiful, so it is leather for her. Why not go for a leather skirt or a nice leather purse that she can keep all of her essentials in? Make sure it's 100 per cent leather – no mixes or fakes for this woman. She will also appreciate anything that can help her keep up her beauty regime, so if you can find a foot spa or a massage machine, then get it. You too can share in the pleasures of a gift like this, and it could even lead to romance if you throw some candles into the shopping basket. She loves food but is prone to putting on weight, so if you go for chocolates or champagne, then choose quality over quantity. Even better, buy some chocolate body paint. It's sure to provide you both with some very interesting memories. If it's your auntie, mother or sister you're shopping for, then stick to slippers. These home bodies love their abode and will get plenty of use out of them. (Their old ones are sure to have holes in the soles!) Chanel No. 5 is the most popular perfume with a Taurean woman, so why not buy a bottle of this scent, and perhaps get the body lotion too? The Bull loves to spoil herself and body creams are a luxury that's sure to earn any extra Brownie points you may have been seeking.

Gemini

For him

This is the man who is known to be the biggest flirt in the zodiac and so you may be a little resistant to the idea of buying anything that will help him in his exploits. Believe me, though, there is nothing better than to show him you trust him, so don't be afraid of buying him the new shirt that he is likely to have dropped a million hints about owning. Bear in mind that he is dress-conscious and has a mind of his own, so don't choose things that he has not seen or commented on; it will only prove embarrassing for you when you have to march it back down to the shop and change it for him, which he will not hesitate to ask you to do. If you know he really needs clothing, it would be far better to give him a voucher so that he can choose for himself. The latest electric tooth-brush would also be good for a Gemini man – he never stops talking so is unlikely to find the time to use a manual toothbrush. Music also appeals to him, but once again listen for the hints. His tastes are alternative to say the least and what you think he will love he may well hate!

For her

This is a woman who is likely to get some very varied gifts on birthdays and at Christmas, and this is because people see her in so many different lights. She loves to come across as businesslike and wouldn't mind something like a leather briefcase, or better still a designer one, so that those she meets will know she means business and is a professional woman. If you've got the cash, then go for a laptop; she'll love it and love you for buying it for her. A mobile phone could cost you a small fortune if you agree to foot the bill, so why not get right to her roots, because if she really values you she will prefer something personal and slightly sentimental. A small piece of antique jewellery would be a perfect choice. So would a diary or address book that you have somehow had person-alized, or even a framed picture of a memory that you have shared together.

A word of warning: if you're married to the woman, don't just give her money; she won't appreciate it. You see, it's far too impersonal and she will also end up spending it on others instead of herself. The best present of all for a Gemini woman is to make the effort to get on with her friends, who are certain to be a mixed bunch, and give her a happy Christmas to remember.

Cancer

For him

He is romantic, so the thought counts far more than the gift for this man. It doesn't really have to be a big or expensive present, but it should be something that looks as if you have put a lot of time and thought into it. What you buy depends on what his interests and hobbies are. You see, the Cancer man will have hobbies that he discovered years ago that remain a passion. He doesn't discover a new interest every day, so you will have to try to find a gadget he hasn't yet got for a skill that he probably thinks he perfected long ago. Most men born under the sign of Cancer are DIY enthusiasts, or at least like to think they are. Many are keen gardeners too, so there should be an idea in that for you to look into. Fishing and golfing are another possibility, so why not arrange a holiday that has places for him to indulge in his favourite pastimes as well as the romance that is so important to anyone born under Cancer? This very emotional sign would also appreciate a picture of someone he cares for, but don't be fooled – you'll have to put it in a very expensive, top-class frame or you may find yourself getting the cold shoulder, as he will think you should surely know better than to give him something half done.

For her

This is a woman who loves to pamper herself and a set of expensive bath oils are sure to meet with her approval. Be careful about going for face masks, though; she may think you don't believe she is beautiful enough for you already. A gift for her house or flat would be appreciated, or anything decorative to hang on the wall; a clock would be good as she's always running late both personally and professionally. A new duvet cover should go down well, and you may even get the chance to experience your new gift with her for being so thoughtful!

If it is a family member that you are buying for, then why not have a piece of jewellery that has been handed down made into her size? This emotional sign reads deeply into everything and will know that you think the world of her to give her something with an important memory or meaning attached to it. Also choose a card with meaning, as she will read the words more than once.

You may want to buy her favourite song on CD or MP3.

She is not as free with her own money as she is with others' and she will probably have a stack of albums she is dying to hear again, so pick up a copy of her favourite hits. It's sure to be an artist from yesteryear!

Leo

For him

This is a man who won't mind if you spend money on things that other guys would deem feminine. You see, Leo men really are in touch with their feminine side and are not afraid to look after themselves. Some skin products by trusted companies such as Aveda or Clinique will go down very well indeed. You may also want to consider a day out at a beauty salon. This is a man who probably has very good skin, hair and nails, and so he will show an interest in a gift that helps keep him in tiptop condition. The Leo male is a natural flirt and anything that helps him look better is sure to stroke that ego of his. He often has a fetish for shoes, so why not invest in a new pair that he has seen? A shoe-care kit or a quality set of shoehorns will not be laughed at by the Lion. He also loves his sleep, so pick up a nice pillow for him to dream away on. There are plenty of good ones on the market that are sure to do the job. If you choose an aftershave, make it light and lemony. He won't like anything too heavy.

For her

This is a woman you don't want to upset, so think very carefully before investing your money on just anything for her. Lesson number one is that you shouldn't break the bank on a present for her: she can't stand people who mishandle their finances, even though she is probably lousy with money herself. She loves to look good and will not turn her nose up at a designer jumper to keep warm this winter. The latest hair products could be a good idea too. She will not want to part with her own cash for them but won't mind you doing so on her behalf. She loves to change her look, so don't choose anything that is dated.

She will not like anything that is too difficult to work out, so forget puzzles or presents that she has to put together herself. Keep life simple for her and she will keep you in laughter and joy with her infectious sense of humour. A funny video or a movie that she deems a classic would go down well, and if it's perfume you're wanting to buy, then pick something that is happy and summery to go with the image she likes to portray to the world. Make it a well-known and expensive brand, so she can tell all her friends!

Virgo

For him

This man will probably already have a list of the presents he would like, how much they are and what shops they are available from. Take it, but then throw it out of the window and take this one with you instead. These are men who like to think they are in control but really they need looking after, as they are only little boys at heart and need to be loved and nurtured. Buy the Virgo man something that will show him you are around for more than just a day: underneath that confident exterior he is actually a very fragile character and lacks self-confidence more than you would ever imagine.

He loves a good book, but preferably something based on fact so he can talk about it afterwards. Buy him stuff for the upkeep of his health and you'll be making a rod for your own back, as he is also a hypochondriac. You could go for vitamins so he knows you care. Satin bedcovers could be a winner if you've got the nerve, or maybe a throw or rug with an earthy pattern or animal design, but don't go too wild – he likes natural, not bizarre!

For her

Like the Virgo man, the Virgo woman thinks she knows what she wants, though she doesn't have a clue. You see, she really needs pampering but she will think she wants to be organized and so while the new Filofax or latest mobile could be on Santa's list, you may want to head instead for the lingerie department and pamper her rotten. She'll never do it herself. This earthy sign of the zodiac will want to know that you are serious about her and so you will need to buy something that you can both use over the years but that also signals coupledom or family values. If you do give in and buy her a phone, make sure it's pay as you go: this sign could run up a bill that could well bankrupt you – she is the agony aunt of the zodiac and will use any means possible to counsel and put the world to rights. She needs to learn to relax and so a weekend at a beauty spa would hit the right buttons. Just check her diary for free dates – this is a woman who has plans right up until 2012, but will never stick to them. She's a born organizer of others, but unfortunately not very good at organizing herself.

Libra

For him

This man is addictive and so rather than just buying one gift for him, you will feel like buying several. You'll need to make a plan so that you don't break the bank, and remember that you don't have to spend a fortune to show a Libran you love him. Invest, if you can afford it, in a piece of artwork; this is a sign that will love anything that is beautiful and they are often budding artists themselves. Whatever you buy your Libran man must look good, so forget spending a fortune if you don't have wrapping paper to match. If he has shown any interest in music, then look to a guitar; he should have a natural talent for it. Don't go for anything louder, he may just have a contradictory aspect and could end up driving you round the bend playing the bongos badly!

The air elements love to talk to friends about the gifts they have received, so do yourself a favour and get something you and he can be proud of. If you don't buy him a present he can show off, he will sulk for days or even weeks. The Libran man likes to look and feel good, so go for a scent that is classy not cheap, or he may just decide to wear the image you've painted him with!

For her

The Libran woman is going to need something that epito-mizes good style and taste. She loves to wear nice clothes. Why not go for a small item by her favourite designer? She will not tolerate anything that she deems tacky and would rather go without than be embarrassed by something that she believes to be so obviously not her. She will also appreciate a meal out at her favourite restaurant. Flowers are a good choice, or an unusual plant – unusual being the key word; don't let her think you see her in the same light as everyone else. Taking her to an exhibition by her favourite artist would also be good, or a concert, or buying her an album by her favourite band; this woman is no wallflower, at least not if you really know her.

Underwear is only worth getting if you are willing to spend the money, and forget about perfume unless you are prepared to go for the real thing. Eau de toilette is just that to her, as past friends and loves are sure to tell you. The sure winner for this very exhilarating air sign, though, has got to be a new coat. She never stays in for long and is bound to need a new one for the adventures her life takes her on.

Scorpio

For him

This man, you will have to admit, has alternative tastes. What he loved last year he will hate this year. You will know what he is into as it will dominate his life and you may have trouble finding something he has not already got, because when he does something, he gives it 100 per cent. He is not afraid to spend money, yours or his. Steady on the drink as a gift: he doesn't handle alcohol too well, and if you buy him champagne, it really is a gamble whether you'll end up with him laughing or crying on your shoulder. Your best bet for him is some new undies, but check his size; he'll be devastated if they're too small and insulted if they're too big. If you can find something different and unusual, then buy it; he will hate to be the same as others and you'll wish you'd got it when it's disappeared from the shelf, only to find he bought it himself on one of his many shopping trips.

For her

This woman will know what she wants you to buy her, but forget asking – she'll expect you to guess from the very confused signals she's been giving since January. The best idea is to take her away for Christmas and really blow her mind. You see, she will believe that you can't pull the wool over her eyes, so it is all or nothing if you want to surprise her. Don't drop hints: she'll only imagine something you can't afford or couldn't possibly have organized in time. This is a lovely woman but one who will expect the best, so go for a piece of jewellery that you know she will value. She'll keep it with her for life and it will be well worth the investment.

A word of warning: don't buy lots of little things. She already has cupboards full of rubbish she's been hoarding and meaning to throw out. Nice cushions that she can lie about on would be a good idea. If you imagine a harem or a den of iniquity, then you'd be thinking along the right lines – only in terms of colours of course! She will love you to buy her something that makes her feel sexy; the way that others view her is more important to her than you can imagine. If you want to go for alcohol, don't go for a case of red wine, just one good bottle. She doesn't know the word 'limit', but is all too familiar with the word 'excess'!

Sagittarius

For him

The latest computer program could be spot on for this man. If he doesn't have a computer, then think about sending him on a course. He will also appreciate anything that can help him speed his journey to success, and self-help books are something that he may be too embarrassed to buy himself but is sure to appreciate from you. In fact if you look at the latest novels, then you would be on the right track. Wrap up a range of the latest blockbusters, but be warned it will probably only take him a week to read the lot. This man adores life and loves to work and play hard.

Book a table at a nice restaurant, but make sure it's a social place so that he can see plenty of faces and do the networking that is second nature to him. Other quick-fix options are any gadgets that can make life at home a little easier for this modern sign. The keyword really is speed. If you can find a remote that flicks through channels more quickly, then get it. He'll love you for life, if he can find time to tell you!

For her

Look for the latest beauty creams and you will be on the right lines. Even better, though, would be a gadget that does something new. This woman is born ahead of her time, so she wants to be the first to learn about something that can improve her life, skin, nails or just about anything. She could probably do with a new purse. Even if she bought one last month, she is sure to have used it so much that it needs repairing. A good party is likely to be her first choice as a gift, so why not give her tickets to an event? She's sure to have told you of a dozen already. Her music taste is often wide and varied, so she is bound to appreciate some more CDs to top up her ever-increasing collection. If you have any extra money and are willing to splash out on her, then buy this woman a piece of exercise equipment; she has an excess of energy to burn off. Invest in a treadmill and give us all a break from her exciting but very demanding personality.

Capricorn

For him

This is a man who will be very offended if you buy the wrong thing and won't be afraid to get you to take it back. Keep away from gifts without meaning, as he will go on for years about how you deliberately chose something that reminded you of an ex. He loves to read, so books are always a good buy. He doesn't often splash out on hardbacks, so you can be sure that he won't have read the latest title by his favourite author. He will love nice smells, but don't bother going for a new scent, as he will have his favourite. A good idea would be to get the hair product or lotion to match the aftershave. He loves to smell good all over and this flirtatious sign will know just how to greet people, so will want his neck and hair to smell nice. Chocolates are also a good bet, but don't expect him to share them, and exercise equipment is only worth investing in if he has asked for it. Capricorn men don't mince their words and you could end up wasting a fortune if you don't check with them first.

For her

This woman will love things for the home, so why not offer to contribute to a new sofa for her or even a new bed? Like the male of this sign, she will tell you if your gift does not meet with her approval. You would be wise to buy something she has asked for, as she will be very surprised if her gift is something you haven't discussed. Don't even think about choosing a new outfit as a present without her. The best, and I think most obvious, present is to take her out for a day of shopping and dress her from head to toe. If she feels good, then so will you. Top it all off with a meal at her favourite restaurant. She'll have several regular food haunts.

A nice wooden box that she could keep all of her mementoes in is another idea and is perfect if you won't get the chance to see her before Christmas. At least she'll have another place to store all her junk – sorry, treasures. Good-quality glasses or cups will also be appreciated, preferably in the pattern she collects but has not got round to completing.

Aquarius

For him

He is nostalgic, romantic and slightly sentimental, so give him a gift to remember you by, like a framed photograph of the two of you together or a book that means something to you, with some heartfelt words written on the inside. Aquarians love words and will certainly remember yours. Why not browse the bookshops and find out what the latest best-sellers are? You may just be able to add them to his collection before he does.

A keepsake, say a small box to keep things in, or perhaps a print of a painting will be appreciated. A money clip or a pair of cufflinks will also be things he can use and treasure over the years, and he's sure to love showing off these gifts to friends. Remember, though, that the loving words you write on any card will be just as important to him as the gift itself, so make them count; they could be worth far more to your future together than you can imagine.

For her

A meaningful but flippant and slightly sexy gift is what the Aquarian woman needs to go with her outrageous yet seductive nature. Perfume is a sure-fire winner, but just make sure she doesn't have hundreds of bottles already sitting on her bathroom shelf; there's a good chance friends and close ones will have cottoned on to her love of scents over the years and you don't want to end up buying something she's already got. A set of underwear will also gain you a high score in the popularity stakes, or maybe even a daring nightie or an outrageous top or skirt, as Aquarian women like to be noticed when they walk into a room. Avoid a sensible or practical gift, though. She won't thank you for a cookbook, bathroom scales or a new work briefcase, so don't kid yourself. Go for what she really wants and who knows what rewards could await you in return!

Pisces

For him

The Pisces man just loves surprises and is a real practical joker. You can get away with buying him very little if you make a big enough presentation and laugh out of it. Any small gift wrapped in layers and layers of paper that take ages to unwrap will delight him, or even a comic motto that he can put on his desk. If you are not one for jokes, then try something artistic, such as a nice jumper, but it will have to be tasteful; these are men with an eye for style, so any tacky clothing will be taken straight back and you could end up being traded in in the process! Something small, delicate and beautiful in the antique line will appeal to him much more than you think. These are men who really do prefer quality to quantity. They usually have quite a sweet tooth too, so some chocolates from Switzerland could do the trick if you're looking to seduce.

For her

She is a clever, sensible and practical type who will appreciate a clever, sensible and practical gift, provided of course that it is different. To get her something that everyone else has got is a sure recipe for disaster. A cookery book would go down well, but it would have to be written by someone she admires or has commented on seeing on television, otherwise it will be thrown in the cupboard with the rest of them she is sure to have collected over the years. Something to wear is also a safe bet; like her male counterpart, she can never have too many clothes. You see, behind that practical manner lurks a party animal with a thousand places to go and people to see. An easel and paintbrushes, a knitting machine or even a dressmaker's dummy may sound as if you'd be insulting her, but think again – she is naturally a dab hand at making and designing things and so if she has not shown an interest in the past, you could well be opening up a whole new world to her.

Part 3

MONEY AND CAREER

Chapter 8

MONEY

'Money can't buy friends,
but you can get a better class of enemy.'
SPIKE MILLIGAN

Were you born to be the next Bill Gates, or are you destined to pay off loans for the rest of your life? Do you check the price on your grocery bill, or do you use your credit card more than your brain? Maybe you're one of the signs who can no longer get a credit card. It's no laughing matter when the debts have got so bad that you can't see a way out. I've had clients who were determined to hide their financial problems from their loved ones, for fear that it would mean the end of their relationship. Their partners often think they're having an affair before they contemplate that a financial worry is the thing that has come between them. Keeping secrets of whatever kind causes damage to a relationship, but don't be one of the signs who allows money to end it. Not when there is a way out, no matter how bad things have become.

Some of the greatest and most famous faces of our times have survived bankruptcy, a word that is scary to say let alone contemplate. Businessman Richard Branson, founder of the Disney empire Walt Disney, film director Francis Ford Coppola, composer George Frideric Handel, talk-show host Larry King, businessman Donald Trump and actor Ray Winstone all went through this very tough experience, but they came back bigger and better than before. My aim of course is to turn your life round before you reach bankruptcy, but if you follow my advice, I can get you back where you belong regardless of how far you've fallen.

Do you know what is one of the biggest causes of financial problems? Lack of communication. Taureans, Virgos, Capricorns, Cancerians, Scorpios and Pisceans are prime candidates for burying their heads in the sand when things start to go wrong. Aries, Leos, Sagittarians, Geminis, Librans and Aquarians continue as if their finances are getting better by the day. They think that if they continue at full speed, they may just have a miraculous change of fortune along the way. Let's have a look at your sign's strengths and weaknesses so we can get you into the black and out of the red for good.

Aries

Being ruled by Mars, the planet of change and unpredictability, life is never as you planned and the majority of the time you kind of like it that way. Unfortunately your tastes are more expensive than the average sign. You can't help it, really; you just know how to walk into a shop and pick the most expensive item. You were born to expect quality and could probably tell a cheap imitation from a famous label any day.

What some of us would regard as an expensive, non-essential item, you will see as a necessity. Your enthusiasm for life in general is, however, infectious and you are very good at encouraging your friends and family to spend money they should be saving. 'Come on, you only live once' is one of your favourite sayings, and if there's a sign to make you feel that a social outlay is essential to your career, then this would be you.

The thing about you, Aries, is that you may claim that you

are broke, but as your life is one big adventure you will always find the money from somewhere to splash out on a little luxury. My mother had an Aries client who was about to be made bankrupt and was most put out by the fact that the bailiffs called her on her mobile in the south of France and interrupted her afternoon cocktail session with a girl-friend! To this particular Aries, holidays really did come before sorting out her debts. We never found out what happened to her, but the lack of contact probably meant that she was off on another adventure. (I am not advising this, by the way!)

Indeed entertainment is your main outlay. You would rather keep the same clogged-up hoover for fifty years than miss a Saturday night out at that must-be-seen-at party. You have a habit of changing your mind as often as the wind changes direction. Halfway through an evening you can decide you want to do something different, and if you don't get your own way you can become really difficult. This is where your secret supply of credit or loans comes in handy. It may be worth your while warning any new partners not to hurry home after you if you rush off following an argument. You're more likely to be sipping cocktails at the latest wine bar than sulking on the sofa.

So you see, my friends, yours is an expensive lifestyle. You can be a bit of a snob in many ways and woe betide a loved one who buys you an inferior label. Items must be from a credible and preferably designer source. You also have a talent for getting your loved ones to pay for things.

So the big question is, can you keep hold of your funds? If you have surrounded yourself with people who have taught you the value of the pound, then yes, but if you have surrounded yourself with faces who encourage you as much as you encourage them, then you could already be in trouble. The sensible of your sign do actually have money saved away;

if you can afford it, you will try to invest it in property or some fund that doesn't allow your impulsive nature to withdraw it too quickly. You are a little slower than other signs at putting fabulous ideas into action. You need to stop talking the fabulous talk and walk the walk. You have a really good brain – use it!

You'll be pleased to hear there are some famous Aries with money, one of whom is Elton John. (We all know how he's supposed to have spent thousands on flowers, though, so just watch out that those weekly carnations don't turn into daily bouquets of roses.) Then there's Mariah Carey (who has managed to work out how to get other people to pay for her flowers!) and Sarah Jessica Parker, from the popular girlie series and film *Sex and the City*. Her character, Carrie, has to be held responsible for a legion of women spending their mortgage or rent money on Jimmy Choos.

Just remember to keep putting a little of your money away on a regular basis, and if you have financial worries, then read the Rules on page 178. Make sure you don't give in to your weakness for overspending in the name of a good time. The majority of you live a long and healthy life, so do make sure you don't burn your bridges.

Taurus

Being ruled by Venus, the planet of love, your passions usually cost you the bulk of your income. You also seem to spend more when you are in love and need to learn that you don't have to buy things all the time to assure others of your affections. Financial problems have often started for Taurean clients of mine when they have got into debt for their close ones. Know a Taurean well and you will know that there is always a way to manipulate them. I've seen the most professional and worldly of Bulls lend money to family members who obviously have no intention of paying it back, but being a sucker for a show of waterworks, Taurus has handed over wads of cash.

When you become focused on what you are doing, you are capable of making an absolute fortune, but when you lose sight of your goals, then finances can start to dwindle. Earth signs such as you can and should be very good at saving money. You know that life is about planning, and this is something you do well. I must say that you don't mind spending your cash on nice food and drink, though, and this can sometimes be your downfall when your income dictates otherwise. It is well known in the world of astrology that Taureans love three things in life: food, sex and money, and sometimes all three mixed together! Socializing, however, doesn't cost you as much as people would think, as you prefer to see friends at home, so that you can hold court in the manner to which you have become accustomed.

You do, in your defence, think before you act. You're not as impulsive as Aries, for example, but you are far more emotional and here your problems begin. You want life to be beautiful and perfect, but what appears picture-perfect is not always what will make you happy in the end. Learn not to listen to what others tell you is the ideal. You are an individual with individual needs and you must work out what feels right to you. Wouldn't life be boring if we all craved the same job and the same-looking house and the same number of children? Dare to be different. By being youself you'll have people admiring you for the glow that's sure to adorn your very gorgeous face.

You don't mind putting your money into the family, and if you can invest in the younger generation, then so much the better. Family values mean the world to you, and even though you're known to have a mean streak towards those who are not part of your 'inner circle', for blood relations you would usually go to the ends of the earth.

You love to buy things for the home and your abode is often a place of great comfort. If there is a new and better sofa about or a bigger TV, then you have to have it. This is how you can start to spend more than you can really afford, though. Typical is the Taurean who complains about an item they bought last year because a new and better model has come out. You can start to sound quite immature to friends who have less than you, and it's not uncommon for you to lose friends over money. It would be hard for you to fall out with people over much else in fact, as you're such an amiable and welcoming character when things are going well for you.

The best way for you to keep hold of and improve your funds is to plough them into your property, as not only does this give you pleasure but you can see just how much you have to spend should you need it. Money is no good to you sitting in a bank. You like to be in control. You're also not averse to a pension fund, which the air elements would probably run a mile from. They don't have the patience to wait for things to mature, but you do.

It can take a long time for you to tell someone you have got into debt, as it's hard for you to admit. They say that the bigger you are, the harder you fall, but some very famous Taurean faces have overcome their debt problems. Think about how much tax and VAT you pay when you are earning a fortune, and think how much scarier it must feel when the bill could wipe you out because you've had a bad year. I've helped well-known faces out of trouble and I can help you too. Turn to the Rules on page 178 and realize that life can and will be fun again.

You'll be pleased to hear that there are some famous Taureans with money, including David Beckham, who is known for buying his wife expensive gifts. His homes have definitely seen a large amount of his income too, so much so in fact that his home in England used to be called Beckingham Palace. Then there's Jack Nicholson, who did a typically bullish thing by sinking his money into his own restaurant.

Gemini

Mercury is your ruling planet and governs travel and communication. You love excitement, and for you it is essential to keep up with the latest trends and fads. Your finances are eaten up by your social life. If friends have done something, then you want to do it too. There is nothing you wouldn't do for a true mate either, which can unfortunately include lending them money. More often than not it's harder to get back than you'd thought. When the mood and timing are right, you'll lend sums that many signs would consider unthinkable. Some Geminis may well have had one too many drinks, which made them feel like the Bank of England. Certain friends will swear the money was a gift. (I won't say which signs, for fear of ruining several close friendships in your life!)

You are lucky enough to be able to enjoy yourself anywhere and you can easily adapt to others' plans, even if it means giving away the tickets you have just splashed out on. Many of your sign actually spend a lot of money on books too, as you like exploring life. Trying out foreign shores, foods and fashion are other outlets for your spending. Did you know that a large percentage of Geminis either think about or actively attempt to live overseas during their lifetime? Your dual nature is always thinking that the grass is greener on the other side.

I'm afraid that you're not the best sign when it comes to handling money, but the good news is that as fast as you have lost your multi-million-pound fortune, you can make it again. Your gift for being able to talk your way into and out of anything is more valuable than any Swiss bank account.

You love to relax during the day and let your hair down at night, which doesn't really leave a lot of time for work, does it, Gemini? What your sign is good at is delegating your responsibilities. Due to your element of air, you keep abreast of the latest things and so are the first with the inside scoop on where money can be made.

I used to have a best friend who was a Gemini. She always gave the impression when we went out together that she was rolling in money. We would walk into a restaurant and the waiters and the owner would gather round and ask what they could do to improve her experience with them. She didn't have a penny; she was broke. Somehow, though, she had an air of class and riches. She led a really good life because people gave her free meals, free drinks, even free holidays and flights because they thought she was wealthy and successful. Her clothes may have looked designer, but she knew how to mix cheap with an average or expensive item (complimentary of course) to make her look like a millionaire. She has ended up with a millionaire who is madly in love with her and is rapidly spending every penny he has. I'm not worried, though, and I don't feel any need to warn him, as I know with her by his side he'll always be able to get a good meal or a nice bottle of wine on the house. How could he not with her charisma? It's like having a celebrity on your arm.

This is not to say that you should go out asking for free things, or building up debt. Be cleverer than that. Turn your charm into a multi-million-pound industry and make enough money so that you can relax and slow down a little. Think of how good it will feel to know you are in control of what happens and that you have made the riches that your sign has the potential to produce.

You don't mind a gamble with your money, but your sign is also prone to be nervy and tense, leading to problems when you back out of deals just as you have signed on the dotted line. Your intellectual and very eloquent way of attracting new faces into your life always saves the day, though. And you know what I love most about you, Gemini? Your sense of humour. You can laugh through any situation and charm your way into new ones.

The Rules, on page 178, will show you how to get rid of debt and get your dream business off the ground. Your sign is very good at communicating, so you can overcome your financial worries and turn them into gold.

Some famous Geminis with money include Noel Gallagher, whose ability to write great songs took him to a life of riches and brought him to the height of London society during his heyday. Then there's Mel B. of Spice Girls fame, who has proved that comebacks are possible. She's got the cheque to prove it and was, incidentally, born on the same day as Noel! Both of these examples came from no money to an abundance of it and you can do the same.

Remember to keep putting your money in the bank and you'll be able to indulge your dreams in times to come.

Cancer

Your ruling planet, the moon, can at times make you a little too cautious, but it can also push you to the other extreme: when there is a full moon, you will do what you want when you want, even if it means putting your money or that of your close ones on the line, and if there is a new moon, then you are great at thinking of successful new ways to replenish your funds. Write down the full moons and new moons in your diary. You know what they say, forewarned is forearmed!

As your sign is that of a nurturer, you will tend to put your children first in the financial-needs department. You won't mind spending your last penny on the best schooling for them, but you'll agonize over installing a new heating system in the house. You are, it has to be said, Cancer, a little mean when it comes to paying for the things that you need. If close ones want money from you, however, then you are a push-over, provided they have learnt that emotional blackmail is the way into your purse or wallet. You love to help the disadvantaged and I have met many Cancerians who have signed away a large portion of their wages to humanitarian causes.

When things get really bad, you tend to go into hiding, and you even hide from your own emotions, pretending that everything is all right when it obviously isn't. You can't bear to let down your loved ones, and you feel that anything that has gone wrong in your life is a personal reflection on those you care for. This is silly of course, for your loved ones will want nothing more than to help you. The more you shut them out, the less they will think you need their assistance.

Communication can be somewhat of an issue for you. Some clients of mine born under the sign of Cancer would rather divorce than let their partners discover that they have got into debt. This is crazy, firstly because it would probably cost more to get divorced than it would to get out of debt, and secondly because if your partner loves you, they will want to help with problems, not be shut out. When the mists of depression descend, you find it hard to realize this fact and have the craziest of notions.

You love charm, history and beauty, and would rather buy an antique book than a new one. Most of all, though, you love good company. You are quite picky with your friends and don't like everyone; you suffer from a lack of self-confidence, although from some of the lovely clothes you wear one would never guess this. Your nature is such that not only are you capable of enjoying yourself without any money, but others are willing to pay to be in your company.

You have a generous nature and a sense of fun, and won't think twice about buying tequila sunrises for the whole bar, until you see the size of your bill. You also love culture, and if you do go away on a holiday, then you will make sure it is somewhere a bit different.

No matter how much you owe, it is not too late to take action. Think positive and make a start today by promising that you will face your worries, not hide from them. I know from experience with your sign that the first step is talking and the rest comes naturally. Trust me, I've seen it first hand and I've also watched the relief when you are able to talk with others instead of fretting alone. Debt can't kill you, but worry can. The Rules (see page 178) will show you the light at the end of the tunnel. Life will get better with every minute that passes; in fact it will taste sweeter and better than ever, my friend.

Some famous Cancerians with money include Richard Branson, who is certainly no Virgin when it comes to making a fortune, and George Michael, who fell out with his record company and lost money in order to maintain control over his songwriting. This shows how emotional this sign can get about their art, and rightly so too. Actor Harrison Ford doesn't need to raid the bank thanks to the adventure films he's worked on. Ex-Beatle Ringo Starr no longer has to have a hard day's night with the money he's earned, and Cancerian Barbara Cartland wrote her way to a cool amount with her novels.

So remember it's never too late, no matter how far into debt you've got. This is the beginning of a brand-new you!

Leo

You are ruled by the sun and usually have a very happy disposition. You are popular in many different kind of circles and are great fun to be around. If you can't afford to go out, then you would never admit it. You would much rather tell others that you have a more important meeting or place to be. You love nice clothes and can make a cheap suit look designer. You are capable of earning millions just from the way you can charm the coldest of hearts. It is a talent you are sure to have learnt at a very young age and will continue to use your whole life.

Your problem with money is that you never do anything by halves, so if you book a nice holiday, you like to have all the trimmings. Don't think for a minute that the champagne that Leo is drinking was free, or that the outfit they are wearing was in the sale; they don't usually know the meaning of the word cheap, unless they are really strapped for cash. You are a clever sign with very alternative ideas. It is difficult to keep you down for long, although when things do go wrong, you feel that there is no way out and don't find it easy to admit that you need help.

You are a born leader and can turn a struggling business into an overnight success. With these leadership abilities, you can talk yourself out of most problems. You are quick at catching on to things and can give the impression you speak a language even if you only know a few choice words.

The real problem for you, lovely Leo, is that you are more often than not too busy having a great time to realize when you've overspent. You also forget to read the small print on things unless you've got enough money to pay someone else to read it for you. You claim you don't have the time to do things that other signs in the zodiac would deem imperative to ensure you don't get conned, or that you're not paying too high a price or interest rate. You are busy, but often you're doing things that should come much further down the line in your list of priorities.

You love luxury and will want to have the best of everything in your home, even if it means getting it on the never-never. The problem with this of course is that by the time you have eventually paid it off, you think it is out of date and require another credit card to keep up with the Joneses or the Smiths. Beware that you don't try to keep up with everyone all the time.

Make sure that you seek help as soon as you realize there are problems. It's often by sticking your head in the sand that you find problems become insurmountable. You *are* capable and you can get out of debt. Don't think just because things have got difficult that you can close your eyes and keep on spending blindly. You are no fool, so don't pretend to be. Read the Rules on page 178 and change things *now*.

The Rules will help you learn to keep making money and not losing it. Try putting some money away for a rainy day. You know you want a designer brolly, Leo, which means you need to start saving right now! Be able to hold your head up high with the power that you will now possess to be a money-maker. That twinkle in your eye will be brighter than ever before.

Remember, life should be about quality, not quantity. With your sunny disposition, you often like to buy things for the character they possess rather than just the price tag. There's no enjoyment in being in debt, but believe me when I tell you that there is immense enjoyment in opening up your bank statement and seeing that you are in the black.

Some famous Leos with money include Madonna, who has managed to turn herself into a multi-million-pound industry. It all began many years ago when she started selling the boyish clothes that she wore on her first album and she hasn't looked back since. Take a leaf out of the material girl's book and start to build on the things you know you're good at. She's never allowed herself to get bored, and when there was a chance she might, then she explored new directions. You can do the same.

Ever wondered about Geri Halliwell's constantly changing style? Well, she is also a Leo and has shown that she knows how to make money from her image. Love her or hate her, this is one woman who will be making money for many years to come.

Virgo

Ruled by Mercury, the planet of travel and communication, you will plough a large amount of your funds into experimenting and exploring life. Although this isn't what you'll really be doing of course, as you find it impossible *not* to plan. You know that by having an agenda you can get what you want.

I've even seen one client go so far as to have a potential girlfriend checked out by a private investigator. As far as he was concerned, this was simply a way of covering his back and not wasting money on unnecessary dates. The way that other people deal with money is very important indeed to you. In fact this could be a deciding factor in whether or not you stay with someone and will certainly be a bone of contention in any relationship. The only problem is, Virgo, you seem to set one rule for others and a completely different one for yourself. You don't mean to be unfair, it's just that you see a risk in everything you do and have to weigh up the pros and cons; it's all part of your lovely nature.

If your Virgo partner tells you that they have stumbled upon a little house for sale by accident and asks you to come and see it, then check their bag. You're sure to find the estate agent's details with mortgage calculations written on the side. They like to research both personal and professional decisions before they go ahead with them.

You are not against putting money into property, but many of your sign are not overly keen on spending on clothes. This is not normally your Achilles heel. If you have bought an item of clothing, or a pair of sunglasses, that cost more than you deem a fair amount, then you will make sure that everyone you meet knows just what you paid, even though you are likely to have got it cheaper elsewhere. You will know the true value and will stick to your story that you paid top whack. Some Virgos may even go so far as to leave the price tag on if they have paid full price. Believe me, I've seen it!

You can enjoy almost any lifestyle, though, and don't need lots of money in the bank to have a smile on your face. Just a small nest egg will do nicely for you, and you will probably pay your money in on the same day every week. Don't get me wrong – yours is not a sign that is boring, but you can be a little predictable.

You hate to be taken for a ride and so naive friends or potential lovers who take you out for dinner and then tell you that they've forgotten their wallet are more likely to end up in McDonald's than in the little Italian they had in mind. You plan carefully and like your instructions to be carried out to the letter. This is because you have tried and tested experiences very early on and actually know what does and doesn't work. In fact when your head is on straight, close ones should go with the flow and follow your lead, as you're sure to have the recipe for success in the palms of your hands.

The wonder of your sign is that you can surprise a loved one with amazing gifts when they least expect it. They had just better remember to tell others who bought the gift and how much it cost! You're not mean; you just attach value to things and want finery to be appreciated and acknowledged.

Life can and should be really good for you, but the worry that you put yourself through over money and the way you are so self-critical about past mistakes can make you ill. Who cares how much you spent on dinner? Well, you do, especially when you've had indigestion just thinking about the price of the desserts.

What other people find hard to fathom about you and money is how you're willing to pay a lot for certain items and yet won't spend a penny on what the rest of us see as essentials. You learn lessons the hard way, and your biggest fear is people finding out you've got bad credit, which in turn affects your health and nervous system and so the downward spiral can begin. But it doesn't have to and I can help you get on the straight and narrow. Follow the advice in the Rules on page 178 and make a fresh attempt to analyze the positive instead of the negative. Half of the battle in life is looking at things from the right perspective. This is the key to your success.

Not a sign to easily admit you have money problems, it takes a lot for you to lay your financial cards on the table, let alone take steps to get help. If you have a friend who is a Virgo, then don't even bother questioning them about their finances; they'd rather run naked around Buckingham Palace than admit their problems to you.

Famous Virgos with money include Wall Street stockbroker and financial whizz Peter Lynch, who made his fortune with his Virgo know-how, Stephen King, who wrote his way into riches and the top of the book charts, and Agatha Christie, who used detective work to make great finances for herself.

If you have financial worries, don't forget to read the Rules. No matter how much you think you've lost, you've got everything to gain by educating yourself and turning your problems into opportunities.

Libra

With Venus as your ruling planet, you can actually be something of a pushover with money, Libra. This means that if any of your close ones want to part you from your cash, then all they have to do is subject you to a bit of emotional blackmail. If a daughter says to her Libran mum or dad how happy it would make her to have that trendy and very expensive pair of shoes, well, she only has to squeeze out a tear and, hey presto, she'll be walking down the street wearing said shoes before the week is out! You love your family and would spend your last penny on them if it made them happy. You know when you are spending more than you can afford, though, as you usually turn a lovely shade of crimson.

You wear your heart on your sleeve, and unfortunately for you, credit cards seem like free cash when you are feeling emotionally vulnerable. The happier you are, the more careful you are, unless of course it comes down to someone putting on the old waterworks and then it's a different story. Emotional blackmail and emotions in general are your downfall. See life, love and money for what they are and you will be one step ahead of the game.

You don't mind letting your loved ones look after your money for you, which depending on what sign you live with can be either a help or a hindrance in your life. You like to look nice and so will pick the best clothes and materials, not always needing to fork out the top prices. Perfumes can cost you more than most signs, as you have to smell good and you use more than most of us. You take for ever to spend money, though, as you will stand there for a good hour or so thinking, Should I or shouldn't I splash out? It's enough to drive your family round the bend. You don't like to be forced to spend your money. You like to do your own thing and tend to expect others to follow you.

You are in love with the idea of love, and romantic places and faces and objets d'art can soon part you and your cash, or your credit card, or any form of finance you can get your hands on. A rich client of mine who was a Libran even bought a beautiful car because he thought it was a work of art in its design. He told me what a great buy it was, but I had to remind him that he didn't have a driver's licence. An independent soul who refused to have a driver, his car sat in his garage at home for him to admire for many years to come. Luckily he was a man who could afford to fritter the green stuff. Nevertheless beware of those shoes you think you want but will never wear, that dress that doesn't fit you now but might and that food that you won't be in this weekend to eat. I find it hard to tell you off because your heart is in the right place, but let's get your finances in the right place too and then you will see what true happiness is.

It's hard for you to admit when you are short of money. You'd far rather try to think of some colourful story about why you couldn't make a party or gathering, as you'd hate to turn up without the right gift, the right outfit and enough money to buy everyone a drink. Your personality is infectious and you love indulging in conversation. It is indeed your love of beautiful objects and people that often breaks the bank for you.

You are one of the worst signs at acknowledging you have money problems, preferring to hide from them and bury your bank statements in a drawer. This is silly of course because problems only escalate if you hide from them, and one of the key ways of getting out of debt is by communicating with your creditors. Your sign is good at communication when the pressure's off. Now all you have to do is learn to do it when the pressure is on, and I'm sure you can. Read the Rules on page 178 for advice on handling your money problems. This will tell you how you can avoid the pitfalls and make up for any mistakes that currently see you in the red. Your life is one of the easiest to turn round. Just try and you'll see.

Famous Librans with money include Sir Bob Geldof, who made his money from his TV production company and then went on to create Live Aid and make money for the Third World, a typical dream of someone of this sign, which he so admirably carried out. Actress Kate Winslet made a *Titanic* amount from her hard work and determination. Anita Roddick, another Libran humanitarian, founded the Body Shop which supported people in developing countries, and she also made a fortune.

Scorpio

Ruled by Mars and Pluto, you can surprise those closest to you by turning any disaster to your favour. Good job too, with the dramas that tend to unfold in your life, Scorpio!

When you save, you're very good, and when you spend, you're awful. Yours is a sign that is notorious for letting your obsession with making money take you over. If you spend, then it is usually a very large amount, and it is only by focusing on your goals and dreams that you are truly able to see that you have control over your long-term security.

You will do your best to support your close ones, and if you make enough, then you will not hesitate to buy a property for those you love. If things don't work out or a loved one does something to hurt you, then they should watch their back, as they could find the joint bank account drained before they know it. You are very quick indeed and you have learnt, usually the hard way, to put your head before your heart.

You are determined and forceful enough to prove that you can make and spend money with the best of them. You are ambitious and hard to stop once you have made up your mind what and who you want. If you say you are going to save up for the house of your dreams, then you will, whatever the odds against you. This determination more often than not pays off. However, you should learn not to let arguments force you to spend money you don't have. Don't order the most expensive drink just to prove to an ex that you are better off without them, and don't make promises you can't deliver to family or you'll let yourself down as well as them. Over-emotional at times, you can over-analyze and put the cart before the horse. Remember what our grandparents used to say: 'Don't throw the baby out with the bathwater!'

I know you can make a fortune if you want to, but I also know you are the kind of sign who doesn't need money to make them happy. You need security, but you want love, security and excitement all at the same time. Not an easy sign to please, but one who will love their close ones until the end of time. As long as they don't betray you, that is!

You can be very secretive with finances in times of trouble, and you do a very good job of hiding credit-card statements from your partner. I even had a friend who was screaming in labour not because of the pain of childbirth, but because she wanted to make sure another friend would open the post before her husband, just in case her credit-card statement arrived before she got home. What an interesting form of pain relief!

You may want to hide your statements when they're in the red, but you will still insist on seeing every single one of your partner's outgoings. This is partly because you are suspicious by nature, but you are also just plain nosy! If you do well, then you will reach the top of your financial game, but you have to make sure you are in a job you love.

Your skill at acting can talk you into many a bank manager's good books, but just remember one of the lessons you will learn when you read the Rules on page 178, is that you're doing them a favour, and not the other way round, Scorpio!

Some famous Scorpios with money include Demi Moore, who at one time was listed as one of the highest-earning females in Hollywood, and actor Leonardo Di Caprio, who certainly knows how to throw himself into a role, so much so that it was reported he got a cut of the earnings from blockbuster *Titanic*, certainly a water sign who knew a winner when he saw one. Rolling Stone Bill Wyman made his fortune with his passion for music and has not stopped making money, and neither has Sir Tim Rice.

Sagittarius

Being ruled by Jupiter, the planet of self-expansion, you are a sign who should know how to invest money and how to get other people to help you. Your sign tends to go from strength to strength, and even if you lose every penny, you are able to rebuild your fortune from almost nothing. Many people watch and study those born under Sagittarius to try to discover just what the secret is to your magic with money. What a lot of people don't realize is that you will borrow as much as you are worth, which is where this feeling of moving two steps forward and one back can come from. Sports hold a fascination for you and you are not averse to the odd gamble. It's often more business debt than personal that Sagittarians build up.

You are a little too opinionated about other people's

incomings and outgoings, however, which can be really annoying. You see, you may be allowed to buy an expensive item, but as soon as others do you will label them frivolous and careless with their cash, unless of course you advised them to splash out in the first place.

I think that it is your optimism in life that really enables you to be such a success. I don't know many signs who are as capable as you are, Sagittarius, of seeing good in every situation, but you have this brilliant way of being able to take charge and come up with ideas just when the rest of us have given up.

Your sense of humour and fun makes you an ideal candidate to head a business and make a fortune. You are also a natural, albeit harmless flirt who won't hesitate to say the right thing to the right face.

You do well heading a team, and spending as one too: you don't enjoy spending your money as much when you are on your own. You are the kind of person who can go out for a washing machine and come back with a car, so keep your eye on your credit limit or you'll end up with a short, sharp shock when the statement lands on your mat. Overspending is appealing to you because you enjoy the rush and the buzz that goes with risk-taking.

So what if you're reading this and you don't feel that you are this Sagittarian at all? Well, that means, my friend, that we have to help make you what you're meant to be. You see, the downside of your sign is that when others don't believe in you, you can think of giving up, but it's when you're at your lowest that you are most capable of turning things to your advantage. You may not admit it out loud but others' opinions of you matter. What good is a million pounds if those around you don't think you're absolutely marvellous for being able to earn it? One of the first lottery winners that I read about turned out to be a Sagittarian and I just knew that this was a recipe for disaster. How could this poor man feel that he had the right to live in a grand house when he hadn't worked for the money himself? OK, I know you're thinking that you could, but you can't! I know this because my Sagittarian clients who have been given their parents' money have spent it quicker than Imelda Marcos in a new shoe shop! You need to feel you earned what people are admiring.

Others must not lack faith in you; they must support you in your hour of need. If close ones are true to you, then you will help them out in return.

Although optimistic in general, when you get into debt you can probably be the most depressed sign in the zodiac, which is why if you're hiding problems with money, I want you to follow the Rules on page 178 and I will help you turn your life round.

Some famous Sagittarians with money include Frank Sinatra, who did the Archer trick of taking something a small number of people were into and making it popular worldwide, as did Sagittarian Mike Stock of Stock, Aitken & Waterman fame, who had the ability to take a nobody and turn them into a somebody overnight. You may mock, but Kylie was originally in their stable – need I say more! Actress Teri Hatcher is no longer desperate for cash since she made it big playing a housewife on our screens for amounts that will have her sleeping like a baby for many years to come. Then there's director and producer, not to mention three-time Academy Award-winner, Steven Spielberg. Now if these people aren't inspiration enough to make it big, then I don't know who is.

Capricorn

Your ruling planet Saturn places more than a few restrictions on your life, but you'll be pleased to hear that you do manage to keep your funds slowly but surely coming in. Well, usually, anyway.

Even though you are slow to get your wallet or purse out, I must say that you always get there in the end, my friend. You don't mean to be tight, but you don't like spending your money unnecessarily. Like your fellow earth signs of Taurus and Virgo, you would prefer to put your money into your home rather than a bank. You like to be sitting on your funds.

You do have a tendency to miss the big deals due to the amount of time it can take you to make up your mind. You like to have stimulating company around you, but you're not always willing to travel far to get it. You have a natural affinity with the good things in life, which can mean the expensive things, but you have the wonderful talent of being able to tighten your belt in some areas to make allowances for the others. You think long term, but you give the impression you live for the moment.

You want to make sure your family are well provided for and will go out of your way to ensure their happiness, even at the cost of sacrificing your own. What Capricorn doesn't always do, though, is check that what they're working towards for their family is what their family really want. Communication is essential but sometimes lacking. This can be rather off-putting for your loved ones when they ask you for money for essentials and you explain to them that the latest car is more important to the children's education and will help them get to school on time and in comfort. Fortunately for you, your way with words means you can make those around you believe anything. Don't be too tight towards your close ones, though; they wouldn't be with you if they didn't love you.

Romance can make you spend more than you intend because when you are in love you tend to take on some of the characteristics of the one you admire. As long as you don't end up signing your whole life away, then this is fine, but Capricorns can lose track of reality when the old love bug bites. Some would say in fact that dear old Capricorn tries too hard and loved ones can be in for a shock when normality is restored. There can often be a confrontation when Capricorn has to placate close ones and confirm that they are still happy.

You must try to stop looking at money as if the glass is half empty or you will have a heart attack from the stress of buying even just a loaf of bread. Approach life and money head on and you will be fine. I want you to read the Rules on page 178 for advice on making sure you are always in the black and never in the red. You have the ability to have a fun life and there is no reason for financial worries to hold you back – not when your down-to-earth nature gives you the skills to face your debtors.

Some famous Capricorns with money include Jim Carrey, whose very Capricorn sense of humour has made him his millions, and supermodel Kate Moss, whose talent for looking good has seen her endorse her own clothing line as well as her own perfume. Carol Vorderman has a typical Capricorn talent for numbers and it's taken her straight to the bank, and Muhammad Ali boxed his way to a fortune, thanks to the earth signs' ability to use their body as well as their brain.

Aquarius

With Saturn as your ruling planet and Uranus as your co-ruler, you are pulled in two directions. You can talk yourself in and out of a fortune. You will have learnt you can do this from a very early age, but somehow can't remember how to make it tip in the right direction.

Try not to surround yourself with negative influences, as you tend to pick up and imitate those who are close to you. You can be easily influenced to be reckless with money by friends. Resist this and leave them to their own devices. You have a successful life to plan! You live for the future and so if there is a new gadget or a piece of equipment on the market, then you can bet that you will spend your money on it. Not really a person to wait for the cash to come to you, you have been known to take out credit too readily. You may say you are keeping it for a rainy day, but what others would call drizzle or simply overcast, you could claim to be a torrential downpour if a new gadget is in your sights.

You are a friendly character who will not mind buying friends a drink even if you are down to your last fiver. You are honest and loyal too, so if you can't afford something, it is not in your nature to play games; you like to play life a little straighter than most. You are versatile, fun-loving and very particular. You won't hesitate to complain if the service is bad in a restaurant, whether it's McDonald's or the Ritz. You love company and will pay more than most to be included in the events that are taking place. If money allows, you wouldn't even mind hiring a plane to take you to a glamorous party, wearing the latest designer must-have clothes.

Try to keep away from long-term service contracts. You tend not to read the fine print and more often than not sign blind, believing that adverts won't lead you too far from the straight and narrow. You learn pretty quickly and expensively that credit-card companies and store cards are not in fact your best friends, although that doesn't stop you forgetting the lesson when tempted again.

You are unpredictable with your finances and should learn to invest more. You're more likely to splash out on an impulsive holiday deal than put down a deposit on a house. The secret is to make you think that you are getting the best deal and to take money from you when the time is right. If close ones can do this, then they may just see you both living in splendour. It is not unknown for you to cut up credit cards as soon as you get them, for you know you can't trust yourself. Loved ones can never fully relax, though, as they can never be too sure you're not planning the next big splurge.

You have a heart of gold, but for now your partner should not allow you to control the money and bills. You can learn, though, and I'm going to teach you, so read the Rules on page 178 and let's make you some money.

Famous Aquarians with money include Lisa Marie Presley, the daughter of Elvis, who has obviously landed on her feet with finances and has continued to make money of her own by endorsing her father's legacy. Another successful Aquarius is Robbie Williams, whose cheeky nature is typical of his sign and who admits to spending his fortune first time round on the latest televisions and stereos, as well as on other things we shan't mention. Let's just hope he can hang on to it this time! Then there's John Travolta, who likes to spend his fortune on planes, which is typical of his sign and their thrill-seeking nature. Luckily for John, his career can fund this, but the rest of you shouldn't go looking at helicopters and the like just yet!

Pisces

With Jupiter as your ruling planet and Neptune as your co-ruler, it's no wonder you seem like a crazy person to the rest of the signs. Drifting in and out of your dream world, making a fortune and then losing it, only to make it again, you would no doubt throw a champagne party while filing for bankruptcy!

Being one of the most dramatic signs in the zodiac, you either have loads of money or not a bean. There really is no in between for you, is there, Pisces? When you have a lot of money, you will not hesitate to spend it on your nearest and dearest, but you can't possibly work out why it is that they won't do the same for you. In fact you think your loved ones are downright mean if they don't give you what you want, but then that's all part of your very dramatic nature.

Your imagination has a tendency to work overtime and so the things that you see as a necessity can raise eyebrows among the rest of us. You like to run away from life from time to time and this can mean taking holidays just when funds are at their lowest, but you really don't care – if you need to run, you need to run, and that is what you will do.

You are spontaneous, and when you feel like doing something, it is important that you are able to do so without interference from others. In fact you may even have broken up a relationship in the past due to the fact that your ex asked too many questions about your finances. Your need to keep an air of mystery requires you to be in charge. Your impatient nature causes you to get bored quickly and so the new designer wardrobe that you bought can often end up being given to the new friend you've just made. They won't complain, though; in fact they're sure to love it.

You love spending money, preferably other people's, and have a natural flair for arranging little surprises, which don't always go down well with those they were planned for. The diamond ring may look lovely on your loved one's hand, but they would much rather you had paid the mortgage!

Your impulsiveness and disregard for money often lead you into hot water, particularly when on holiday. You throw caution to the wind, but you always seem to enjoy yourself.

You love wining and dining and sampling exotic dishes. Gambling and competitive sports also consume a lot of your cash. You don't really like to get involved in anything too energetic, though; you enjoy the anticipation of a new experience far more than the achievement; by then you are bored and ready to move on to something new and probably more expensive.

I don't actually know a Piscean who hasn't at some point got themselves into debt. In fact if there is one out there reading this book, then please contact me – you'll change history. The amazing thing is that you *always* get out of situations by the skin of your teeth and often just in the nick of time. It really is as if you have a guardian angel on your shoulder making sure that your life is blessed.

If your finances seem bad, don't get down – I know you can, but there is never ever a reason to give up. No matter how bad things have got, you are a fantastic sign to be, with great potential. This is why you are going to read the Rules on page 178 for advice on how you can change your life, right now, for the better. You know you love excitement – I can assure you those trips you like to make are far more of a buzz when you're not expecting a knock on the door from a creditor when you get home.

Some famous Pisceans who have (or had) money are jailed Barings dealer Nick Leeson, who took the Piscean tendency to use other people's money more than a little too far, Jilly Cooper, the author whose vivid imagination earned her a fortune, and Beatle George Harrison, who showed his talent to make money with the Fab Four. Not a lot of people know that Michael Caine is a Pisces, but they know he made his mark in the acting industry.

The Rules

Here are the golden rules that will change your life *right now*. All you have to do is be honest with yourself and the true facts and figures and you can solve your problems, no matter how complex they may seem. It's a bit like homework, really, and it will help you digest the facts more easily and thoroughly if you put each point on a separate piece of paper so that you can tackle them one by one. Don't tell me that you haven't got time. I don't care where you are or what you're doing. Even if it means writing the first one on a piece of toilet paper, it's going to change your life!

1. Communication

Write a list of your debts. You cannot solve your problems if you are not totally honest with yourself about the amount you owe. Don't hide from yourself. Bringing things out into the open may sound scary, but you're sure to feel better once you've admitted what is going on.

Talk to your creditors. I know it's all too easy to hide from their phone calls. You believe that if you don't answer the phone, your problems might go away. This is not true, and if you ignore the people requesting their money back, they will think you don't want to solve the problem. I've talked to such creditors and every single one of them has said that if someone who owes money is willing to talk, then they are always willing to find a solution. Pick up the phone and make contact; they're willing to negotiate, no matter how little you can afford to pay back. Not facing up to your problem can cause so much stress, which will catapult you into a downward spiral. By talking you will find a resolution, and if you find you can't talk to them because you are too scared, I have a list of people who are willing to speak on your behalf. Don't ignore them and don't hide. Facing our fears head on will make us stronger.

You are not the first and will certainly not be the last person to get into debt, but you can get out of it by tackling your fears. If you don't, you are only putting off the inevitable and allowing things to get more out of control when you could be paying back a small amount every month and working your way towards a clean credit sheet.

2. Spreadsheet

Write down honestly what you earn and what you spend. It's only by knowing these numbers that you can work out what you can afford to pay back. There are free companies out there who are willing to help you and act as mediator. You don't have to wait until your creditors come knocking at your door asking for money or waving court orders. Even if you are in this situation, there will still be a way forward.

No one can help you if you can't give figures, so draw up a list now. Review the figures on a monthly basis to keep up with any changes that may take place to both your earnings and your spending.

3. Avoid loan sharks, debt-consolidation and debt-management companies

Instead turn to the free help available, companies who won't want more of your money. With companies such as Payplan, who will review the figures that you owe, listen to what you tell them you can afford, talk to your creditors for you, arrange a payment plan and review it until it's paid, then how can you say you can't cope?

Debt consolidation is a bad thing because in most cases it doesn't solve the problem. If the person's difficulty is that they don't have sufficient funds to pay their debts, they will end up taking out interest to pay interest. Fee-charging debt management companies are different from Payplan because they charge the person in debt. With Payplan every penny you pay goes towards reducing your debt. Payplan is free because it is funded by voluntary contributions from the credit industry, and whether or not a particular creditor gives them financial support, they will still help with all of your debt.

Payplan
Offers debt-management services for free. They will help you to set up a manageable repayment plan and review your affairs as time goes on. They won't take away their support until your debts are cleared.

www.payplan.com
0800 917 7823

Consumer Credit Counselling Service
This is a registered UK charity that gives free, impartial help. They will contact your creditors for you, can help freeze interest, stop penalties and get you more time to pay at reduced rates.

www.cccs.co.uk
0800 138 1111

National Debtline
This is a free, confidential helpline serving people in England, Scotland and Wales. They give advice over the phone and can help to set up a free debt-management plan for you.

www.nationaldebtline.co.uk
0808 808 4000

Citizens Advice Bureau (CAB)
Free help is on hand to sort out money issues and legal problems.

www.citizensadvice.org.uk

Equifax
Find out your credit rating through Equifax. This is essential if you have had bad credit and want to know if this is a good time for you to apply for a mortgage or a new bank account. Each time you apply for credit it appears on your record, so you don't want to be applying dozens of times only to be declined. Find out if you have a clean sheet, and if not, when you will have.

EquifaxCredit File Advice Centre
PO Box 1140
Bradford BD1 5US
www.equifax.co.uk

Advicenow
If you are scared that you don't know your legal rights, Advicenow can offer up-to-date advice on legal issues.

www.advicenow.org.uk

The Samaritans
And last but never least, if you just need to talk to someone about what you are going through, the Samaritans offers twenty-four-hour help if you are feeling you can't cope and you need some emotional support.

www.samaritans.org.uk
08457 90 90 90

4. Stop paying the minimum repayment on your credit card

Remember that credit-card companies and lenders are not doing you a favour; you are doing them one! It is a common myth to think that if you stop using your card and keep making the minimum payment every month, you will pay off your debt. Credit-card companies want you to pay off the minimum amount so you pay the highest interest charges. Start paying as much as you can afford until it is cleared. Make sure that if it is a loan, there's not a penalty for early repayment.

If possible, switch to a cheaper credit card and you may be able to get 0 per cent interest balance-transfer offers. Cut up the old card if you do this or there is no point, and avoid using a credit card altogether if you can. Once you have worked out your budget, you will know how much cash you have to spend. This is the way to start getting in the black. You must stop spending money you don't have, and in time you'll learn the pleasure of spending money you do have. Also remember to try and pay off the cards with the highest interest rate first, rather than thinking of what items you bought with the card. It's all too easy to pay off the card with the highest debt first – make the card that charges most interest your priority.

5. Move your mortgage if you are on a lender's standard variable rate and change energy supplier

Deals change and it's imperative you keep up with the times. This is where the free help on offer comes in handy again. Too many of us become lazy with our mortgages, but if you tell your mortgage lender what rate you can get elsewhere, they're sure to take steps to avoid losing you. Check penalty fees on your mortgage if you redeem it early. Regular reviews are essential.

uSwitch (www.uswitch.com) is a free comparison service

with impartial advice on energy suppliers. Make sure you're with the company that offers the best rate.

6. Involve loved ones

Talk to those close to you; don't ignore them. They're unlikely to abandon you due to your debt problems, but they will if you shut them out of your life. Once you have called the advice lines, at least you will have some solutions to tell your loved ones. They may just pleasantly surprise you with their support and understanding. After all, a problem shared is a problem halved, as I've often seen with clients and their families. You will feel like a weight has been lifted from your shoulders.

7. Avoid store cards

They may seem like a great opportunity with exclusive offers, and they may seem like an easy way of getting your favourite luxuries and fashionable gadgets and clothes, but they can carry an interest rate in excess of 29 per cent. Don't think that the smiling face at the till has your best interests at heart when they ask if you would be interested in a card. It's more than likely they're on commission. Just say 'no'. This is becoming one of the quickest ways for people to get into debt. Plastic doesn't seem like money, and shop staff can feel like your new best friends, but they're running a business. If you save up for the items you want and then go back and get them, you will feel proud of yourself.

8. Get used to using cash

Why take out a load of cards in case of an emergency? What kind of emergency could possibly require you to have to use a credit card there and then? Any holidays or purchases can wait a few hours while you calm down and decide if they are a necessity or an impulse-buy.

9. Stop hiding from your bank statements

Many mistakes happen in banking (especially when Mercury is in retrograde!). Fees are added incorrectly and most banks are only too happy to pay these back. You can also negotiate for certain charges to be deducted if you feel they are unfair. Too many of us still believe that banks are doing us a favour. They're not. It's a business, remember, and they make money out of us.

Don't be scared of your bank statements; keep them somewhere handy and regularly read and review them. It's the only way you can work out a realistic budget. I hope that you will get used to using cash and still write down your budget, but in the beginning you're going to need to turn to your statements to identify the leakages in your finances. Remember that credit isn't cash. Keep your budget under review and you will find a manageable solution. The companies that can help can only do so if you give them true figures of what you can afford. You don't want to jump out of the frying pan and into the fire by making promises you can't keep.

10. Keep your priorities in order

Life is for living and that means learning. Don't be embarrassed by your debts. Credit is pushed on us these days and it's often hard to refuse the very lucrative offers of more glamorous lifestyles or quick-fix solutions. Now you have woken up to the business that is giving credit, you have the power to win the game and to get back in the black. Honesty, courage and determination will help make your life more enjoyable and rewarding than ever before.

Remember, live life, enjoy it, be positive and disregard the negative. Those who have made a success out of life have persevered. Try and try again.

Chapter 9

CAREER

Many top politicians and world leaders have long realized the value of astrology. Winston Churchill discovered that Hitler had a team of astrologers working out prime times for him to invade. What did Churchill do? He hired his own astrologer, Louis de Wohl, to work out Hitler's chart. He discovered that Hitler would always try to invade on the seventh day, which he thought brought him luck. Not so, though, for Churchill was prepared. I'm not saying it won the war, but it certainly proved a case of star wars!

Ronald Reagan used an astrologer from San Francisco called Joan Quigley to clear every major move and decision he made during his time at the White House. According to former White House aide Donald Regan, Quigley drew up horoscopes to make certain that the planets were in favourable alignment for the president's enterprises, and on days when Mercury was in retrograde Reagan put a big cross in his diary and avoided travelling. Reagan also admitted reading horoscope columns and was a fan of, well-known astrologer Carroll Righter and his stars led him right to Washington – can't be bad! He was even introduced to his wife Nancy by an astrologer. You too can use the stars to aid your career.

Are you in the right job for your star sign? Maybe you've been selling clothes when you should have been selling shares. When we are young, it's not easy to know what is the right profession for us. We go through school being given tasters of different subjects and are then expected to decide what we want to spend the next forty years doing. It's never too late to change, though. We often spend more time at work than at home, so read on to find out where your true talents lie. My advice could even see some of you handing in your notice today, or pushing the boss aside for the position that you realize was destined to be yours.

Aries

Fortunately for you, people love you and you usually love people (or are very good at pretending to!). This is a great asset for you as you can make total strangers feel as if they have a bond within five minutes of meeting you. When you are in charge of people, you tend to take a personal interest in their well-being, going out of your way to make sure that they get your full help and support.

One of the biggest mistakes you are prone to making is having *too* many friends at work. You can't be a best friend one minute and then be reprimanding someone the next. All too often you try to play both sides and it can create difficulties in the workplace.

Your sense of humour is verging on the naughty and you may have been accused in the past of showing an unprofessional side. It is hard for you always to act like the ultimate professional as you have a cheeky glint in your eye and often come out with the wrong thing at the wrong time. Overall, though, your dry wit and sense of humour are likely to go down well with colleagues, and you won't be against taking the blame for something that was not your fault in order to help someone else save face.

As a boss you are an employee's dream as you will hand out a salary advance with great ease (as long as the money is not yours, that is), but you will expect anyone you employ to put their heart and soul into your business. You can take time off, but your workers have to keep the ship afloat for you. It is one rule for you and another for those you employ, but you do it with such charm and grace that somehow you manage to get away with it.

If you don't like someone, you can't do business with them, and you would rather go without and let your finances and career suffer than tolerate someone you deem to be a fool. This is why your sign can never work for someone you don't like. It would show and you'd end up giving the game away before your first day on the job was over. You are perfect in social jobs. You know how to make people feel at ease and can create a great atmosphere. You carry a joke well while still getting the job done and could, when the mood beset you, sell ice to the Eskimos.

Always full of great ideas, it would not be going too far to suggest that you would make a great inventor or innovator. You certainly have the ideas; the problem is whether you'd talk about them so much that someone else would patent them before you. Less talking, more doing is the best advice for you. If not, you could end up making a lot of money for other people. You see, dear Aries, the truth of the matter is that you really could do any job you put your mind to. You just seem to spend too much time planning; you should trust in your instincts and jump instead of just standing on the edge. Some of the richest Rams in history have made their money this way.

It is also not unusual to see lecturers born under the sign of Aries. After all, you could talk the hind leg off a donkey! A friend of mine once said they were an airline pilot when asked what job they did, when the truth was they just had a very strong interest in flying.

Motor mechanic is another good job for your sign, as you

are naturally mechanically minded, but by no means down at the local garage. It's Formula One all the way or nothing for you. You are far cleverer than you let on. You prefer to let people judge you and then you quietly set out to prove to them how talented you are. You are able to see through flattery and false praise and you know exactly who your real allies in business are. This is not to say that you won't be nice to those you know are waiting to watch you fall. In fact you believe firmly in the old adage: keep your friends close and your enemies closer.

When you make a mistake at work, you can guarantee it will be something silly. Often you are too busy looking at the bigger picture to take care of the finer details, which is why you need a second in command so someone else can finish what you've started.

You play every game in work to win. With your ability to understand and manipulate a situation with complete professionalism when the mood takes you, you're a force to be reckoned with. You have a combustible personality and can be an explosive employee. You are unintentionally insensitive from time to time.

Public-service jobs are popular with your sign, such as teaching, the armed forces, medicine and anything that can offer up an adventure or new challenge. You need a career that is not a nine-to-five; in fact the very thought bores you rigid. If you could, you would work hard when the mood takes you and party when your job is done, but unfortunately that's not always the way work pans out. It is more usual for your sign to find their perfect career after discovering what *doesn't* work. You realize slowly but surely that you have a natural ability as a leader and it can take five years or more to accept this fact and act on it.

The truth is, you can be the biggest asset or the biggest

liability for an employer, but you have to have your heart in what you do and this is the key to your success, my friend.

The best career for this sign would be anything that involves fast-moving action. A sports commentator or presenter would be great for them, or a lecturer, but the best has to be an inventor with the original ideas this sign comes up with.

Ideal careers for an Aries: entrepreneur, lecturer, property developer, teacher, inventor or sales manager.

Taurus

Well, seeing as we know that the three favourite things in a Taurean's life are food, sex and money, your career choices are interesting! You can bet that the owner of your favourite restaurant is likely to be a Bull, and it is more common than not that a Taurean will have a brush with the food trade or think about it at some point in their lifetime.

Seeing as you also love money, it's not unusual for younger Taureans to go into banking or dealing with money and cash registers in their late teens. When you feel confident in your surroundings, then you attract both luck and opportunity. However, if you have to go away to do business or feel that you are out of your depth or dealing with people who speak a different language, then you become easily unnerved and edgy. This is why some of the most successful meetings for you will be done over the phone rather than in someone else's office. It is also why a large percentage of Taureans choose at some point to run a business from home.

Taurean bosses can be like a best friend to their employees one day and a tyrant the next. Your mood can change in seconds, which makes you hard to work for and best kept at arm's length when there is a deadline to meet. You want respect; in fact you demand it. You want things done your way, or the highway, and you're not afraid of making enemies if it helps to get the job done. You may bark orders at people, but you'd seldom get physical. People often say that your bark is worse than your bite, although I'm sure you beg to differ. Work is important to you because it is the way you get your money, which is also important and which turns your dreams into a reality. If people mess with your dreams, they mess with you. You will, however, always offer an ear for people's troubles and it is this glimpse of humanity that earns you respect and loyalty. You are good at keeping hold of the reins and not losing control, unlike some of the more impulsive signs of the zodiac.

You are ambitious and will aim high in life, and if you have a successful team around you, then you will get there too. Your staff, if you have them, will love you one day and hate you the next and yet they'll still turn up for work because they'll know they're on a winning team.

As an employee, you are loyal, reliable and a great team player. You won't start on something until you are fully prepared and no one can rush you to start before you are ready. Your system of organized chaos works so those above you should not knock a plan of yours because you have probably already applied it to numerous things throughout your life. Your temper needs reining in, but your artistic streak needs encouraging further.

Your creativity and love of beautiful things could well take you into the world of fashion. You are notoriously strong-willed, so it's vital that you are given firm rules from the start in any new business partnership. You are practical and grounded and this will ensure that you are an asset to any company or project.

Singing and dancing appeal to some Bulls, as you're good with your voice and more often than not light on your feet.

Singers Bono and Joe Cocker are typical Taureans. You can't deny that Taurean footballer David Beckham is light on his feet, although we'd have to ask his Aries wife, Victoria, if his singing in the shower is up to scratch.

Ideal careers for a Taurean: clothing designer, chef or restaurant owner, banker, artist, builder or advertising director.

Gemini

You have your own way of going about a job, but it works, Gemini. Notorious in the media industry, it is guaranteed you will have a brush with someone famous in your lifetime. You attract attention and look like you should be someone even if you're not.

Your tendency to use people from time to time can get you a bit of a reputation. Someone who is your best friend in business one day can turn out to be your arch enemy the following week. Your reputation often precedes you and it's no surprise. You have made your way up the career ladder in a way that probably sounds a bit like a fairy tale. There will have been a social opportunity here, an accidental meeting there, and before you knew it the big boss was asking if they could personally groom you to take over their position.

You can draw a crowd with ease, which makes you perfect at selling people things that they don't really need. If you can work on commission, then all the better as you have a competitive edge and are willing to work hard to get what you want.

You are in your element in a busy office, surrounded by people and bustle. Variety really is the spice of life for you, and with a restless and quick mind you like to move on rapidly from one project to the next. Your biggest skill, which I'm sure you know by now, is communication. You would excel in any job in which you have to act as a go-between or convey an idea to an unwilling ear. You are also brilliant at using social occasions to better your career and it's not unusual for you to come away from a wedding or a gathering with several business cards in your hand and a promise or two of a deal or new job. You see, socializing is a vital part of any work to you. It's just as important in fact as the job. There has to be an element of fun to your career, as you more often than not take your work home with you and so you have to feel passionate about it.

People are what interest you, although sometimes you can be curious to a fault. Long social lunches at work suit you right down to the ground. Just beware that your gossiping doesn't become a problem. There is a fine line between intrigue and stirring trouble. You thrive as an active team member and don't always have to be the leader. You know you are an individual in your own right and don't feel the need to fight for the spotlight.

You do need constant pressure or you can become complacent about what you are doing. Jobs with a tight deadline work well for you, or any work linked to sweet-talking your way out of a jam. You need to be able to talk as often and as freely as you want. If you can't have your say, you would rather walk out; you don't see the point in letting your best assets go to waste. Life is for living as far as you're concerned. In fact if you could write a gossip column, you'd make a fortune!

You naturally take charge, though can also be accused of delegating but not actually doing. Once you become aware of this fact, you quickly learn the skill of looking like you're working, but be careful it doesn't take you too long to notice those who may have already guessed your game.

Also bear in mind that working with family or loved ones doesn't work for you, Gemini. You need to have compartments in your life and to pretend otherwise could prove disastrous.

Ideal careers for a Gemini: translator, PR officer, any job in the media or gigolo!

Cancer

Due to your low-key approach to work, you can give the impression that you're not overly ambitious. How wrong that would be, though, Cancer. You are in fact one of the most diligent signs in the zodiac, and with a friendly and approachable nature, you're a joy to work with.

If you become a boss, however, you can get far too wrapped up in the workings of the job to pay your employees on time, and you have to remember to delegate and not try to do everything on your own. Prone both to dishing out and falling for emotional blackmail, you must also be careful that you don't end up being taken in by sorry sob stories or giving away things for free, including your valuable time. It's all very well doing overtime, but if your boss is making a mint out of it, then you need to make sure you get a cut. You don't like to be ruled but often are, due to the fact that some of the stronger signs work out how to manipulate you.

Your home life will always have to come before work, but that doesn't mean that it isn't affected by your job. You take your work home with you and your home life into work, which is probably your biggest disadvantage. You are hardworking and are not afraid of giving up your spare time in order to work your way into the chosen profession you desire. You are sympathetic, tolerant and kind. You like to help people who you see struggling in business, rather than seeing their problems as an opportunity to engineer their downfall. You regard people that you have worked with for a long time as extended members of your family, but this can cause problems as often as it helps you.

It is important for you to care about your job, and to have a career that doesn't ignite a passion in you will seem as bad as a prison sentence. Your work has to be something you would do for free and getting paid for it is just a perk of the job. Life is too important for you to spend it doing something that merely pays the bills.

A BlackBerry is perfect for your sign, as you can pretend you're working and checking your emails when you're not. I'm not suggesting for a moment that you're lazy, Cancer, anything but. You do, however, have to do things your way. Look at Cancerian entrepreneur Richard Branson and you'll see a recipe for great success. Beware of drinking on the job at any social meetings, though: you can't drink much alcohol and probably shouldn't. It lets out a demon who crosses the line.

You are artistic and know the best words to use when the time is right. You are also brilliantly cautious when it comes to business dealings. You like to protect yourself and those around you with a non-confrontational approach that makes you the perfect candidate for sensitive negotiations. If a customer isn't satisfied, they will be by the time they've talked to you. You are the voice of reason.

Your love of family and nurturing makes you ideal for a career in a caring profession or in teaching. Any job you do has to be useful to society and allow you to come into contact with the public on a day-to-day basis. You would probably be happiest running your own small business, as this would give you a certain sense of autonomy and lots of contact with different people without having to be told when and how to deal with customers by a superior. Your most valuable asset is probably your memory; you have the ability to absorb facts and figures with great ease. Given your love of history, a job at a museum would be ideal. Wherever you work, your office is sure to be homely, with comfortable chairs and a picture of a loved one.

Ideal careers for a Cancerian: lecturer, doctor, nutritionist, historian, manager, publisher or retailer.

Leo

Proud, energetic and confident, it is not unusual for those of your sign to be able to speak more than one language. You look at life as a challenge and embrace every hurdle as an adventure and an opportunity to improve your skills. You can give the impression you are the boss just by your superior air. Unfortunately for you, your sign tends to attract a lot of jealousy and competition in business. You can make those around you feel inferior and a wise Lion quickly learns to go out of their way to put others at ease whenever possible. You can succeed in life through sheer arrogance and charm, two traits that you possess in abundance.

Usually one of the youngest signs to apply for their first job, you realize early on the importance of getting out there and making your professional mark on the world. You are a team leader who is not afraid to take risks once in a while or to put your own reputation on the line.

You have a positive attitude to work that is just plain infectious, and for this reason you end up being a role model for many. It is not unusual for a Leo to have a younger person who follows them around, hanging on their every word, while bringing them tea and hoping for a few crumbs of wisdom to help them on their way. Look at the way Leo Madonna turns her legion of dancers into family members when she goes on tour. They even call her 'mama' and emulate her every move, knowing she holds the key to a winning career path. Just take care that you don't fall into a state of complacency, otherwise everything you have worked for could be taken from you.

Ideally, Leo, you need a prestigious job. You cope well under stress and tight deadlines. You are not afraid of staying up all night in order to tie up an important project. Networking is one of your many loves and you are often found in all the right bars after work, meeting people just as powerful and influential as you. Your office will certainly convey your position within the company; an expensive, imposing desk would suit you, or a throne in which to give orders to your empire. Frequent trips to international destinations are just up your street, and only business-class tickets will do.

Any employees you have will certainly get to know their place quickly; you'll make sure of that. Your dedication and drive are contagious, even if your strict rules and discipline are not easy for some of the other signs to comply with. If you say that lunch is at a certain time, you mean it and lateness is not looked upon kindly. You are a good and trusting boss, but will not suffer fools gladly and will not put up with sloppy work. Some would call you a control freak, others a born leader. Only you know how far you have taken your very royal traits. The wonderful thing about you, Leo, is that you take your job seriously. You are the ultimate professional who will remember to give colleagues or staff a birthday card but may not remember to give them time off!

Partnerships don't usually work for you, I'm afraid. You have your own way of doing things and you don't like to share the reins. You are happy to poach staff and jobs from other people because to you this is just the name of the game and part of business fair and square. If you have a boss, they should beware: it's highly likely you've got your eye on their job and you're more than likely to get it too!

Anything of a revolutionary nature appeals to them, as do professions such as judge or police officer, and the girls of this sign make great catwalk models, with their striking and somewhat alternative looks.

Ideal careers for a Leo: politician, art dealer, performer, film director, presenter, architect or manager.

Virgo

You are clever, quick and have a great sense of fair play. You are the good guy in a pool of sharks, out for justice and quick to speak up for those being trodden on. You can't abide liars or lack of loyalty, and you will have planned out your career with great precision right down to which outfit you will wear when being offered your promotion.

You like colleagues to pull together and don't hesitate to point out the weakest link. Quick with words and ready with a solution to other people's problems, you don't always recognize that colleagues' ways can work well sometimes too. Beware that you don't simply become very good at making other people money: you have the talent to be making it for yourself.

You are kind but at the same time hard to work for and with. You can't sit still and you dish out orders, which annoys new colleagues who haven't yet seen the endearing side to your many foibles. With a work ethic that will make the more lazy signs of the zodiac tremble, you want things done your way or not a all. As a secretary, you're great, but the way you reorganize your boss's schedule without asking will make it seem like your boss is your employee. You love to analyze facts and figures, and have excellent problem-solving skills. You are highly organized with an excellent filing system and orderly database at your disposal. You are a realistic worker who knows how to set achievable goals for yourself and your team.

You are also a perfectionist and are liable to criticize instead of encouraging others. You see a glass all too often as half empty instead of half full, and it is important to reverse this outlook sooner rather than later. Believe in yourself and great things will happen. Lacking confidence and believing the negative can be your downfall. Your perfectionism can also lead to health problems if you're not careful, as your health is often a mirror image of your emotional state. Balance is needed if you are to stay happy in your job. Your sign is keen on healthy living and you are attracted to working in the health industry. A job as a personal trainer or a nutritionist would give you a platform to preach about the importance of a healthy lifestyle, as would a job in the medical profession. The more unconventional among you would be interested in alternative medicine, such as homeopathy and aromatherapy.

If you can overcome the temptation to constantly self-criticize and if you keep your eyes focused on your goals, then you can and will make it to the top. You need to like the people you work with and for. You are fair, considerate, loyal and sincere, and expect the same from those around you.

You don't and shouldn't mix business and pleasure. In fact when you have spare time, you should get as far away from work as possible. You're not a sign that should work from home; it will end up making you ill, and you'll never be able to decide whether you should be doing the housework or your actual work. Deliberating between the two will eventually become intolerable.

Time counts for everything for you and you use every minute that you have to put your plans into action. When you're not working, you're planning, and so the circle continues.

Ideal careers for a Virgo: doctor, civil servant, lawyer, copy-editor, personal assistant or chemist.

Libra

Although you look like the first choice to have in charge, you don't really have a clue what you're doing some of the time, do you, Libra? You get by on a wing and a prayer. Don't get me wrong, the brainwork is there, but your charm does most of the work and it's no surprise, as you carry it in abundance.

No one could ever accuse you of favouritism or partiality. You have a sense of justice and fair play that is hard to rival. Any decision you make in the workplace will have been carefully weighed up beforehand. You would be suited to legal work and politics, although you're probably a little too honest for the latter! You like to weigh up problems logically and proceed to give great advice to those around you, albeit a little too airy-fairy for the more serious signs.

You are a dreamer and, unfortunately for you, people don't always take you as seriously as you would like. People born under your sign like to work in a harmonious environment and in beautiful surroundings.

Your sign needs a job that allows you to converse and exchange ideas with a range of people. You are also the networker of the zodiac and the king of schmooze when it comes to any sort of social occasion. You can get away with murder as you really do look as if butter wouldn't melt. You have staff and bosses alike eating out of your hands. You dislike formality among colleagues and are usually on first-name terms with everyone. You make a great teacher and an even better storyteller! You have an approachable manner and find it easy to deal with the public, knowing at just a glance what kind of handling each person will require from you, or what kind of flirting. Dress-designing could be an option, as could writing poetry, following in the footsteps of fellow Libran T. S. Eliot.

Stay away from speculative or risky jobs on the stock exchange; they are bound to end in disaster for someone as emotionally involved as you. You like work that involves a degree of travel, and if something has an air of nostalgia or romance, then so much the better.

You must make more of an effort to finish one thing before starting another. To be quite good at a lot of things may make you attractive to new faces, but is unlikely to make you wealthy. You need to learn that work can't always be fun; sometimes you have to get down to the nitty-gritty. By making the extra effort you can excel as long as you remember when the time comes to listen and not talk, Libra. With your charm, though, you'll work your way to the top no matter how many obstacles you encounter.

Ideal careers for a Libran: judge, diplomat, psychologist, artist or musician.

Scorpio

You are a force to be reckoned with in the workplace – when you choose the right profession, that is. Find your niche in life and you will make a fortune. Get into the wrong job and you will make your boss's life, your employees' lives and your customers' lives a nightmare.

Big business deals are your thing. Once you have a goal in mind, you will stop at nothing to reach your target. You play to win and are determined to reach the top. It could be argued that people born under your sign are only out for themselves, but you are capable of helping others, just so long as it doesn't inconvenience you too much. You have no patience for anyone who displays weakness. This means you will have trouble working for anyone you don't respect. It shows in your eyes, Scorpio; they are, after all, the window to your soul. If you are required to be ruthless to close a business deal, you won't hesitate to pull out all the stops, even if it means a few casualties along the way. Business is business to you and you just hope those caught up don't take it personally.

You set exceptionally high standards for your colleagues and don't suffer fools gladly. More people get hired and fired by a Scorpio than any other sign. You are very particular. If people don't suit you, then you won't take the time to train them your way like many of the other signs would. You are a hard taskmaster who expects the best because you want to give the best. When things go wrong for you, then everyone else had better run for cover, as you will spread your bad mood like the flu. You can forgive mistakes as long as you're not losing money. You remember all who have helped you and all who have crossed you too.

You do know that you can sometimes be too aggressive and inflexible, so need to remember that no one is indispensable, even you! Many of your sign have a natural aptitude for things mechanical, so engineering may appeal.

You are not afraid to take chances and face with bravery things that other signs would run a mile from. Your career has probably involved you taking a few gambles, and speculation and ambition go hand in hand for you. As soon as you have achieved what you wanted, you are off looking for the next challenge. No one could ever say you were dull or uninteresting. They could say that you were unpredictable and obsessed, but these are traits that help you to get ahead of the game. More often than not your sign excels and surpasses their dreams just through sheer cheekiness. You are willing to do what others only dream about.

You work hard and play hard, and can make a success of the most unexpected things. You're a great public speaker, although you probably don't think so. It is this slightly out-of-character nervous disposition that gives you your charm. You can convince people you know everything about anything with the power and energy you exude, and those who doubted you are sure to receive an anonymous clipping about your success in the post, although I'm not daring to suggest you hold a grudge!

You don't usually work just to earn money; you need to do a job that you enjoy. If you can earn a fortune doing what you love, then that is usually an added bonus. As you are one of the most dramatic signs in the zodiac, the most natural thing for you to go into is acting. Scorpios love the arts, so it's no surprise that some of the top male and female earners in Hollywood and Britain are born under this, the second water sign of the zodiac. Julia Roberts, Jodie Foster, Meg Ryan, the list goes on . . .

Ideal careers for a Scorpio: private detective, scientist, manager, actor or engineer.

Sagittarius

Yours is the face that looks cheerful on the first day back at work, Sagittarius, although you may not realize you're wearing a silly smile; it just comes naturally to you. You have a positive outlook and can see opportunity in every setback. This makes you a born leader to whom others will naturally turn for advice and guidance. You are excellent for team morale and at boosting everyone's spirits.

The idea of working on your own does not appeal to you. You're a people person and need contact with others in order to fuel your ambition for work and life. You have a thirst for knowledge, and your inquisitive nature gives you an aptitude for research. You get bored easily, though, and if you swap jobs at the beginning of your career, it can become a hard habit to break.

Money, although important to you, is not the be-all and end-all. It is essentially the experience of a job or profession that you are looking for. It just so happens that you put so much of yourself into what you do that you end up making lots of money from it. You are an explorer, adventurer and traveller of the zodiac who is never happier than when out on the road, meeting people along the way. It would prove hard for you to stay in an office for long; you would feel stifled. You need fresh air to clear your head and bring new ideas, to blow the cobwebs away.

You promise people the earth and then expect everyone else to rake in the sun and moon in order to get it. That said, you'll give anything a go and when the mood takes you, you could achieve things many of the other signs only dream about. Just beware of expending your energy too soon. Work on getting someone to help you who can finish off the great ideas you have, otherwise you'll end up forever talking about what could have been.

You prefer to work odd hours and you get your best ideas at the most strange times. That's why the successful of this sign so often carry a notebook with them or can be found with writing on their hand. These scribblings mean nothing to us, but could be the makings of a grand master plan.

You speak as you find, which makes you plain rude in some people's books, but with your natural good looks and model physique, it's hard for anyone to stay mad at you for long!

Ideal careers for a Sagittarian: travel agent, photographer, ambassador, expedition leader, newspaper magnate or professor.

Capricorn

Status and prestige are very important factors to you when picking a career. You need, you demand in fact, to have respect, for without it life is not worth living. Whatever you do, you will make it sound impressive, though. The list of responsibilities you reel off will give those listening the impression that you have had years of training. If you're the post-boy, you tell your friends you're the head of circulation! A Capricorn without a job is not a happy Capricorn. You need to work to feel a sense of purpose, and luckily for you, your appetite for life will get you back on your feet.

Your ability to persevere, coupled with your practical nature, means that you get there in the end, even when many of the other signs may have given up, though sometimes at a slow pace. It's hard for you to delegate, as you naturally take on more than you should, feeling that everything is your responsibility and yours alone. Learning to delegate can help you find success and can also earn you some very loyal supporters and co-workers.

Think of the goats on top of the mountain and how hard it must have been for them to get there. Well, the same goes for Capricorn. You know that hard work is imperative for you to feel genuinely successful. Unlike some signs, who would take a fancy job without having done a day's work, you want to know you are worthy. You get stuck in where many other signs would shy away, and it is this very trait that gets you such support and admiration.

You have to keep work and home life separate if you are to handle either well. Having a personal phone call in the middle of a meeting can create all sorts of problems for you. Dealing with one thing at a time is how you like to do it.

The temptation to link work and love is your downfall. It's a slippery slope, but your libido finds it too much of a temptation to resist at times. Ask a Capricorn over forty if they've had or nearly had a relationship at work that caused problems and they're sure to look bashful.

You expect people to keep to their word, and if you have been promised something and it has not been delivered, you will not be backward in coming forwards about confronting the person concerned. You'll even go so far as to seek legal help in getting things put right.

You will make it to the top even if it's just through sheer persistence. Just remember to keep flirtations for after hours; you'll always regret it if you don't!

Ideal careers for a Capricorn: computer expert, manager, army general or CEO, travel agent, teacher or estate agent.

Aquarius

It doesn't take a brain surgeon to see that your idea of hell would be working in a cramped office full of people. You like to be surrounded by lots of people, but on your terms! You are a humanitarian who will stop at nothing to help your fellow man. Working for a charity or other non-profit organization would stimulate you immensely. How long you can keep doing this while family shout at you to help pay the bills is quite another matter.

Teaching is another great profession for you. You are bound to get job satisfaction from educating and inspiring a new generation, particularly because you love to be admired by younger people, who can't possibly know as much as you do!

Your profession needs to involve a sense of purpose and needs to be challenging. The corporate world holds no appeal for you and is totally unsuited to your righteous nature. You do, however, have a natural aptitude for all things technical and what you know on the computer is probably self-taught. Computers do often play a major role in your life, and you can bring the most prehistoric business into the twenty-first century. You love gadgets and probably own more office gizmos than you could ever need or use. You are constantly coming up with new ideas for things you can do, but it's rare for them to make it past the planning stage. Cutting-edge ideas and new developments come naturally to you, then just sit there. So what you have to do is learn to take them to the next phase and level. You don't lack ambition, but you do expect to see results a little too soon.

You like everyone around you to be happy in their work and try to make a friend of those you deal with in business, only to reprimand them when they don't do things as you had envisioned. You expect your orders, should you give them, to be carried out to the letter, but then neglect to make sure you have completed your own list of responsibilities. You can't stand moaners or people who are not team-players. You like to be around people in work who can get results. You want to make money and are no fool; you know that brains come before beauty, although if you can get the two together, then so much the better!

Aquarians can be pretty tight-fisted with money in business, which can get you a bit of a reputation, particularly when you do a million-pound deal but then send in the taxi receipt for the cab you took to the meeting in the first place!

You take offence when others tell you how to do your job. Even if you've only been doing it five minutes, you already know the way you want to conduct things. You barely listen, except to your own voice, and you need to learn the art of convincing other people that your new approach was their idea in the first place. Tact, Aquarius, tact.

The more you can travel as part of your job, the better. Travelling from one country to another would suit you right down to the ground, but as soon as family come into the picture, you often feel torn and reach a rather painful crossroads in your life. One of your biggest fears is branching out on your own, but you're a fool not to try. It's what you were born to do, and you're sure to find career success if you do.

Anything run of the mill or predictable is not suitable for you. Constant challenges stimulate you and give you a thirst for life and a desire to go on. A tied-down Aquarian, robbed of an outlet for your Water-Carrier's marvellous sense of humour quickly becomes hard to live with, so mix humanity with change and see if you can't make a fortune and help those less fortunate. One last word of warning: just remember to finish that work you've started this time in case someone actually checks!

Ideal careers for an Aquarian: inventor, scientist, politician, fund-raiser or charity worker.

Pisces

People may tell you to stop daydreaming, but you need to inform them that you actually have some of your best ideas when you drift off. Practicality does not know your name, nor would you recognize it. You are a contradictory sign who has highs and lows in your career that many signs would find absolutely terrifying but that are part of your everyday life. You enjoy giving people pleasure and showing how much fun you can make of things. A lot of artists and musicians are born under your sign, as you have a natural ability to perform.

Yours is the most psychic sign in the zodiac, and if you have a hunch about a good business deal, then you should go for it. It is rare that your instincts will let you down. However, where large amounts of money are concerned, you would be wise to seek a second opinion, lest you end up out of a job and in debt. Your instincts do let you down when you become too emotionally involved.

If you decide you don't like someone, then woe betide them if they cross you, as you will never forget. You need to feel rewarded and appreciated for your efforts, and if those you cross paths with at work fail to do so, there could be a high price to pay. Love and hate come close together for you, both in how you feel about those around you and how they feel about you.

If we're being honest, you do prefer to hear your own voice rather than listen to others, and this is where you tend to miss out on some golden opportunities at work. Your brain never stops working and you retain the most bizarre pieces of information while forgetting things a child could remember.

Creative professions suit you right down to the ground, but hard-nosed business doesn't scare you and your reputation will precede you. You have not usually learnt your skills at school but through life. You absorb every experience like a sponge. You may not live in the real world, but it certainly can be a successful one, if you put your mind to it. Who can resist wanting to do business with a sign that could promise such an unforgettable experience? Well, some would run a mile, but those who do choose to work with you will never forget it.

Some of you see money as the be-all and end-all, whereas the rest of you just want to do what you want to do when you want to do it and are laid back beyond belief one minute and wound up like a spring the next. You go to such extremes that you could be the tea boy one month and own the company the next.

When you get bored, you'd give it all up for the promise of excitement in far-flung shores without a moment's hesitation. My best advice for you, Pisces, is to invest in things that you can come back to, otherwise you'll miss your past achievements.

Yours is the sign who liked a business so much you bought the company. My mother is a typical example of this. She had been out for so many bad meals that my father said to her over another terrible dinner one night, 'Why don't you open up your own restaurant if you don't think anyone else can do it right?' She did indeed open up her own restaurant, called Eva's, which was a fabulous seafood and steak house with live jazz and a chef who would come out and talk to you. She sold it for a profit, but years later always reminisced about how she'd like to be back there listening to the jazz and being part of the hustle and bustle of a kitchen. I don't miss it. I used to come back from a twelve-hour shift of giving palm readings and constructing birth charts to be whisked off to the kitchens because the washer-up or the commis chef hadn't turned up. Still, being a water sign myself (Scorpio), I understood her passion and even laughed at the nightly dramas, and I'm grateful for the culinary skills it taught me!

I digress, my friends, but you get my point. Don't taunt a Piscean by saying they wouldn't be able to run your business. They may just do it, and better than you; in fact I don't doubt it – although for how long and at what cost remains to be seen. Staying true to their psychic intuition and knowing when to get out and make a change is half the battle to a successful career for this very individual and loving sign.

Ideal careers for a Piscean: artist, musician, psychologist, writer and of course restaurateur!

Part 4

HEALTH MATTERS

Chapter 10

HEALTH, DIET AND FITNESS

We all want to be in optimum health, both physically and mentally. What we don't realize, though, is that it's hard to be fit mentally if our bodies are not at their best physically. Skipping meals, eating too much, stress-eating and choosing the wrong types of foods for our bodies can all lead to problems. I can help to make you fighting fit. Life will seem better than ever before. No more being depressed, no more feeling out of control.

Let's look at what you're eating and where you're going wrong. We'll also discover the right foods and exercises for your star sign to ensure you have the energy and the health that you need to make the most of your life. Your tailor-made plan can help you turn your life round and reach your full potential.

No wonder we feel depressed when we're missing out on vital nutrients. How can we expect to function well when we can't think straight? Mothers spend time and care giving their children the right foods because they *know* that diet plays a key role in development, yet when our own lives are going out of control, many of the signs seem to punish themselves as a way of telling others that they are unhappy, though half the time close ones don't even notice! There are certain signs of the zodiac who choose to head straight for the bottle or the larder as soon as they confront a problem, while others abstain from food and see it as a hidden enemy. Virgos and Scorpios in particular under-eat if they become sad, while Taureans, Aries and Pisceans often head straight for the chocolate.

Our bodies are all too often trying to tell us that something is wrong weeks or even months before we're willing to admit it out loud. Many of us ignore the warning signs and wait until something shuts down before we give ourselves an MOT. However, by recognizing the clues your body is giving you, you can overcome your problems and obtain both the health and mental agility you need to make a success of your life. Without a healthy body you cannot find a healthy mind.

Everything has a place

We've all looked at photographs of celebrities in newspapers and magazines and wished we had their figures. However, looking good is not just about being super slim; it's about being healthy and being the right weight for your height. Being underweight can cause just as many problems as being overweight.

Good health is about mentally adapting to the changes we face in life, which many people don't make a priority. They're too busy making sure that everyone else in their life is happy to think about themselves, or they're too busy doing what looks right instead of what feels right. How will close ones feel if what you're doing makes them happy but you miserable? Putting others before yourself will have a knock-on effect on your relationships.

Let's start by taking a look at what your ideal weight should be for your height and age. Remember that if you do feel you need to start a weight-reduction programme, you should aim for a sensible weight loss. About a kilo a week is ideal, as otherwise you risk starving your body so that it stores fat when you eat.

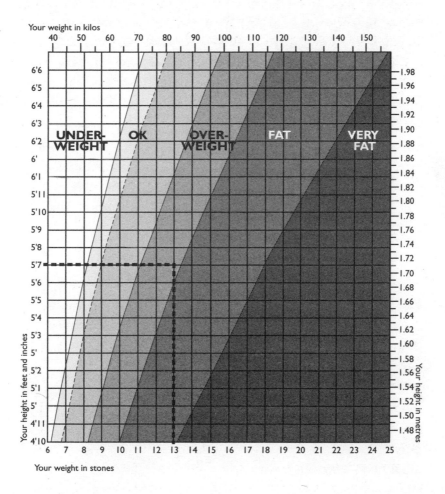

If you're using the BMI chart, you must be aware of your body shape. The index doesn't take into account if you're an apple, a pear, square, muscular and so on. You can use a BMI chart as a base, but using a tape measure is the best way to monitor changes. When you increase muscle mass through exercise and lose fat through healthier eating, your shape can change rather than your weight, as muscle weighs more than fat.

Did you know that it is generally thought that the average person is about twelve kilos overweight, which, if you want to visualize it, is the equivalent of twelve large bags of sugar. Next time you are in the supermarket, pick up a bag and you will soon see how being just a little overweight can make you feel uncomfortable, awkward and off balance.

The majority of us are carrying around more weight than we should. That's why it's so important that we try to educate ourselves about exactly what we are putting into our bodies. When we reward ourselves with a piece of chocolate, why does it seem like a reward? Why should our five-a-day of fruit and vegetables be a chore? Relearn to value food for the energy it can give you. Why so many of us think we should stop learning when we leave school is crazy. As one chapter of your life closes, allow another one to begin.

An astonishing 60 per cent of people go to the supermarket when they are hungry. This means you're likely to buy more food than you would normally. Plan ahead and write a list. I'm sure the Virgos among you probably already do, and in aisle order too, but you Geminis and Aquarians don't. Librans get seduced by the beautiful colours and presentation of foods, and Scorpios go off on a tangent when one item they like the look of makes them decide to cook a completely different meal.

Did you know that your star sign rules a part of your body and when you get stressed, that part will start to suffer as a way of telling you that you need help? Let's take a look at the tell-tale signs you need to recognize and learn how you can get yourself in tip-top condition with your health, diet and fitness regime. It's the key to unlocking the real you and to reaching your full potential!

Aries

Aries rules the head, brain and face.

People may think you have a cool, calm exterior, but underneath that smile you're a bag of nerves. Even the way you hold yourself may seem like the height of coolness to some of the signs, but it is only a cover and inside you are fervently planning your next move so that you don't give the game away.

You need to be in charge and when you lose control, you lose your cool. Your very hectic lifestyle, along with your lack of planning, means you are more susceptible than some to stress. Problems that affect Aries people sign when life begins to take its toll are eye strain, insomnia and headaches ranging from mild to full-on migraines. This is linked to the fact that your sign often suppresses emotions. You must learn how to let off steam if you are to maintain the right physical and psychological health. The best advice is to try and treat headaches naturally first, rather than through medication. If you take away the stress, the headaches should disappear. Of course, getting rid of the stressful factors in our lives is easier said than done. Try getting plenty of fresh air. We spend far too much time indoors or in cars. You could also try drinking herbal teas instead of overdoing the caffeine. Infusions of valerian or lime flower made from a tea bag or one teaspoon of each herb per cup of hot water work well for your sign. Juniper oil diluted with two tablespoons of olive oil offers great results for you, and this treats nervous strain well too. Massage this oil into your temples to relieve migraine. Juniper berries are good for all kinds of Aries inflictions, including nervous strain, eye strain and stomach ailments. You can chew the berries raw or you can steep a dozen juniper berries in 900 millilitres of boiling water for ten minutes and drink, adding honey to taste. Most good herbalists and health-food stores will stock what you need. Some of the best solutions are the simplest, Aries.

Those typical of your sign are often too busy to remember to eat properly. A good breakfast, a light lunch and a light dinner usually work best for you. You are prone to a deficiency in potassium phosphate, which can contribute to the nervous problems you tend to suffer from – eat more fruit, pulses and cereals. You can boost your immune system and your all-round health by stocking up on tomatoes, lemons, celery and grapefruit, and resist the urge to opt for fast foods.

Because many fire signs such as you suffer from insomnia, you can develop a tendency to eat in the middle of the night. The fridge-raider at three in the morning is often an Aries. There you are, cheese sandwich in hand, denying you were ever on a proper diet or claiming that you are just having a well-earned night off. You are smooth talkers, so you can often convince your nearest and dearest that you are right, and that doesn't just apply to diet and exercise.

DIET

As I have mentioned before, your sign all too often runs on nervous energy. You also have trouble finishing what you have started, be it a diet plan or a business deal. If you have support, then you find it a lot easier, so joining an online diet club if you need to or a fitness group will help you to keep motivated. Watching other people's progress will also bring out the competitive streak in you, which will help you to keep up with any new regime. Try not to pitch yourself against others, though, as any threat of real competition from some-one who is losing more weight than you is a sure-fire way to knock your confidence and convince you to give up. You need a little leeway for the times when your very busy life has other areas that require your attention.

The secret to keeping weight off is to look out for the calorie and fat values usually found in the nutrition panel on food packets and read them carefully. Remember to note whether this is given by weight or by serving size. Know exactly what you are putting in your mouth, Aries.

If you go out to work, then taking a home-prepared meal can help you to shed any excess weight. Only you can decide to make this commitment to try to lose weight; you have to do it for yourself. It's your life and you must take control of it.

FITNESS

If you are an unfit Aries

You have probably failed in the past because you need change and get bored by routine. That's why you're best to try an exercise that can constantly stimulate you.

Start off with five to ten minutes of exercise twice a week if you have never done anything before, and then build up to twenty to thirty minutes three times a week. From here the sky is the limit, and your new fitness kick could lead you into many exciting sports. Try a boxercise class to get rid of all those pent-up emotions. Power-walking would be an ideal way to start. Just imagine you're walking towards your new future, and set yourself a distance as a goal, with a prize at the end of it – even if it's trying a new healthy dinner or buying a copy of your favourite magazine.

If you are a fairly fit Aries

I know you can excel because life is often one big competition to you, and I just know you're not going to take a challenge such as this lying down, are you, Aries? Start off with a celebrity fitness DVD from your favourite personality, but one which can take you to the next level. Once you feel confident with this, you should look at body-pump classes, which are sure to prove exciting and stress-relieving for your sign. You don't have to join a gym to do a class; you can often pay separately at your municipal gym. Running is also good for you, but short distances at a good speed will eventually turn out to be your best choice. It's important to use the right equipment to avoid injuries, so make sure you go to a proper running shop to buy the correct footwear. Hop on a treadmill and hit 'random' for a real challenge.

If you are a very fit Aries

You need variety, which is why a triathlon is ideal for you. Plenty of change and yet the ultimate challenge. Once you have started to become good at a sport, you can become complacent, which is why you always need to up the stakes. Fast sports attract you as you like to make an impact. There is no reason why you couldn't become a professional sportsperson; just look at motor racing's Mark Blundell, golf ace Sevvy Ballesteros, footballer Robbie Fowler, round-the-world yachtswoman Clare Francis and sprinter Linford Christie. If these Aries can do it, so can you!

Taurus

Taurus rules the throat.

The Bull is probably happiest when sitting down to eat. Nice food is a great love of yours, but you also know you have to be careful not to over-indulge. You can become fixated on a dish and eat nothing else for weeks on end. Just look at famous Taurean footballer David Beckham, who admitted that he used to have an addiction to SuperNoodles and on a supermarket trip would buy twenty at a time! It's not always good foods that your sign craves. As a result of this many of your sign suffer from acid indigestion and weight problems. Exercise is essential if you are to keep your body and mind fighting fit, but it's something that you either over-indulge in or under-indulge. You find it hard to reach a happy medium. Moderation *must* be your keyword. You have to learn to eat little and often. Hurrying meals is natural to you, but you need to remember to chew before you swallow and shovel in the next mouthful. Surely from the very romantic reputation you have you should know that it's not just love that can give you more pleasure when indulged in slowly, Taurus!

It is common for your sign to be deficient in sodium sulphate, which can lead to rheumatism, arthritis and stiffness. You should steer away from fat-laden foods and go instead for fruits. Strawberries and pomegranates are great for this deficiency, so make them a regular part of your diet. Remember that prevention is better than cure! Apples are also fantastic for your sign and ward off rheumatism, gout and bladder problems.

You Taurus types are also prone to sore throats and do not cope well with smoky atmospheres. Unfortunately for Taureans, products such as chocolate and cream exacerbate the problem of throat infections in that they are mucus-producing foods. Romanies have traditionally recommended that Taureans drink an infusion of blackcurrants, blackcurrant leaves and boiled water to soothe a sore throat.

DIET

Because moderation is an issue for your sign, it is often the amount of food you eat rather than the kind of food that is the problem. You must be careful that you don't turn to comfort-eating in times of stress or strain, particularly sweet foods. You love the home and you also love to entertain, so you always make sure you prepare plenty of food, which you usually end up eating yourself to make sure it doesn't go to waste.

Singer and actress Cher, who is a Taurean, once said that when she can't get her favourite jeans on, she knows it's time to diet. This is her guide, but many of us keep clothes we will never get into. Do a reality-check – look at the graph on page 215 and work out the healthy weight for you.

You, along with Virgo and Capricorn, have a tendency to go for the most fattening dish on a menu and so you will have to retrain your mind to get flavour without adding inches and the threat of heart disease. I don't write about health just so you can look good, it's about being healthy inside too, and I want you to be able to live long enough to see your dreams come true.

FITNESS

If you are an unfit Taurean

It's well known that many Taureans suffer from a slow metabolism. If you don't do any exercise at the moment, then find a passion that keeps you active, such as gardening. You could also always bring out the romantic in you and sign up for a dance class. You do have a brilliant sense of rhythm and you just have to look at the craze for dance programmes on television to see that they can transform someone's figure in a matter of weeks. Even just walking the children to school can be the perfect starting point.

If you are a fairly fit Taurean

If there is a social or family matter that calls, then you will more often than not be tempted to put your fitness routine second. However, if you're not fighting fit, then how can you help your close ones fight their battles in life? Yoga and Pilates can become a passion for you and will firm up all your best bits. These are also exercise forms that will become a way of life for a sign such as you, so should hopefully become a priority. Hatha yoga is one to look into, as it will suit your star sign. It concentrates on posture, something your sign doesn't usually make a priority.

If you are a very fit Taurean

Rock climbing and hiking are a must for the fittest of Bulls. Your love of the earth can see you excel, and even mountaineering could be on your list of sports to conquer. There's an array of charity treks that you can sign up for, giving you the perfect inspiration to take sport to the next level. You share the same sign as famous cricketers Phil Tufnell and Brian Lara, footballers David Beckham and Neil Ruddock, and boxing legends Sonny Liston and Sugar Ray Leonard!

Gemini

Gemini rules the chest, shoulders, nervous system and lungs.

You are renowned for having an unpredictable, hectic and very exciting lifestyle. Unlike some of the other signs, at times you really seem to thrive on stress, Gemini! Active lifestyles such as yours deplete energy levels; therefore it is imperative that you get enough liquid into your body. Energy drinks are good, but you should also consider drinking the juice of a parsnip, a carrot and half a cucumber before you tackle the day. I promise you this simple but odd-sounding concoction is just what your sign needs to take on the world and start your day on a positive note.

You must learn to communicate with your body and stop and rest when you need to. Pushing through is second nature to you but doesn't always leave you fighting fit and ready for round two. I often think of you as a very good short-distance runner. Learn to be a long-distance runner and beat the competition. Your dreams are always big, and now it's time to make them attainable.

Geminis are prone to swollen glands, asthma and allergic reactions due to a deficiency in potassium chloride. Herbs such as comfrey, tansy and even sweet liquorice are rich in this mineral. Unlike Taurus, you Geminis should be guzzling more mucus-producing foods, such as organic milk. However, beware of fatty foods. You have a tendency to put on weight in certain areas, making your body look out of proportion.

Like Aries, you suffer from nervous strain, and juniper berries or juniper oil are the ideal remedy for this. See the advice for Aries on page 217. Yoga is the perfect way to unwind after a stressful day at work. Finding a new pace of life and slowing down when the body requires it are the best ways for you to maintain high levels of fitness and health.

You can always find the energy to go that extra mile if it's to impress someone. Well, now it's time to impress the most important person: yourself. Show the world that you put yourself first and then others will learn to treat you with the respect you deserve.

DIET

What I love about you is that you go into things with such a good heart, but air signs such as you don't always have a lot of willpower, which is why motivation is so very important for you. You could even think about starting your own diet group; it could certainly turn into a money-spinner with a sign as business-minded as you. You are good at getting other people motivated, you see, which in turn can help you to achieve your goals and dreams. You'll be pleased to hear that even though it's hard for you to start, once you get the initial weight off, you manage to keep it off. Your sign has also usually been vegetarian at some point in their lives. Fresh air and exercise are vital for Gemini. It should become an essential part of your diet regime and for the healthy life I know you really want to live.

FITNESS

If you are an unfit Gemini
I know that your social life has probably interfered with your gym life, but I'm also sure that at some point you have taken out a gym membership, so I know the good intention is there. Get down to the gym this week and discover how social the classes can be! A challenge such as the cross-trainer will give you a buzz, not to mention being great for fat loss and cardiovascular training.

If you are a fairly fit Gemini
Cycling is great for you – fresh air, speed, excitement and changing scenery. It will tone up your legs and your bum, and is brilliant for the front of your thighs too. Cycling to work can and should become a way of life for your sign, unless of course it's geographically impossible. If you have to take the bus to work or when you go out, then get off the bus two stops early. Within a month you'll feel the benefit in both your lungs and your mind.

If you've started something, then I know you can get to the top. Circuit training is great for you, as it gives you the chance to show off the natural skills your sign possesses, as Geminis are great at keeping up with constant change and pace. You could also try competing in a half-marathon, as you're more capable than most of raising the sponsorship money. As long as eyes are on you, then you will rise to the challenge. Make this the beginning of a new way of life and look up some alternative sports such as flying; there's an adventurer and explorer in you dying to get out.

If you are a very fit Gemini
Hang-gliding and extreme sports will call out to you once you know your mind and body are up to the challenge. You need to push the boundaries in order to deal with the stress that you all too often attract into your life. You could also try skiing or snowboarding, which you don't have to travel abroad to do. Join the ranks of famous fellow Geminis such as footballer Lee Sharpe, cricket's Mike Gatting and Ray Illingworth, fitness guru Diana Moran and tennis ace Steffi Graf.

Cancer

Cancer rules the stomach, breasts, digestive system and liver.

They don't call you crabby for no reason. You can be moody and irrational, and this is all too often reflected in your health, which is a mirror to your emotional state. When you get stressed, it is often the stomach that first shows signs of a breakdown. You always have so much going on in that head of yours, namely the past, present and future, that you forget to eat. In fact with the amount of emotion running through your body you probably already feel full! When you do eventually get round to looking after yourself, the temptation to over-indulge and to stuff yourself with the wrong foods is all too strong. You then spend the next few hours not relaxing but fretting over what you have put into your body. You are a perfect candidate for indigestion. This can be easily remedied by using peppermint oil. Place one or two drops in a small amount of warm water and sip. Do this three times daily, preferably with meals. Do not exceed this dose. You can also take peppermint in tablets, capsules and powder.

Make peppermint tea by infusing a tablespoon of the leaves in a cup of boiling water and drink two or three times a day. Those suffering from liver damage, inflammation of the gall bladder or obstruction of the bile ducts or gallstones should consult a doctor before using peppermint, as should anyone suffering from gastrointestinal upset. For children, chamomile is a better choice.

You can cleanse the liver with an infusion of fresh or dried sage in hot water. Take a handful of fresh sage, well washed, or a teaspoon of dried sage, and 600 millilitres of hot, not boiling, water. Place the herb in a jug, add the water, cover and leave for twenty-four hours. Keep in the fridge and drink one glass each morning. Don't strain it, though: it's essential you leave the sage in the water. You could also try milk thistle, which is available as a supplement from health-food shops.

A lack of calcium fluoride means that Cancerians suffer from nerve and muscle problems. You can ward these off by stocking up on plenty of organic milk, watercress and oily fish like sardines. You should stay away from sushi – raw foods can cause you all sorts of stomach problems, so you should make sure food is thoroughly cooked before eating.

Because of irregular eating patterns, you are also prone to migraines, so ensure you drink water throughout the day and avoid tea or coffee; if you are only 2 per cent dehydrated, you can lose up to 20 per cent of your concentration. Eating little and often, which will prevent blood sugar levels from dropping, can prevent migraine too, and incorporating more ginger into your diet also works a treat. Give yourself a schedule and plan ahead with your food. It can save you a lot of trouble (and stomach aches).

DIET

If you don't believe that you can lose weight, then you won't. Support, encouragement and self-belief are half the battle for you water signs. Even just having a phone number you can ring for support or a website address where you can chat to other people can be enough, but you do need to have some sort of network structure to be able to reach your goals.

One of the main reasons you tend to put on weight in the first place is contentment. Self-control is a crucial word for you to learn and one that you will come to know well in your lifetime, I'm sure. A healthy body gives a healthy mind, and water signs such as you always feel so much better when you are looking good. Your close ones will also be happier because you are happier, and arguments are less likely to ensue.

FITNESS

If you are an unfit Cancerian

Drink plenty of water when you exercise to keep your body well hydrated. No fizzy drinks, though: we want you to have a natural high! Look to cycling in the gym for ten minutes and then work up to changing machines every ten minutes, so that after a few weeks of just the bike you can alternate between rower and runner or stepper, leading up to twenty and then thirty minutes of cardio. Slowly but surely you will up your fitness and improve your mood, ready to take on the world. You've failed previously because you haven't believed you can succeed. Now believe you can and see what a difference it will make.

If you are a fairly fit Cancerian

I know you can excel, especially if you find a sport that you enjoy. With your often curvy figure, look to weights to make a difference where it counts. You'll soon start to feel sexier, and before you know it, you can join in a body-pump or weights class and achieve the tone and confidence that will see you going for jobs and relationships you would previously have shied away from. Hiking is also therapeutic for you, my friend. Get your boots on and blow away those cobwebs. Nordic walking improves endurance, fitness, strengthens muscles, increases mobility and aids circulation, not to mention releasing pain and muscle tension in the neck and back. Get yourself some poles, find a group and get walking!

If you are a very fit Cancerian

Push the boundaries and try turning gentle swimming into a power swim. It's what your sign is made for and will give you the physique of your dreams. You can also look to kayaking and windsurfing. Your fitter body will open up a whole new world and can make all the difference. Team this with healthy eating instead of emotional eating and join famous Cancerian sports figures such as footballers Jamie Redknapp and Gianfranco Zola, cricket legend Sunil Gavaskar, golf ace Nick Faldo, boxer Steve Collins and even lord of the dance Michael Flatley.

Leo

Leo rules the back, spine and heart.

You love to live life to the full. If the mood takes you, then you will be open to a party at any time of the day or night. You often experience extremes, though. When you are happy, you are ecstatic, and when you are low, it's hard for close ones to know what to say to lift you up. Of course, these extreme characteristics are sure to take their toll on your health. Ease up on your schedule. Leos are all-or-nothing people, and while it is great to give everything 100 per cent, sometimes you need to say 'no' to things.

You are an ultimate professional when you're working, and even when you're partying. Over-exertion on your part links most commonly to back problems. Some astrologers argue that this is because you're naturally supposed to be on all fours, but whatever the reason back pain is very common for Leos. Massages can help this, as can making sure you've got the right sort of mattress. Avoid strain on the back by working to develop good posture. If you work sitting down, ensure your chair is correct for you.

You feel full of energy and vitality when the weather is good, but when it's cloudy and dark, you can become depressed. You love sunshine and good food, but when you get offered this, you often take it to the extreme and overindulge. You are prone to a deficiency of magnesium phosphate, which is needed for healthy lungs, muscles and nerves, not to mention the brain. This mineral can be found in plums, bran and even cocoa. You Leos are also lucky creatures – you rarely have alcohol problems and have mastered the trick of appearing sober, no matter how much you have had. In fact, you are more likely to get hooked on caffeine than alcohol, as Leos tend to be quite partial to cola and coffee. This doesn't mean you get the green light to over-indulge in the old vino either, though. Moderation is and must be the watchword for you, Leo.

Any foods that put a strain on the heart are not good for you. Make sure you eat meat in moderation and the best cuts only, and watch against over-indulgence once you hit fifty. Excess weight on a Leo is a lot harder to shift as you get older and yet that is precisely when we have more time to overindulge.

DIET

The big no-no for your sign is caffeine. It will keep you up all night and make you high as a kite. This is where your problems may start, as then you won't know or care what you are eating. Although caffeine is reputed to be good for you before a workout, if drunk afterwards it impedes your digestion, so cut down to reach your goal weight.

The majority of the time you are actually pretty good; it's just that when you have a bad day, you tend to go overboard. If you have eaten one thing that is bad, you see no reason to stop. Never go food-shopping when you are hungry. The people you see buying ten things that don't add up to a whole meal will be a fire sign such as you. Many Leo children find themselves underweight with all of the running around that they do, trying to find out what the world is all about. Why is it that as a child taking the stairs seems like a fun option to beat our family or friends who have taken the lift, yet as we get older we forget this? You always were a child at heart, Leo, so rediscover some of that enthusiasm for physical activity. It's the key to the body of your dreams.

FITNESS

If you are an unfit Leo
Now is the time to change. After all, your body is meant to be fit – you are a Lion, and without air in your lungs, your body and mind start to shut down. You need to tone your entire body and mind for a really dramatic change in the way you look. Don't overdo things; start by looking at simple measures if you are a really unfit Leo, such as carrying your basket at the supermarket instead of using a trolley. Doing speed housework could be fun, and when your confidence grows and we start to bring out the leader in you, head down

to a tai chi class. Before you know it, you could be teaching it. Visualize your goals. Boxercise classes are great for you too. You have a great body, you just don't know it yet, so are already one step ahead.

If you are a fairly fit Leo

Up the tempo of any classes you have attended and take things to the next level. I know how much better you'll feel when you start to see a change in both your body and your mood. Even alternative sports such as archery and javelin-throwing will bring out the beast in you. You want excitement, so look up local places that can make your weekends alternative yet healthy. Ice-skating may seem like a chore but is sure to end up as a passion with the natural ability you will have for it.

If you are a very fit Leo

Long-distance running is something you are probably already good at. Keep going and make runs more interesting by heading somewhere new. Decathlons and even iron-man competitions could and should be on your list of things to do. Join the ranks of famous Leos such as cricketer Dominic Cork, boxer Chris Eubank, tennis players Anne Hobbs and Jim Courier, and racing driver Nigel Mansell.

Virgo

Virgo rules the intestines.

Your sign is reputed to be a hypochondriac and born worrier. Your cupboards are usually full of medicines, potions and lotions for things you've had or thought you were coming down with. The good side to all of this of course is that prevention is better than cure, and as you take your health very seriously, you are already likely to be a mine of information about it. You don't actually have many health problems, but when you do feel ill, the whole world gets to know about it.

It is normally work that affects your health, causing stomach and bowel problems. This is because you worry and get stressed a lot, and even if you don't work, there is always some drama in your personal life causing you anxiety. This can often be because you get involved too readily in the problems of your nearest and dearest. Having said that, you Virgos are usually very healthy, though you need to keep the digestive and nervous systems in good order. Juicing an apple with some strawberries, blackberries, raspberries and lemon can make a great stress-buster for your sign. Taken regularly, this will soothe the most frayed of nerves.

You are more likely to be vegetarian than any other sign in the zodiac and are fussy about what you eat. You can lack potassium sulphate, which causes colds and coughs – in fact Virgos catch colds more easily than other signs. You really need to eat more tomatoes, lemons, apples and grapefruit to ward off these ailments. Dress for the weather – you can still look good in a scarf, you know. If you think you've already picked something up, then go to bed, drink plenty of liquids to avoid fluid loss, caused by sweating, and to flush out those toxins, hug a hot-water bottle if you feel shivery and call your doctor for advice if your symptoms persist for more than a few days.

In addition you need to get more fresh air, and for an earth sign, walking or running are ideal exercises. Health-conscious Virgos find that alcohol gives them kidney problems, and they are far more sensible than the rest of us. You usually alternate drinks with water when you go out and suffer far less the next day. Those of you who do choose to be drinkers know it comes at a price and can suffer from kidney and liver problems more than the rest of the zodiac, so often learn the hard way.

DIET

The key for your sign has got to be quality, not quantity. Healthy foods are essential for earth signs for optimum results. You spend so much of your time worrying about your close ones that you get embarrassed when it comes to you because you know you have left it too late. It's never too late, though, and the beauty of your sign is that you more often than not like the healthy fruits and vegetables that the rest of the zodiac turn up their noses at.

The other good point is that if you promise yourself, you will stick at something. You are your own taskmaster and so can excel where others fail. My advice to you, my friend, is not to be quite so hard on yourself. Even the top diet experts treat themselves every now and then.

FITNESS

If you are an unfit Virgo

Pilates would be a nice start for you, Virgo. It's designed to tone and sculpt your entire body, strengthening core muscles and increasing flexibility, and can also help you lose weight. You can start off with a DVD at home if you like, but when you see the difference it can make, you'll want to pop down to a class and make a major change. It's great for improving the condition of your body. The trampoline could also be fun for your sign and is a great starting point to get the blood pumping round your body.

If you are a fairly fit Virgo

It's probably been hard for you to take things to the next level because you are scared of failure and of people laughing at you behind your back. You go about things in such a practical manner that there is no reason for you to be worried or scared. I'm sure you're among the best in the zodiac at preparing yourself for any challenge. The best activity for you now would be skiing either at a sports centre or on snow if you want to get on the piste. Another great exercise would be a spinning class, which is a stationary bike class to music, because this really gets the body working hard.

If you are a very fit Virgo

Find which sport is your passion and enter it professionally. It's a fantastic thing if someone of your sign can turn a hobby into a career. Fencing would appeal to you, as would kiting. With your sign, you've got to enjoy what you do and any sport must have a social aspect to it. Olympic gold-medal cyclist Chris Boardman did just that, as did fellow Virgos yachtswoman Tracey Edwards, tennis aces Tim Henman and Greg Rusedski, ex-motor-cycle champion Barry Sheene, footballer David Seaman and Grand Prix champion Damon Hill.

Libra

Libra rules the kidneys, lumbar region and skin.

Without balance and harmony in your life, you become a very unhappy Libran. You need to work, rest and play if you are to function at your best. You are a great social animal and are all too often the last to leave a party. You love rich foods and have a wickedly sweet tooth.

You should take care of your kidneys by going easy on the booze at those late-night parties you love to frequent. You handle beer better than spirits, though should beware of the effect this can have on your waistline. You poor Librans get worse hangovers than other signs. You should try juicing a bunch of grapes with a nectarine after over-indulging. You should also get into the habit of drinking plenty of water throughout the day to flush out any toxins from your system and cleanse the kidneys.

Your sign can have a deficiency of phosphate of soda, which means you should eat more spinach, lettuce, apples and strawberries to maintain the balance of fluids in the body. You seem to thrive on vegetables grown above the ground, like mushrooms and bamboo shoots, which make for delicious stir-fries.

Fresh air and exercise are vital for you, Libra, especially with your element of air. Blowing away the cobwebs after a stressful day can help sort out all manner of problems. You should join a gym so that you can exercise and socialize to your heart's content.

DIET

One of your main problems is that you don't like to stick to one method of dieting for too long. You would prefer to mix and match. That is why when someone asks a Libran which diet they're on, they often um and ah before they answer.

One of the main issues for those of your sign when trying to lose weight is that, like Taureans, you have a sweet tooth and cannot resist the chocolates. What you must learn, though, is that if you don't pick it up and put it in the trolley, you can't eat it! Fresh raw foods are good for your sign and can help you to maintain lasting weight loss. Anything that is grown in the open is good for your element. Explore the flavours and stop thinking that you are only prepared to pay a decent price for a pretty bottle or package. Look beyond the appealing packaging and go back to nature. Fresh fruit and vegetables can be just as exciting, and are worth the extra pennies too.

FITNESS

If you are an unfit Libran

Your health is often a mirror image of your emotional state. You know deep down that you need fresh air and exercise to think straight. Get outside, go sightseeing or walk and eventually jog around places that inspire you. It's important to avoid injuries, so make sure you go to a good running shop and buy the correct footwear. There are so many different intensities that you can jog at. Start today with walking and reveal a new you. Even just walking the dog (or a friend's dog) is a great way to start. Feel and see the benefits that the fresh air can have on your sign. With a beautiful view as inspiration, you're sure to want to take things to the next level.

If you are a fairly fit Libran

Jogging is something that your sign should really enjoy. It is a pursuit that is indulged in by people of all fitness levels. You are prone to dips in energy levels, so find the best time of the day to exercise and stick to it. Exercise at least three times a week.

Look to new classes to inspire you. The latest fads catch your attention, so opt for a class that's only just begun and you're sure to be top before the month is up. You should also try hot yoga, which is a series of poses (something you like to do) done in a hot room. The room is usually maintained at a temperature of about ninety-five degrees. As you can imagine, a vigorous yoga session at this temperature causes sweating, which rids the body of toxins. It also makes the body very warm and therefore more flexible.

If you are a very fit Libran

Then it's time to really tone up as well as hitting the cardio and getting hot under the collar. Don't be afraid to look to weights – they don't have to add pounds; they can define muscle and give shape. Your sign, the Scales, is all about balance, so you've got to make sure that as well as cardio you are toning. Perfection is but a step away. You could even get into power-plating, which with each vibration forces the body to perform reflexive muscle actions twenty-five to fifty times per second. This results in an improvement that doesn't take months to achieve, just regular commitment. How can you not want to join the likes of fellow Librans footballer Paul Warhurst, Olympic gold-medal rower Matthew Pinsent, rugby's David Campese and tennis aces Jana Novotna and Thomas Muster?

Scorpio

Scorpio rules the reproductive system.

You are intense and powerful, a real force to be reckoned with. You are full of energy and do not do anything by halves. Like Pisceans, you are the extremists of the zodiac – for example, Scorpios who smoke and drink will usually do so to excess. Your addictive personality can cause you lots of problems. Eating disorders are not uncommon among your sign and usually surface during the teenage years. Scorpio rules the reproductive organs and the womb, meaning people born under this sign are subject to menstrual pains, urinary infections and water retention. To combat water retention, you must eat foods rich in potassium such as potatoes, bananas and tuna (no more than three times a week if it's tinned tuna). Try a juice-booster of an orange, a pineapple, a plum and a tangerine. It's sure to put the spring back in your step and that glint in your eye.

Scorpios can lack calcium sulphate, which is needed to keep the lungs healthy and ulcers at bay. Many foods are full of calcium sulphate, including cabbage, kale, milk and onions. Contrary to popular belief, your sign does not thrive on stress; in fact it affects you badly, as you are an over-emotional sign. Wherever possible, you should try to avoid stressful situations, and when you do feel anxious, you should try relaxation techniques. A bath with aromatherapy oils is great for both body and soul, and will set you up for a good night's sleep. Scorpios are renowned for reacting unpredictably to alcohol – a drop of wine can leave you legless one night, whereas after drinking a bottle of whisky the next, you could still be sober as a judge. Focus is what's needed and then you can excel in whatever you put your mind to.

DIET

Your sign spends more time talking about what you're going to eat next than actually eating. It's not unusual for Scorpios to turn to their partner as they dish up that day's dinner to ask what they're going to be eating the following day.

Because water retention can be a problem for your sign, you need to be careful with your intake of both salt and alcohol. Sugary fizzy drinks, such as cola, can make you look far bigger than you are through bloating. You may want to avoid bloating foods such as beans, cabbage and onions three days before a big event. Just this simple deduction from your diet will offer you dramatic results. Drinking plenty of water is also important for you.

The problem for you, Scorpio, is that if anyone tells you that you can't have something, you want that food all the more. Fish is a key food to keeping you slim, as it suits your sign better than red meat.

FITNESS

If you are an unfit Scorpio

You have probably failed before because you have become obsessed with a particular exercise and have then grown so bored that you never want to go to that class or see that teacher again. Exercise can and will become a way of life for you. Start by treating yourself to something relaxing at the end of a workout. Get down to the gym and try a different class every week; you'll soon find which one becomes your new best friend.

If you have not done any exercise for a long time, then try a gentle aqua class. Don't take the car to the car wash; wash it yourself. Build up to a healthy active lifestyle. Promise to take the stairs, not the lift, and book a private swimming class. I promise it will be well worth it. Get some lessons on technique and before you know it you'll be beating everyone in the pool with your perfect front crawl.

If you are a fairly fit Scorpio

It's time to make sure you keep variety in your routine so you don't get bored. Naturally good at running, you should join a running club so that you can explore new places. It's important to avoid injury, so make sure you buy the correct footwear. Pilates would also help you to release your pent-up feelings and would probably save your close ones from an ear-bashing about the day's problems.

Variety is the key for you, as once you've mastered a sport, you'll need a new challenge. Cycling becomes mountain biking, swimming becomes competitive, and running turns into a marathon! Just make sure you plan something as a reward for yourself afterwards. Having an incentive will always see you go the extra mile. Make it a healthy treat, though, Scorpio!

If you are a very fit Scorpio

It's time to push the boundaries and enrol in a marathon in a foreign country. Run the five volcanoes in Italy, get on your bike and cycle the Nile or run the Great Wall! With a taste for excitement, you're sure to push yourself harder if you don't know what's round the corner. In fact with your determination it won't be long before Everest is on your agenda. You crave a challenge, just like fellow Scorpios top swimmer Sharon Davies, cricket's Courtney Walsh, rugby's Austin Healey, goalie Ian Walker and footballer Ian Wright.

Sagittarius

Sagittarius rules the hips, thighs, nerves and arteries.

Lust for life and optimism characterize your sign. You are extremely versatile and move quickly from one idea to the next, constantly needing to grow and expand. Adventurous Sagittarians relish a challenge and love exercise, sometimes to excess, so the poor body suffers. You are constantly on the move and often do not warm up before doing strenuous sports, meaning your body can be prone to sprains, thigh fractures and even hip dislocation. Swimming is the ideal exercise for helping pulled muscles and ligaments get back into shape.

When it comes to colds, you have a particularly weak resistance and only need to spend a short while in a smoky, crowded room before catching a nasty bug. I'm sure you were one of the signs who rejoiced when the no-smoking ban came into effect. Indeed more fresh air is the best preventative measure, and you must not forget to wrap up warm come winter. You could try to incorporate more onions, barley and cherries into your diet, which will help to boost your immune system and ward off colds.

Because you always have somewhere to go and people to

see, you are all too often impatient cooks. You frequently eat on the run and this almost always means that you eat fast food. It is very important that you take time out to ensure that you have a balanced diet. It is likely that you will suffer from a silica deficiency, which may well show itself in your appearance – brittle nails, poor skin and hair. You can remedy this by adding raw oats to a smoothie or eating parsnips, asparagus and the humble cucumber, which will give your health and appearance the boost they need.

DIET

Your sign is known as an initiator of action but not necessarily as a great stayer. You like constant change; it keeps you feeling alive. If you begin anything, it will be with a great deal of energy. People around you will believe you could make it to the stars and back again should you so desire. You inspire others, but don't always put as much effort into inspiring yourself. There is hope, though – you just have to want to change your life and you will find that you can. Many fire signs go on binges. They starve themselves for a couple of days and then go mad eating all the wrong things. Starving your body teaches it to store fat. Learn to eat the right foods and you won't need to calorie-count again.

FITNESS

If you are an unfit Sagittarian
Start off with your best asset: your legs. These are what give you an edge over the other signs. You already have a level of fitness to tap into of which you are unaware. Look to fun sports that will see you moving more on your feet, such as dancing, ice-skating, hockey and basketball, and take it from

there. Once you've got into the game, you'll get into the zone and you'll be looking for the next challenge.

If you are a fairly fit Sagittarian

Horse riding, tennis and archery are all things you'd be good at. Once you've begun any sort of exercise, you'll find that you have the kind of body that feels ill when you don't keep it up. You thrive when you are giving your body what it needs. Yoga is also good for you and can help you focus on the jobs you have ahead of you in life. Look to Ashtanga yoga if you want to take things up a level, as it is a vigorous and more athletic style of practice.

If you are a very fit Sagittarian

Rock on with rock climbing and discover the excitement that can come from taking risks. You do it in work and now you can do it in your spare time. Close ones will love the new you and I'm sure your love life will benefit too. Desert running and boxing should also be on your list of things to try. Join ranks with fellow Sagittarians at the top of their game, such as cricket legends Imran Khan and Craig White, squash ace Jahangir Khan, ski ace Alberto Tomba, footballer Ryan Giggs and boxer Gary Jacobs.

Capricorn

Capricorn rules the knees, skeleton, bones and skin.

With Saturn as your ruling planet, you are self-controlled and self-disciplined, and this is often reflected in your health. You are proud of your body and will be the first to notice when you have put on some weight.

You Capricorns need to watch your calcium level, as your joints and bones are particularly weak. Make sure you're eating plenty of green leafy vegetables and some nuts and seeds. Desk jobs exacerbate stiff joints: you really do need to keep moving! This does not necessarily mean to say you should go out and get a personal trainer to whip you into shape, though. Gentle exercise, like walking or swimming, is the best way to maintain fitness without putting too much strain on your joints. Knees are particularly weak and can be strengthened by adding more parsley to your food. Both parsley and devil's claw are good for aches and rheumatic pain, and can also help gastrointestinal problems. Sprinkle them over meat and vegetables for a quick and easy vitamin boost.

Like Sagittarians, Capricorns are vulnerable to chills. Glucosamine may help to relieve osteoarthritis of the knee, and studies even show the supplement can be good for mild to moderate arthritis. Do not take this if you are a diabetic or suffer from a seafood allergy, and always consult a qualified practitioner before you take any supplements. It can also help to slow down the progression of arthritis by helping to keep joint cartilage healthy.

You must remember to wrap up warm and get more fresh air. Your lungs are generally not as strong as those of people born under other signs, though a tea made with half a teaspoon of lungwort, half a teaspoon of ribwort (available from a good herbalist) and boiling water can work wonders on your respiratory system.

DIET

In general Capricorns are self-controlled, but eating can be an addiction for the earth sign such as you, just as smoking or drinking is for some of the other signs in the zodiac. You also spend a lot of time thinking about what you are going to eat or cook next. Many earth signs eat more food the more weight they gain. It is a kind of self-inflicted punishment for gaining weight in the first place. Change this habit now and work out a plan of action for yourself. Your sign naturally savours flavours and should really be able to stop eating when you are full. It is normally emotional pressures that tip you over the edge or that can see you reaching for foods you know make you lethargic. You are more aware of your body than many other signs, which is why it is so important you distinguish good foods from bad. You have an instinct for knowing what you should and shouldn't be eating and must rise above any emotional stress.

FITNESS

If you are an unfit Capricorn

Cycling is great for your calves, and if you're overweight, then it's perfect, as there is less pressure on the joints than in many forms of exercise. If you haven't cycled in years, then hop back on. Bikes now come in every shape and design you could imagine. Just call your nearest cycling school and get hooked up with some fellow enthusiasts. Make sure you have the saddle at the correct height or ask the professionals to show you. This is a sport that can help you lose the pounds without putting too much pressure on your body.

Rambling is also great for your sign; you get to see beautiful countryside while exercising your body. You are a sign that needs to stay hydrated, so make sure you take plenty of water with you. Up the intensity and make your trips longer each time. You'll soon be ready for the next level of fitness.

If you are a fairly fit Capricorn

You often drag yourself down with the belief that you can't do the things that lie ahead of you when in fact you could, if you took it in stages. You think of everything at once and need to learn only to worry about what is happening now and not what is round the corner. You are a natural climber, so get on the stepper at the gym; you'll find it soul-building to realize what a natural aptitude you have for exercises which the other signs find a struggle. Martial arts would also be great for your sign. You are a perfectionist and will rise through the ranks quicker than other less dedicated signs.

If you are a very fit Capricorn

Walking and climbing appeal to you, so take these to the next level and make your goals and destinations more extreme. Tobogganing, skiing or snowboarding should be on your list, and body-boarding is something you'd be a natural at. Weights are also something you can now incorporate into your regime to make your body the temple it should be. Meditation will allow you to focus on life and ensure that you are making the right decisions. With a good base of training, you can try any exercise you please. The sky's the limit. Join the leagues of high-achieving Capricorns like motor racing's Michael Schumacher, football's Lee Bowyer, rugby's Gavin Hastings, tennis ace Christine Truman, jockey Richard Dunwoody and soccer legend Eusébio da Silva Ferreira.

Aquarius

Aquarius rules the circulation and the ankles.

Those born under this sign are prone to ankle sprains and other leg problems. You often feel cold even when the weather is warm because of your poor circulation, and the fact that you love wearing skimpy clothing does not help matters. A tea made from angelica leaves will not only stimulate circulation but also blitz a stinking cold. Exercises like swimming and aqua aerobics are best for building up leg muscles and improving the circulation. Comfortable rather than impractical shoes are a must if you want to avoid those painful ankle strains. When it comes to fashion, you are all too often willing to pay a high price just to look good, but ill-fitting clothes can have disastrous consequences for a sign such as you, so be warned. Tight jeans, shoes or even just the wrong kind of products can cause skin problems. A high price tag doesn't always mean quality, Aquarius.

Like all air signs, you should have a light and nourishing diet. Fast foods can leave you feeling bloated and lethargic. Substituting them for something like a jacket potato with beans will see a slow release of energy that will last you throughout the day while still leaving you feeling full.

You really are sensitive creatures and can suffer from periods of nervous tension, which will affect the digestion. It is important you find a partner who can help you to lift yourself out of the depression you all too often find yourself in. Women are also prone to severe period pains. They should drink lots of water and avoid alcohol.

Although you are social animals, you should not and must not sacrifice your sleep. You need to make time for relaxation and pampering yourself. Valerian tea before bedtime is preferable to a stiff nightcap if you want a deep, satisfying sleep. Remember that you can't take on the whole world's problems yourself! Enjoy today and stop living for tomorrow.

DIET

You annoy the rest of the zodiac because there are parts of your body that look as if you have worked out even when you've been doing nothing. You are a great conversationalist, but you also have the ability to talk on subjects you know nothing about. Sensitive and impulsive, it's vital that the decision to do something about your diet and fitness must be one you have reached on your own and not one that you have made due to pressure from friends and family.

FITNESS

If you are an unfit Aquarian

Camping is an ideal way to get you into the idea of using your body and being at one with the elements. Just putting up the tent is sure to get the blood pumping. Outdoor exercises are ideal and bring out the adventurer in you. Rollerblading would be great for you, as you'd enjoy the social aspect. Why not team this with a competitive sport and look at ice hockey once you're ready to take things up a level?

If you are a fairly fit Aquarian

With your love of the outdoors you may want to start cycling. Work up to longer distances and even turn it into a weekend away. First of all I want you to aim for thirty minutes of continuous steady cycling and get used to the feel of the bike. Once you get used to this, you can incorporate some bursts of flat-out cycling and then continue at a lower intensity. Surfing or diving will fare well with you, as will parachuting. Do it for your favourite charity and feel extra good about your challenge. It should give you the incentive to actually do it instead of just thinking about it.

If you are a very fit Aquarian

Scuba-diving and gliding are exercises that allow your sign to express themselves and to experience some extremes. You need to get your circulation going and any sort of adrenalin rush is sure to keep you coming back for more. Don't rule out skiing either – you're sure to have a natural affinity with the sport. If fellow Aquarians boxer Nigel Benn, footballers David Ginola and Robbie Earle, ballet dancer Mikhail Baryshnikov, golfer Nick Price and boxer Prince Naseem Hamed can excel in their sports, then so can you!

Pisces

Pisces rules the feet.

Pisceans believe in suffering for their beauty, and strangely it is usually the feet that suffer. Your most common bad habit is buying shoes that look spectacular but are extremely bad for your feet. You must watch out for swollen ankles and water retention. Regular visits to the chiropodist are recommended, as is investing in a foot spa. If you can find a willing participant, a foot massage with essential oils will perk up the most tired and swollen of feet. Generally speaking, Pisceans create many of their own ailments by living life to the extreme. You love intense experiences, whether they are good for you or not. Moderation is not in your vocabulary! Pisceans are dreadful dieters; you are prone to snacking and have varied eating patterns, which results in digestive problems. You also tend to turn to food to make your worries go away instead of eating when you are actually hungry.

Pisceans are often lacking in phosphate of iron, which is needed to make red blood and increase good circulation. This can be found in most leafy green vegetables, raisins, dates, figs and nuts. When it comes to alcohol, Pisceans are extremely weak. You are not very good at judging when you have had enough, and those who over-indulge can suffer from liver ailments. Restraint should be the watchword for Pisceans everywhere, and that is in *all* aspects of their life.

DIET

We all know by now that you have an addictive nature. If I told you that you were not allowed my apple, you'd want it more than anything else. The problem is that it's not usually something as healthy as an apple that close ones are trying to keep away from you. It's probably that extra glass of wine or beer or that big dessert. Your figure can and should be fantastic. You have such a determined mind that you could easily excel in anything you put your mind to. Bananas are good for you, as they have a high potassium content and can take the place of sweet foods that are packed full of calories.

FITNESS

If you are an unfit Piscean

Dancing will appeal to you, as you are naturally good on your feet. Why not pick up one of the dance DVDs on the market? Or get down to a class and learn some new steps. The social aspect will appeal to you, and with your addictive nature it won't be long before you're ready to take things up a notch. It's never too late to start ballet either, you know. There are classes for all levels, so there's no reason not to start or to pick up where you left off as a child. You could also try Pilates, which involves rebalancing your body and stretching to build up muscle tone.

Besides burning calories and reducing your body fat, aerobic exercise is a fantastic stress-buster. It can help rid you of all the problems your day has heaped on you. Any class you do should give you plenty of variety, as you are prone to boredom. You can be sure that you will be working on lots of different muscles, ensuring an all-round programme.

If you are a fairly fit Piscean

Instead of swimming as a hobby, get into it as a sport and try alternating between the water sports. Scuba-diving would be good, especially as you'll get to visit some very exotic locations. You know you are good at whatever you decide to do, so make up your mind and increase the level and intensity. Challenge a friend and you're sure to find the inspiration to throw in a couple of extra sessions.

If you are a very fit Piscean

You want something with a hint of danger. Swimming with sharks, diving on the Great Barrier Reef or white-water rafting! You also want speed and action and would be great at a competitive sport, such as semi-professional or even professional football or boxing. Just remember not to take it too personally. Be inspired by fellow Pisceans motor-racing legend Alain Prost, soccer legend Denis Law, football's Ole Gunnar Solskjaer, boxer Barry McGuigan and basketball's Charles Barkley.

A new you will emerge

As your fitness levels increase and your body starts to take shape and become lean, your self-confidence will grow too. No longer will you be looking to other people for happiness; you will find what you need within yourself. You will, however, recognize who or what was dragging you down and then it will be 'Goodbye, past, and hello, new and improved future.' For example, I know many of you think you couldn't end a relationship that you rely on right now even though you know you should, but once you start to boost your self-confidence by becoming fit in body, the mind will follow and you will be able to sort out your life.

Quick health checklist for your shopping trolley

Coming from a Romany family, I have been brought up with the belief that herbs and vitamins are vital to our health. Further study over many years of writing books and working with health experts has only increased this belief. Of course, firstly we should all look to vitamins in our foods, and if we are not getting sufficient, then supplements are a good way to ensure we are mentally and physically able to tackle all that life throws at us. Read the checklist for your sign and see if you're getting enough of the right vitamins. It could turn out to be the key to the energy and vitality you've been looking for.

Aries

- Magnesium can help with tiredness.
- Try feverfew and evening primrose oil for headaches.
- Take B2 and B3 for the metabolism, nervous system, vital organs, eyes, muscles, skin and hair. These can be found in brewer's yeast, wholegrain cereals, liver, rice, nuts, milk, eggs, meat, fish, fruit and green leafy vegetables.
- For nervous problems and neuralgia, take B1 (thiamine). B1 is in brown rice, peas, beans, breakfast cereals and Marmite. It should aid your nervous system by releasing the energy you need.
- B6 can be found in wholemeal bread and wholegrains, liver, fish, bananas, wheat bran, yeast extract and brewer's yeast, and will promote healthy skin and nerves, and help hormone production by increasing antibodies.
- Drink peppermint tea for stomach problems.

Taurus

- For that vulnerable Taurean throat, baptisia or lachesis are fantastic and are what many of the top homeopaths recommend. They are also good for toxic intestinal conditions. Available from all good homeopaths and health-food stores.
- The best drink for a Taurean is water and plenty of it. This is the simplest and most effective health measure, and the cheapest. There is no excuse for not drinking lots of water, so give it a go. You will end up feeling and looking 100 per cent better.
- To reduce catarrh, turn to zinc, which can be found in seafood, beef, pork, dairy products, green vegetables and cereals, or take supplements if you must. The recommended daily intake is 15 milligrams.
- Vitamin C, which helps the body fight infection, can be found in blackcurrants, kiwi fruit, peas, potatoes, Brussels sprouts, broccoli and oranges. You can also take supplements. The recommended daily intake is 60 milligrams.
- Sniff tea-tree and eucalyptus oils, and take garlic supplements to ward off colds if you spot the symptoms in time.
- For digestion difficulties, try peppermint tea.
- If you've overeaten, try the herb centaury.

Gemini

You are one of the signs that can really benefit from taking vitamin supplements on a regular basis because no matter how much you try, you don't eat when you should.

- For eye strain, try bilberry extract and vitamin B-complex.
- vitamin B1 (thiamine) is good for nervous problems. Take a supplement or eat foods such as brown rice, peas, beans, breakfast cereals and Marmite.

- All the water-soluble vitamins (B-complex and C) are good to take on a regular basis. The body doesn't store these and they need constant replenishment, something Geminis need to bear in mind.

Cancer

- Honeysuckle is great to help a Cancerian who is having sleep problems. Fill a pillow with fresh honeysuckle and you can guarantee that your dreams will be sweet.
- The herb feverfew is great for migraines but needs to be taken regularly to get the best results. You can get feverfew in tablet form or tincture, but the fresh leaves are better. A couple of leaves a day eaten in between some bread work well. You can also soak a cloth in an infusion of feverfew and place it on your forehead to relieve headaches.
- For stomach problems, try taking digestive enzymes (extracted from pineapple and papaya) or peppermint oil.
- B2 detoxes the liver. For liver problems, get Bio Light liquid from your health-food store. It's a great detox and comes in several flavours.
- Nervous exhaustion can be tackled with vitamin B-complex and vitamin E. The nervous system depends on an adequate intake of those vitamins.
- Take vitamin B1 (thiamine) daily to help with muscle coordination and the nerves. It also acts as a general pick-me-up when energy is flagging or in times of stress, which can produce symptoms such as irritability, headaches, loss of appetite and indigestion.
- For the blues, 50 to 100 milligrams of vitamin B6 can help (but not if pregnant).

Leo

- If you suffer from strain on the heart, try co-enzyme Q10. This substance is found in all the body's cells, particularly its heart muscles, nerve tissue and blood. It aids the transfer of oxygen and energy between the blood and body's cells and between components of those cells. If you are deficient in Q10, often an affliction of athletes and the elderly, take a supplement of 10 to 30 milligrams daily. It is widely available in health-food shops and chemists. It occurs naturally in peanuts, spinach, bran, beef, sardines and mackerel.
- Antioxidants – for example, vitamins A, C and E, beta carotene and lecithin – are found in parsley, garlic, fruit and vegetables and fish oils, and should help fight free radicals, which are thought to damage the body's cells, making you prone to disease and the effects of ageing.
- Eat more fresh tuna, salmon, pilchards, sardines, herring and mackerel. They are all particularly good for you, as of course are fresh fruit and vegetables. Only have two to three portions of oily fish a week, preferably organic or wild.
- For over-exertion, rest! Restore your energy reserves with iron and good nutrition.
- Weak circulation can be treated with vitamin E or ginkgo biloba, which are especially good for those with cold hands and feet or poor memory and concentration.

Virgo

- Herbal remedies work well for Virgos and should always be tried. If you're not eating the diet you know you should, then take a one-a-day multivitamin and mineral tablet.
- Zinc lozenges are good for Virgo throat problems. Or try a horseradish throat remedy of half a teacup of fresh (and only fresh) horseradish soaked well in vinegar for twenty-four

hours, making sure the horseradish is immersed. Add a tablespoon of glycerine, mix well and take half a teaspoon in a glass of hot water when necessary. Sip very slowly.

- For stomach problems, look to the probiotics acidophilus and bifidus.
- A bout of flu means you may have to forget about work for at least a week. As a precaution or when winter looms, take echinacea, zinc and vitamin C.

Libra

- Cranberry is good for cystitis and kidney infections. Why not include cranberry juice in your shopping trolley? Make sure it's low in sugar and additives. Cantharis is a good homeo-pathic remedy for cystitis.
- If you are having problems with your skin, you need vitamins A and E. You can find vitamin A in cod-liver oil, liver, butter, cheese and eggs. Pregnant women must be careful about taking too much vitamin A. Vitamin E is found in vegetable oils, peanuts, eggs, wholemeal bread, wheatgerm and green leafy vegetables. Eat plenty of these and consider supple-ments. Evening primrose oil, vitamin C and beta carotene are also good for the skin. Aloe-vera lotion or gel is nice to apply to soothe and moisturize the skin.
- If you suffer from diabetes, ask your doctor about taking chromium.
- If you do take pills such as headache tablets, go for the lowest dose. Medicines affect Librans more quickly than most. You might find your headache is cured with just one tablet. Or try the herb feverfew, which is fantastic for headaches. Of course, if your problems persist, then consult your GP.

Scorpio

- If you want to ensure a healthy heart, make sure your diet includes essential fatty acids from either oily fish such as fresh tuna, salmon, pilchards, sardines, herring and mackerel or plant oils such as flaxseed. Also for the heart, co-enzyme Q10 is valuable. It can be absorbed by the body from peanuts, spinach, beans, bran, beef, sardines and mackerel. It helps to release the energy in food for use by the body's cells. Pregnant women should not take it as a supplement.
- For organ problems, make zinc a regular part of your diet. This is found in seafood, beef, pork, dairy products, green vegetables, seeds, nuts, pulses and cereals. It is particularly easy to add green vegetables to a dish or a meal, and there are so many different varieties around that you need never eat the same vegetable twice in a month, let alone a week.
- For nasal catarrh, take supplements of zinc, vitamin C and garlic. For relief, sniff tea-tree or eucalyptus oil.

Sagittarius

- For stress, try getting some fresh burdock root if you can track it down. Scrub the root clean, chop it up and then boil it in two pints of water for fifteen minutes. Strain and, when cooled, drink a glass three times a day. You can make up a new batch as and when necessary.
- Elderflower tea is good if you are recovering from a cough or a cold or are feeling a little run down.
- Fennel tea relieves indigestion, especially that caused by stressful mealtimes. Its lovely aniseed taste helps you digest food more easily, and it takes away that bloated feeling.
- Try peppermint tea if you have over-indulged in alcohol or are just feeling sickly. It will bring you nicely back down to earth.

- Camomile tea helps relieve anxiety attacks and should help you sleep more easily.
- For lack of sleep due to pain, try cowslip tea, available from all good health-food stores, which is fantastic.
- Rosehip tea contains vitamin C and has a pleasant taste.
- If you are pregnant, stick to camomile, lemon and lime or peppermint tea to be on the safe side.
- If you suffer from nervous exhaustion, improve your intake of the B vitamins. Good sources are brown rice, seeds, beans, breakfast cereals and Marmite.
- For blood disorders or anaemia, you need iron and vitamin B12. Please consult your doctor or a health professional, who can tell you the correct doses. Iron can be found in beef, pork, liver and kidneys, canned pilchards, sardines, eggs, fortified cereals, spinach, cocoa powder, tomato purée, apricots and green leafy vegetables. B12 can be found in meat, poultry, fish, eggs, cheese, milk, molasses and breakfast cereals.
- Rheumatism can be helped with evening primrose oil and starflower (borage) oil. Devil's claw also works well. Look to your local health-food store for supplies.

Capricorn

- For skin disorders, try zinc, which can be found in seafood, beef, pork, dairy products, green vegetables, seeds, nuts, pulses and cereals. Also try vitamin A, which can be found in cod-liver oil, liver, butter, cheese and eggs. Pregnant women must be careful not to take too much vitamin A. The B vitamins, vitamin E, antioxidants and evening primrose oil are also important for the skin.
- For chills, take ginkgo biloba.
- For rheumatism, ask your health-food store for devil's claw, evening primrose oil and starflower (borage) oil.

- Treat liver problems with Bio Light liquid, available from health-food shops.
- Make sure you get enough calcium. It helps to keep your teeth and bones strong.
- Magnesium, vitamin C (found in blackcurrants, kiwi fruit, peas, potatoes, Brussels sprouts, broccoli, guava, peppers and oranges) and vitamin D (found in kippers, mackerel, eggs, milk and some fortified margarines) are also important for you.

Aquarius

- If you suffer from bad nerves, try ginseng, a plant that has long been used as a nerve tonic. It is also a stimulant. B-complex is good for nerves too.
- For bad circulation, try ginkgo biloba (from your health-food store) or fish-oil supplements. Better still, add ginger to your cooking and eat plenty of tuna, salmon, pilchards, sardines, herring and mackerel. Only eat two to three portions of oily fish a week (and only one of tuna), and where possible, buy organic or wild. Vitamin E, found in vegetable oils, eggs, peanuts, wholemeal bread, wheatgerm and green leafy vegetables, is also good for the circulation.
- For cramps, look to magnesium supplements and eat more seafood, pasta, peas, soya beans, nuts and wholemeal bread. Try brewer's yeast too.
- For nervous indigestion, try peppermint tea.

Pisces

- For rheumatism, try evening primrose oil, devil's claw or starflower (borage) oil from your health-food store.
- For any chest problem, the essential fatty acid omega-3 is helpful. It can be found in oily fish and ground linseeds,

which you can try sprinkling over your cereal. Some of the other fats, especially too much saturated fat, can be harmful to the body, but omega-3s are beneficial and are especially good for the heart. Evening primrose oil is also good, as is antioxidant vitamin A, which is in cod-liver oil, butter, cheese and eggs. Pregnant women must avoid taking too much vitamin A. Avoid caffeine if you suffer chest pain.

- For chills or feet problems, try ginkgo biloba, as it helps to maintain healthy circulation.
- For gout, avoid meat and alcohol, and try zinc, vitamin B6 (found in wholemeal bread, liver, fish, bananas, wheat bran, yeast extract and brewer's yeast) or calcium and magnesium.

Health questionnaire

If you feel that all is not as it should be in your life, then ask yourself the questions below and answer with honesty. After you have written down your answers put them somewhere safe. When you have followed my health plan for a month, you can ask yourself the same questions. Keep answering them each month until the answers give you confidence and boost your self-esteem. If you follow my advice, it won't be long before *all* your answers are self-confident ones!

1. What or who is the main reason you want to get healthy and improve your diet?
2. What do you think will change about your life if you get healthy and improve your diet?
3. Do you like who you are?
4. Do you recognize the things and people you need to remove from your life that are bringing you down?

5. What are the goals and ambitions that you know will make you happy?

Remember that if you keep to an improved health and fitness regime, the answers to these questions will change as time goes on. You'll start to make the answers fit your life, instead of relying on those around you to affirm your identity and dictate your mood. You'll soon see that a healthy body does equal a healthy and happy mind. With this proven, there really will be no going back!

Chapter 11

HIGHS AND LOWS

We're only human and so we're bound to go wrong
once in a while. Life is, after all, a learning curve. Remember
that experience is what makes us wise, and without going
through the hard times we wouldn't recognize the good times.

Did you know that some signs in the zodiac have more
addictive personalities than others? Strange but very, very
true. Scorpio and Pisces are actually two of the most
addictive. In fact many famous stars born under these signs
have fought problems with drink and drugs, but have also,
you'll be pleased to know, won! Leos think life is a competition and get upset if they don't achieve things in the time
they have allotted for themselves. Taureans and Virgos hate
to let their loved ones down and blame themselves before
others. Geminis think life is a race, while Capricorns give
themselves too little time to complete what lies ahead. These
signs can show addictive behaviour when they get stressed
and must learn to recognize when they hit pressure points
so that they can keep their lives from spiralling out of control.

Aries want to save the world and change it, Aquarians want
to understand the universe before they've had a chance to
understand who they are, while Cancerians and Librans want
to solve the problems of people they don't even know.
Sagittarians, meanwhile, want to excel in things they know

nothing about. We're a confusing bunch, and that's before we start mixing together!

Whatever it is that you think you may be addicted to – drink, drugs, alcohol, bad relationships or overspending – you have to know that you are not alone. There are many people out there fighting the same battle as you, and there is far more help on hand than you think. If you want to go to a support group, that's great, but if you'd rather pick up the phone and talk to someone anonymously, then that's all right too. There is no hard and fast rule. If you embark on a road to recovery that makes you feel positive and good about yourself, then you know that it's the right route for you. If you don't feel that you're going in the right direction, then think about what and who isn't quite working. There are plenty of organizations out there to help you find your recipe for success and I have listed them later in this chapter.

The first step is believing in yourself. There is a whole future out there ready for the taking and anything is possible with just a little support and determination. If your partner or friends and family are not giving you the support you need, then move on and find someone who can. If you are with someone who has an addictive personality, then take the first step together. If they don't, then take it on your own. They should soon follow when they see what amazing progress you are making.

In this chapter we'll take a look at some of the traits that the various signs possess so you can recognize yourself at your lowest and embrace your highs. Addictions are often our way of saying that we need help, and it's important that we look at the root of the problem so that we don't solve one problem just to inherit another.

There is always a way to communicate, no matter what your sign. Some people like to sit and talk about their problems, while for others it's a personal journey they need to travel alone to discover what makes them happy. Years of experience have taught me that problems in our bodies and minds are warning us that something needs to change. I have seen clients who could not move for back pain and yet when they made a change in their life, the pain vanished virtually overnight.

We can blame a person or a situation, but we all hold the power to change, no matter what our sign or age. Taking action can and will help us move on to bigger and better things. Life is about balance. It's about making ourselves happy, giving something back to the people we love and acknowledging when there's a problem before that problem becomes bigger than us.

Aries

You know you are at your lowest when you feel totally irresponsible and become reckless. Aries such as Robert Downey Junior and Butch Cassidy allowed the negativity of their star sign to rule for a while.

Turn to your positive qualities and light up the lives of those around, like Aries Andrew Lloyd Webber, or create a more beautiful world like Aries Leonardo Da Vinci.

Taurus

You know you are at your lowest when you feel stuck in a rut and unable to think about tomorrow for worrying about the problems that today may bring.

Actor Al Pacino, star of *The Godfather*, is a Taurean and may have only been acting in many of his Mafia-style movies, but he's sure to have drawn on a few of his sign's traits for inspiration. Even the late, great actor Marlon Brando, who was also in *The Godfather*, was as famous for the controversy and excess in his personal life as he was for his on-screen success.

Turn to your positive qualities and be clever with your life and words, such as Taurean William Shakespeare. Be courageous and strong, like Pope John Paul II, who was always there for his faith and was deeply committed to the love of his life, God. Her Majesty the Queen has always followed her belief that life will and should go on, no matter what problems and dramas face her.

Gemini

You know you are at your lowest when you feel it impossible to let go of the past or of relationships that are not working. Gemini Marilyn Monroe had a string of lovers who were no good for her and who led to her decline.

Turn to your positive qualities, like Gemini Kylie Minogue, who faced the world when she became ill and fought her way back to health with the power of positive thinking.

Cancer

You know you are at your lowest when you feel emotionally empty and full of self-doubt and loathing.

Turn to your positive qualities, like Cancerian Helen Keller, who became blind and deaf at the age of nineteen months and went on to learn to read Braille. She graduated with honours and began a life of writing, lecturing and fundraising.

Leo

You know you are at your lowest when you feel that what you have is more important than who you are. Leo J. D.

Rockefeller allowed arrogance to prevail and take the limelight away from his best traits.

Turn to your positive qualities and reinvent yourself, just as Leo Madonna has done time after time. Know that life never has to be boring. Stay open to change; it's what your sign thrives on and what attracts success to you.

Virgo

You know you are at your lowest when you become self-critical. Virgo Nicole Richie may have come from a famous family, but she had her fair share of rehab before she realized that a simple life was not so hard to find. Actor River Phoenix died far too young, due to dabbling with narcotics.

Turn to your positive qualities and become a saint! The late Mother Teresa, who was a Virgo, certainly did a good job of showing off the best of this sign's traits.

Libra

You know you are at your lowest when you feel moody, lazy and unable to put others first. Rebel Tommy Lee, who is a Libran, had a reputation for this in the past.

Turn to your positive qualities and join the ranks of the late Linda McCartney, who was a typical Libra – charitable, animal-loving and a humanitarian.

Scorpio

You know you are at your lowest when you feel jealous, aggressive, ruthless and dangerous. The late Scorpio Ike Turner allowed these traits to come to the fore, so much so that he became known more for his turbulent relationship with his ex-wife, Tina Turner, than for anything else.

Martin Luther King and Gandhi certainly made the best of their positive Scorpio traits. Focus on your positive qualities and join the ranks of Scorpio Marie Curie. You can heal yourself and the world!

Sagittarius

You know you are at your lowest when you feel like taking gambles and living life in the fast lane. Sagittarian Frank Sinatra was no stranger in the night to this feeling in his heyday. Archer Britney Spears also went off the rails and lost control when success got too much for her to handle.

Turn to your positive qualities and join the ranks of Winston Churchill, the great prime minister. Walt Disney put a smile on children's faces, and still does with the most famous cartoon character in history, Mickey Mouse.

Capricorn

You know you are at your lowest when you feel your temper getting the better of you. The late, great Elvis Presley allowed his Capricorn addiction to food and drugs to take his life.

Turn to your positive qualities and become like Capricorn Isaac Newton. You too can change the world!

Aquarius

You know you are at your lowest when you feel unable to listen to advice and you do the opposite of what you know deep down to be right. The rebel in Aquarian Paris Hilton came into play when she featured in steamy videos on the Internet, and again when she ended up in jail for her illegal antics. Let's just hope she can manage to stay focused on her many winning attributes in the future!

Turn to your positive qualities and work to make the world a better place. You have a natural commitment to humanity, just like Aquarians Oprah Winfrey and Charles Darwin.

Pisces

You know you are at your lowest when you dice with drink or drugs. Piscean actress and director Drew Barrymore was on cocaine and alcohol before she reached her teens. She now talks openly about it and has certainly turned her life round.

Turn to your positive qualities. You are an artist with a natural ability to paint and draw. Be inspired by Piscean Michelangelo and his artwork in the Sistine Chapel.

Helplines

We all need a helping hand from time to time. If you do, then call today: the sooner you start, the sooner you can see results!

Alcoholics Anonymous
Get help with drinking problems.

www.alcoholics-anonymous.org.uk
0845 769 7555

Recover
Rehab and detox for getting off drink and drugs.

www.recovernow.co.uk
0845 603 6530

Frank

An honest website with information on drugs and help on beating them.

www.talktofrank.com
0800 776 600

Shelter

Emergency access to refuge services.

www.shelter.org.uk
0808 800 4444

The Samaritans

www.samaritans.org.uk
08457 90 90 90

Women's Aid National Domestic Violence Helpline

Nationwide telephone support provided by highly trained staff and volunteers backed up by a wide range of leaflets and resources.

0808 200 0247

Man2Man

Abuse helpline for male victims only.

0208 698 9649

Gingerbread Lone-Parent Helpline

An information service for lone parents, organizations, local authorities and the media.

0800 018 5026

NSPCC
Free confidential service for anyone concerned about children at risk. Offers counselling information and advice.

0808 800 5000

The Pink Practice
A counselling and psychotherapy practice for lesbian, gay, bisexual and transgender people in Leeds and London.

www.pinkpractice.co.uk
0207 060 4000

Refuge
Twenty-four-hour national crisis line that provides advice and support to those experiencing domestic violence. Refuge can also refer women and children to 250 refuges nationwide.

0990 995 443

Relate
Local Relate centres provide counselling for couples with relationship problems. They also offer psychosexual therapy and relationship and family education.

0300 100 1234

Chapter 12

FINDING YOUR CONFIDENCE

Each star sign is unique, and many of us can't see our good points for the many bad points that others all too often remind us about, so here is a little helping hand for those days when you're lacking inspiration or when tiredness and pressures make it impossible to see the wood for the trees.

Aries

Remember, no matter what anyone else thinks of you, you are living a life of which you can be proud. You are a person who is liked and who enjoys life, but your problem has all too often been that you've rushed into things. It's seemed to others that you've been callous when you've broken up a relationship or spent money that wasn't yours, but in my experience and knowledge of your sign, you have never, ever maliciously set out to hurt or upset anyone. Use your quick thinking to improve your life; it is an asset, not a failing. You are better than the other signs in the zodiac at coming up with a solution when things go wrong. You just need to stop looking to others for ways of turning something bad into something good and to trust in your own instincts. They may have got you into hot water, but they can get you out of it too. Don't run away from things any more either. Stop seeing the past through rose-tinted spectacles and allow your ruling planet, Mars, to help you get in touch with your inner self and your emotions.

You are dreadful at saying things you don't mean and then regret. Sometimes people of your sign spend their whole life making up for mistakes which only took them five minutes to make. Slow down and enjoy the view, and take a big breath before you make a commitment or a promise. What sounds good today may feel different after the sun has set. Read Chapter 15 and make tomorrow better today.

Taurus

If a relationship of yours has broken down, you know it's taken a long time and a lot of honesty to reach this sad point. Don't blame yourself: you don't give up on love easily, and your sign works harder at relationships than any other. You do, however, have a tendency to tell pointless lies, and this is something that can often spiral out of control and get you into a lot of trouble with your partner. You have a great sense of pride and this is what I hope will get you through any break-ups or problems. You know deep down that your loved ones want to see you get yourself together and strive for bigger and better things.

Just for the record, I have never known a Bull to repeat mistakes. You learn from every experience, so what you need to remember is that you've learnt your lesson and can now move on. People like you. You're popular, and you're funny and charismatic, so how can you not rise from the flames? Come on, think about it – don't you want to show that ex-partner or colleague how well you're doing without them? Your stubborn nature alone is reason enough not to give up. If you're feeling sad, you can shake it off with the power of your mind and by practising the Five-Step Plan in Chapter 15 daily. I know you will do just that!

Gemini

When you suffer a heartbreak or a disappointment, you can go to extremes. It is not unusual for Geminis to emigrate following a broken heart. You are a dual-natured sign whose instinct is to go to the opposite extreme in order to solve a situation, but that doesn't hide the fact that you are running away. You can move countries later, Gemini, when you've achieved enough for your friends, family, ex-lovers and ex-colleagues to attend your send-off with champagne at the ready. You need to be able to hold your head up high, and the Five-Step Plan in Chapter 15 will help you to do just that.

The great thing about you is that you're able to visualize, and with the power of your imagination you can sell yourself the ultimate game plan for your future. That plan has to start with sticking things out so you can clean up any mess that's been made. You do this by taking what went wrong and changing it into something that will work for you. Still living in the house you once shared with an ex? Don't move out and put it up for sale looking empty and unloved. Do it up and sell it for double the price, then show your ex how much you made. (After their name is off the paperwork of course!) If you've lost your sense of humour, then find it again. I know it's there somewhere and it really will be your saving grace, no matter how challenging the situation.

Cancer

When you're happy, you're ecstatic, and when you're down, you're inconsolable. You want friends and family to rally round, but the problem is that they can only do so for so long. It's not unknown for you to lock yourself away for a year after a relationship has broken down, even if it only consisted of a few dates! Think positive, as positivity is what will get your sign through any disaster. Read the Five-Step Plan in Chapter 15. It will give you the tips you need to see you through your problems.

If you begin the morning with a smile on your face, it will set you up for the rest of the day. It's when you start off your day with groans and gripes that things begin to go downhill. Remember that when there is a full moon, it affects you more than most, as the moon is your ruling planet. Luckily new moons also offer you inspiration, so note your ideas in a diary and use new moons to formulate plans. They're sure to be successful.

Get over that ex and don't fixate. One client of mine would still send her ex-partner pizzas and taxis that he didn't order a year after they broke up. Instead of ordering food for exes, go out yourself and eat. Don your party gear – you sparkle socially and it's time you realized it.

Leo

You are such a proud character that you hate to feel you've failed at anything, be it making a meal or losing a million. There is no difference, to you, between a minor and a major mistake, but it takes you a while to work out where the blame should lie. Why? Because pride is so strong in your character that you need to look elsewhere first. The problem is that even if you aren't to blame, you still end up shouldering some of the guilt. You don't let the past go and can't forget anything that has gone wrong. You carry the memory like a war wound but never really learn from it. Sometimes you can be like a child who walks into the same door time and time again. Read the Five-Step Plan in Chapter 15 and learn to watch for the warning signals.

Give yourself time to be happy without worrying if everyone else is happy first. Stop setting impossible standards and agree to disagree if you can't make a loved one or a colleague see sense. Stop worrying how your life looks to everyone else and start focusing on what makes *you* happy.

Virgo

You worry about things before they've even happened. It's not unusual for you to be angry with a loved one for something they might do but haven't yet done. Friends and lovers wouldn't be in your life if they didn't want to be and you should start enjoying them, rather than worrying about losing them. You give advice with the best intentions, but you should try taking your own. Stop right now and take in the view. Think about the things that are going on in your life and allow yourself to enjoy what you've done, where you are and what's on offer. You're allowed to have fun and must stop feeling guilty when you do.

Read the Five-Step Plan in Chapter 15, which can help you to appreciate who you are and value your many skills. After all, Virgo, if you don't put yourself first, then why should anyone else? You're worth more than you think. You are kind and compassionate to others, so start to show the same respect to yourself. You arrange things around what others might like, but all they really want is for you to be happy, so plan for yourself for a change, and that means dressing for yourself and not for an ex. The results will be tremendous.

Libra

It's awful to see a sign such as you broken-hearted or down on their luck because it affects you in every way. While some signs feel bad but put on a brave face, your every movement and word tells the tale of what you've been through. Because of your sign, you have no choice but to love completely and to give your heart and soul to any project you commit to. This is why you fall harder than most when things go wrong, but it is also your hidden strength. You see, Libra, even after a disappointment you don't lose faith. New projects don't scare you as much as they do many of the other signs. Where some see fear you see excitement, and this is the very strength that can carry you through any problem and on to better things.

Read the Five-Step Plan in Chapter 15 and allow yourself to grow as a person. You have so many attributes that I'm certain you can't yet have discovered every single one of them. Family often let your sign down, so promise yourself that you will learn and move on. It's all about focusing on the positive and not the negative, my friend. You'll always be a sign who can make new friends and you'll always be capable of carrying on, no matter how it may feel when you're going through a tough patch. Just remember that success will be all the sweeter if you've had to fight for it, so pick yourself up, brush yourself off and get going. There's a future waiting to be lived!

Scorpio

When things go wrong, you feel that life has never looked so bleak. Well, not until the next time, anyway. You see, a strange thing happens when you have a crisis: you forget that you've ever had a problem before. You are winded, shocked and deeply distressed. You have been through difficulties before, though, and you are probably one of the most able signs at coping with what's ahead. In fact turning disaster into opportunity is your talent. Don't be afraid to look to the past or to talk about it. Just remember not to wallow in what was. Take the lesson that's there to be learnt and move on. Don't go all out for revenge either, as there's nothing to be gained; you're just wasting time that could be spent enjoying a better future. Little do new partners realize that when you say you're ringing a friend, you're actually giving an ex nuisance calls.

Focus is the watchword for you. When you're in a constructive mood, you can change the world. When you're in a bad mood, you can ruin it. Read the Five-Step Plan in Chapter 15 and digest it. Make it your daily ritual and learn not to look back.

Sagittarius

When you know what you're doing with your life, you're one of the happiest signs around, but when you lose what you thought was going to be a staple in your life, it can be a really distressing time for you Archers. You love wholeheartedly, and you trust your loved ones implicitly. Actually, you don't have a choice: if you didn't trust them, you'd have a breakdown, as your life is so very busy that you just don't get the chance to watch your loved ones all the time. Work means the world to you and so if someone betrays you in your career, it can sometimes feel like adultery has been committed. Your sign will work with the same faces for years. You know you will go far and trust those you do business with to know this and offer you loyalty in return. The problem comes when people want a piece of the pie for themselves and undermine you because they want to try to be you. They can't and they won't, and that's what you have to realize. Follow my Five-Step Plan in Chapter 15. It will teach you that by simply carrying on you can walk out of the woods and back into the sunshine that is and should be the life of a Sagittarian.

Capricorn

It's hard for you to make a change for anyone, as you're quite a stubborn sign and it takes a very long time for people to earn your trust. When you're hurt or let down, it can often take you a few weeks to acknowledge to yourself what has happened. It's as if you've been winded, and deciding what the next move should be is usually something on which you have to seek advice and support. You fail to realize, though, that every setback is a learning experience that shows you where not to go next time and what not to do. I always advise your sign to take a holiday or a break after any shocking news or when you're feeling down. By changing the scenery, you can gain fresh inspiration and uncover new options. It is harder to do this if you stay at home, where you are reminded daily of what happened. The past haunts you, but it doesn't have to. The Five-Step Plan in Chapter 15 will help you turn every negative into a positive. There is nothing that has happened to you that hasn't made you stronger, and you are better off without anyone who has left your life. Time out, a fresh approach and on to a better footing for you, my friend.

Aquarius

You need to talk about what's gone wrong and find it hard when loved ones refuse to talk about a problem and just up and leave. You need answers and closure, and if you don't get them, then it's not unknown for you to choose the same types in love just so you can get the opportunity to work out what went wrong or even to right that wrong. You have an addictive personality and so you need to be careful that your behaviour doesn't become self-abusive. Remember that if something hasn't worked out, it wasn't meant to be. Blaming yourself is wrong. Lessons must and will be learnt in life, and you are a kind character who wants life to be full of laughter and fun. If someone has brought you down, then you weren't meant to be with them. They didn't bring out the best in you. Cut your losses, but don't cut off your nose to spite your face, not when there are so many signs out there who can help you turn your life into a spectacular one. Read the Five-Step Plan in Chapter 15 and make tomorrow better today. I know you are going to be tempted to skip through it, but don't. You are one of the signs who should read a step a day and do only one a day for five days. Armed with this plan, you need never look back again.

Pisces

The first indication that something is not going right in your life is when you start to let yourself go off the rails. All too often with your sign loved ones blame you for the breakdown of a relationship or for work problems, but what they've failed to realize is that the reason this has happened is because there was a problem there to begin with. You simmer and bubble, and when you are ready, your actions have even the hardiest signs in the zodiac running for cover. It's not surprising you've got a small circle of close friends: not many people can cope with your intensity. I'll tell you a secret, though – every other sign in the zodiac wants to be you and wishes they had your zest for life. They know you'll make it without the help of anybody else, no matter how down on your luck you are, how much money you've lost or how disastrous your love life. Within the year you'll have that ex begging for you to take them back, you'll have the bank willing to give you the account of your dreams, and you'll have achieved a dream. Read the Five-Step Plan in Chapter 15 for the future you know you deserve. It will help you navigate a less bumpy transition to the top and focus on the future instead of the past.

Steps to confidence

We've all had those days when we couldn't cope. Sometimes we blame it on others, and sometimes we blame ourselves. For some of us, it's the simple day-to-day things that can become too much – the school run, family pressures and financial worries. Some very powerful people cope very well with the daily pressures of their high-powered job and yet can't cope when it's time to come home and make their relationship work. What we need to know is that there are tools we can use that are individual to our star sign and personality that can help us to avoid the pitfalls and show us how to make our life a success.

Fire signs (Aries, Leo and Sagittarius)

You often fly off the handle and then regret what you have said but are too embarrassed to say you're sorry. Learn to count to ten before you react and promise yourself you will try to think before you speak. It could save you a lot of red faces, my friend.

Earth signs (Taurus, Virgo and Capricorn)

You often expect your close ones to know what you want. However, our loved ones are not all mind-readers (unless they're water signs, in which case they may have a hunch when you're unhappy!). Learn the skill of communication and try to keep others informed how you're feeling so that they can be there for you.

Air signs (Gemini, Libra and Aquarius)

You talk yourself in and out of a whole lot of trouble. You seem to spend too much time running away from your past and looking for a new future. You need to learn to put more time and energy into the here and now.

Water signs (Cancer, Scorpio and Pisces)

You don't have to stay in a situation that makes you unhappy. Don't wallow in self-pity and don't hold others responsible for your actions. Be assertive, and learn to love yourself. Depression doesn't suit you. Beat it and don't let it beat you. Think positive and life will be positive.

Pointers for bad days

Don't ever let anyone – no matter how important they are to you or how high up the career ladder or popularity stakes – tell you that you can't have a good life or that you won't ever be anything. Every time someone says 'can't', then come back with a 'can'. Every time others see failure, you must see opportunity. I want you to focus only on the positive. You hold the power to turn any experience to your advantage. See any problem as a challenge, not a failure. Look to the good points you have, not the bad points. They are a thing of the past, not the future.

If you're having a low day, then follow these helpful pointers:

1. Remember that experience is what makes us wise. Without the mistakes you have made how would you know not to go down that path again?
2. Learn to focus on your good points. We all have some, whether it's great teeth, a sense of humour or a listening ear. Acknowledge what yours are and say them out loud when you look in the mirror each morning.
3. Friends are there for a reason. If you're having a bad day, call up or text a friend and let them cheer you up. We all need a reserve team to keep us feeling good. Why not choose someone whom you can acknowledge as your feel-good buddy and offer to do the same for them? Know that when you hear from them, you will think of something great to say to them. Even have a codeword for these times. Spreading positivity can become infectious, you know!
4. Spring-clean your life. If you're unhappy, make it your goal for the day to rid yourself of one thing that is not working for you. It could be a top you don't like that it's time to give to the charity shop or deleting the phone number of someone who no longer makes you feel good about yourself.
5. Replay a memory in your head that you know makes you feel good. Sit with your eyes closed and play this moment in your mind as you would a DVD or a song. Let a smile wash over you and acknowledge that life can and will be good for you again.

6. Think of something you want to do. I don't care how extreme it is; it depends how wild you're feeling. I want you to do something to ensure that what you want is one step closer to happening. If you don't try, then how can a job you want be yours, how can a relationship you cherish improve, and how can financial problems disappear? You may need to call the bank today to arrange to see the manager about your financial troubles. You may need to pick up the paper to see what more interesting jobs are out there. You may need to call a friend to ask them to put the word out that you want more than friendship from someone. Taking a step towards one of your goals can make it happen. Doing nothing cannot.

Life Signs is here to give you the confidence to be the best your sign can be. I know from experience with my clients that part of the reason so many people don't obtain their dreams is because they don't try. Start today and you'll be amazed at the result.

Part 5
LIFESTYLE

Chapter 13

AT HOME AND ABROAD

We've looked at relationships, we've looked at finances, and we've looked at health, diet and fitness, but what about you? What about your surroundings and your things? Do you wonder why you can't think straight in your home but can find clarity in other places? Your star sign, your life sign, is not just about making things right in your head; it's about making sure that your surroundings work for you. Why is it that we need a holiday to recharge our batteries but when we come home we feel a sense of impending doom at opening our own front door? It needn't be like that.

With my help you will slowly but surely be able to tailor your life to make your home a happier place, to ensure that when you go away, you pick a destination that can give you what you need.

Are you stuck in the Eighties, or are you a Noughties guy or girl who should be heading back to the Swinging Sixties? We'll take a look at what you like to wear and what you should avoid. You can even learn how to look your best after a split. So let's start off with fashion signs to see what's really at the back of your wardrobe, what you should be carting down to the charity shop and what you need to invest in to make it to the top.

Fashion

Aries

With at least as many shoes as Imelda Marcos and a wardrobe most people would die for, you are the trendsetter of the zodiac. You aren't afraid to try new and daring outfits, safe in the knowledge that people around you will soon be following suit. When you see something that catches your eye, you don't hesitate to spend some of your hard-earned cash to look the part. You won't think twice about piercing your belly button or cutting up an expensive pair of jeans if that's what the fashion magazines deem to be cool.

Your wardrobe is a treasure trove, full of all shapes, sizes and colours, though you aren't the sort to go for a sharply tailored look. Male Aries tend to love clothes specially designed for sports or camping and are bound to have one phenomenally expensive pair of trainers in their collection. Accessories are another of your weaknesses – belts, bags and especially hat shops are your personal Mecca.

True to your fiery nature, if you want to knock them dead crimson is the only colour to wear – you'll make an impact that won't be forgotten.

Taurus

You are the typical designer diva who would never dream of rooting through a charity shop to find a funky outfit. You value the highest-quality fabrics and are willing to spend a small fortune on that perfect garment, even if it means you will be living on bread and butter for the rest of the month. Having said that, no one can deny that you have a great eye for style and colour, which means that you rarely appear in a fashion disaster.

People born under your sign never have the problem of knowing what to wear to a formal occasion. Dinner with the French ambassador? You will have at least five outfits that would be suitable. Your logic is that fashion fads come and go, whereas well-made clothes will last you a lifetime. Although you rarely have the confidence to wear something offbeat, when you do pluck up the courage, the effect is fantastic.

Taurean men love to wear blue, whereas Taurean women dress to impress in feminine colours such as pale pink and baby blue.

Gemini

When you open your wardrobe, the clothes probably all fall out into a crumpled mess on the floor! You can be incredibly fussy and indecisive about your clothes – in fact you probably only wear about 10 per cent of your wardrobe. This is because you tend to get bored with the latest fashions and embrace any new trends at the drop of a hat. Unlike Taureans, the label of a garment is the last thing you look at – how it looks and feels is more important than whether it says Gucci or Pucci.

You are one of the more experimental signs in the zodiac and are willing to try out all manner of new trends, though you do shy away from constricting clothes – Tom Jones with his leather trousers could never be your fashion icon. Clingy clothes are simply one of your worst fashion nightmares. Provided you get up early enough in the morning to decide on the day's outfit, you are generally pretty well dressed. Try being a bit more spontaneous when it comes to clothes and you will be surprised at the results.

Gemini colours are generally citrus tones like yellow and orange, which can be worn to brighten up a dark suit.

Cancer

It could be said that you are attached to certain items of clothing as much as you are to your loved ones and your pets. This is because you associate clothes with specific land-mark events in your life. There is no doubt that you will have kept the jumper you got engaged in and the dress you wore to your graduation party because of their sentimental value.

Women born under Cancer are some of the most feminine in the zodiac. They manage to look womanly even wearing the most masculine of clothes – wellies and combat trousers make no difference to them. However, Cancerian women should really try to look as feminine as possible; it will give your confidence a boost. Invest in some silky lingerie to look your best.

Cancerian men don't tend to make much of an effort with their clothes unless there is a special occasion. When you do bother to dress up, you are bound to outshine those around you. You usually have a rule of thumb for dressing that dates back to a compliment you were given in your teens, and as the years go on you may need to reassess this rule in case it has become outdated or no longer flatters you. You are the sort of people who find a style you like, then stick to it throughout your life. Some experimentation is what's needed – wearing something a little more daring than you are used to could really pay off.

Silver, blue and green are the colours best suited to you.

Leo

No bargain-basement shopping for you, Leo. If it doesn't cost a small fortune, then you probably won't buy it. Fashion magazines are your bible and you tend to follow whatever they say. As for comfortable clothes, forget them. If the trend requires painting yourself blue and wearing sheepskin shoes, that's exactly what you'll be doing. You aren't afraid of wearing daring outfits and often customize a plain garment with funky accessories. If you weren't so attached to labels and designers, you could save a fortune by using your creativity to create fantastic outfits from garments picked up in thrift shops.

Male Leos tend to be a tad more conservative than the women, preferring expensive clothes that will stand the test of time. Leos have a weakness for costly, not to mention flashy, jewellery and love to show some skin. Don't forget your sign rules the back, so for women, going strapless or even backless is a great way to attract attention. So long as you keep your outfits dramatic, you won't fail to make a great impression.

Your best colours are those guaranteed to make you stand out – glitzy golds, oranges and bronzes teamed with black are the order of the day for either sex.

Virgo

Known as the perfectionists of the zodiac, woe betide you if you try to talk a Virgo into buying an outfit that doesn't match. They will know exactly what accessories go with the outfit they have chosen, right down to the correct scent to set it off. Usually seen going for greens and dark browns, true to their element of earth, they like to feel comfortable, practical and stylish all at the same time. Somehow, as if by magic, they manage to do this.

You will note that their homes are an organized mess, so their hanging space will consist of their wardrobe, the dressing table and the bed, but they will take great offence if you try to tell them this is not the norm.

Known more for telling friends how to dress, they believe

they are trendsetters, but they always manage to retain a certain amount of class as they don't go for fashions that are too OTT. Instead they look as if they have the secret style the rest of us are longing for.

Virgos won't spend more than they think is fair on an item of clothing, but if they do splash out, then they will go out of their way to let you know just how much they paid for it. The men of this sign get good use out of their suits, more so than the women, but at least they're in style when the cut comes back into fashion ten years later.

Libra

Librans are probably the most stylish dressers in the zodiac. They adore quality and beautiful-looking clothes. They wouldn't even be averse to planning a holiday around where all of the best clothes are to be found. Yes, this is the sign that will long for their coat to slip down so that the designer label shows. The secret they have is that they are also dab hands at tracking down designer goods in second-hand stores, and as they wear it so well, they make it look double the price it was to start with. The women of this sign are suckers for super handbags, and if it is a famous label, then so much the better.

Generous to the bitter end, clothing will be top of their list for friends and family too, so if you don't feel too pleased with the tie they've bought you, check again – it's likely to be top of the range and made in Italy, one of their favourite countries.

Blues, pale greens and pinks usually adorn their attractive bodies, and the males of this sign are likely to have a tie collection that other men would die for.

Scorpio

Scorpios love to look sexy, if you're trying to sell them a suit or an outfit that is designer but doesn't look sexy, then you may as well give up, for they have to look and feel a million pounds. Fabrics and the feel of a material are important to them, and if it comes in red or maroon, that's even better.

The women of this sign usually have enough nail varnishes to fill ten beauty salons, and they are not cheap brands either. These are, I'm afraid, all in dramatic colours. They love great shoes, and the higher the heel for the women, the better. Leather holds a great attraction, and Scorpio women also like to wear chokers, which may create a misleading impression as they will not be dominated. When wearing make-up, they concentrate mainly on the eyes, as they know these are their best feature, and they are not averse to large amounts of black eyeliner. Even the men don't mind a smudge or two to give their eyes definition – just look at Leonardo Di Caprio; at recent awards ceremonies, you may have noticed his eyes have been more defined than usual. Scorpios use fashion to give out a message, so read it and decide. But don't take too long, as they don't like people who can't make up their minds.

Sagittarius

The Archer has fantastic legs and will go to great lengths to show them off. One of the main problems they have with their dress sense is that they buy clothes in such a hurry they don't always have time to get a whole outfit, so they can end up dressing as if they represent every season. Fire signs are always in a hurry, but they do have this knack of being in vogue and turning more than a few heads with their clothes, whatever their age. Tina Turner is a typical Sagittarian dresser: her clothes are made to show off her fine muscles and yet give her the ability to run, dance, jump, whatever her energetic sign requires.

Just beware of catching them at home when they are not expecting you, though. Sagittarians hate being restricted and you may well find them wearing their birthday suit.

They prefer rich purples and dark blues. Rich is of course the operative word for this ambitious sign who always manages to dress like the boss, even if it's their very first day at work.

Capricorn

Capricorn is an earth sign who gives people the impression that they have been someone, are someone or will end up being someone. They have an air that makes it hard for you to be rude or cheeky to them, and this has as much to do with their dress sense as anything else. They can usually be seen in conservative colours – chiefly dark green, grey, brown and black. They are not avid followers of fashion but will have worked out their own style over the years. Even the young Capricorn will not feel the need to fit in with the rest of the crowd and will have their own sense of fashion, albeit strange at times. They worry about getting cold in winter, so even the good-looking eighteen-year-old will be found with thermals in their drawers ready for the chilly season.

They are practical and will want labels that are trusted. High-street stores are fine by them, but they will know the beauty of a designer piece too, usually jewellery. Look at their watch and you'll get my point. As they are slow to make up their mind, you may want to take a chair with you when going out shopping – you could have quite a wait if they haven't made a list!

Aquarius

Aquarians spend more of their time chatting about what they are going to buy than they do getting out there and buying it. When they do go shopping, they don't mind buying quantity over quality, and for the women of this sign, the smaller the item of clothing, the better. Remember, they have been known to suffer with circulation problems and this is no surprise considering the short skirts and the high heels they favour. This is usually only a phase, as when the first blister kicks in, they start to see the point of proper clothing and seek to wear things that scream comfort, with a sexy edge to it of course. They can usually be found going for electric blue and turquoise. The women like floaty skirts that you can see through, and the men love linen shirts. If a T-shirt has writing on it, then so much the better. After all, Aquarians don't have time to talk as much as they'd like, so they try to get their point across with their clothing.

They don't need designer clothes, but they do have to have trendy gear. They are forward-thinking and like to be at the front of any fashion revolution, even if it means going overdrawn. Bangles, peace beads and lots of necklaces appeal, and the child in them is fascinated by way-out hair dos, which often turn more heads than any item of clothing that can be seen adorning their beautiful bodies.

Pisces

Think Piscean and you must think of the sea and floaty materials, which for the men is often represented by linen trousers or even flares. Pisceans like to wear dramatic, over-the-top shoes or no shoes at all. They're accustomed to taking off their footwear to feel the earth under their feet. They believe that shoes are for looks, not comfort, so it's no surprise they want to kick them off after ten minutes.

Soft shades of green can often be seen adorning their attractive bodies, and they like to wear things that give them a slimline shape or that allow the light to catch them and show the contours of their bodies. Pisceans get obsessive about clothes, and if they choose a new fashion, they will throw out everything they have that represents their old style. They are true chameleons. Gypsy styles suit them, and that's probably because they spend most of their time counselling and giving readings to friends. They are, after all, the most psychic sign of the zodiac.

At home

The water signs, Cancer, Scorpio and Pisces, should live near the water if they can, but there are ways for them to find tranquillity if they can't get away from the city, whether it is walking in a park or sitting in a garden. Fire signs, Aries, Leo and Sagittarius, need a fast pace and hustle and bustle to feel alive, and earth signs, Taurus, Virgo and Capricorn, find living in temporary or rented accommodation can send them crazy as they need security. Air signs, Gemini, Libra and Aquarius, need a modern style of living, as they like to keep up with the times.

Clues you have entered a fire sign's home
The fire signs, Aries, Leo and Sagittarius, are always keen to make their homes look good, but all too often their enthusiasm wanes, leaving jobs half done and homes looking as if the builder has had to leave for an emergency call-out. They

mean well, but they need to be balanced by a sign who can finish what they've started. Bright colours suit them, but they can be a little too adventurous with fashion and style in the home, making the more old-fashioned and traditional signs feel uncomfortable. Chrome and glass will be a favourite choice for them, and they dislike clutter and gadgets, so their kitchen often has a minimalist feel.

Clues that you have entered an earth sign's home

The earth signs, Taurus, Virgo and Capricorn, can't help but keep belongings and objects that have personal meaning. The table or chair that they bought for their first flat will still be in their house twenty years on. It reminds them of where they came from and how far they've come. Don't get me wrong, though: this is a most fashion-conscious element. They have a flair for design and know how to make a home a home. Big armchairs and oversized items will be the perfect choice for them.

If your partner is an earth sign and you are not, then I'm afraid you are going to have to give in to their style, as they have a distinct idea of what will and will not work. This is one area where you should give them free rein, as they know what they're doing and are sure to make your home a place of comfort and relaxation.

Clues that you have entered an air sign's home

If it's new out, then the air signs, Gemini, Libra and Aquarius, have to have it. To be living with wooden floorboards when carpet is back in vogue would be enough to make these signs lose sleep. These are social creatures and so they need their home to be a place they can entertain in. They like to change the way their home looks but need to be careful that they don't invest large amounts of money in things they will want to change next year. These signs are not afraid to spend money to impress people. That funny-looking object on the wall is not a work of art; it's probably the latest phone, which they just had to acquire to bring them bang up to date with whatever the latest interiors magazines are raving about.

Clues that you have entered a water sign's home

The homes of water signs Cancer, Scorpio and Pisces will be full of things their loved ones have bought them. Dare to open a drawer and you must be prepared to find some oddity there. Water signs need a relaxing space; they will have to have a sofa that they can sleep on. Objects are not bought for how they look but for how they feel, although if they own an expensive item, you can bet it will be in prime view. The bedroom is a key room for them and should not contain anything to do with work. It has to be the place where they can recharge their batteries. To even think about having a shower instead of a bath is also a no-no. These signs need to soak their troubles away in order to plan their next big step in life. If you're invited into their home, you're lucky: they don't let people they don't like into their private space.

Holiday destinations

We often choose to vist places that please our loved ones, but are they right for us? Should you have been meditating when you were medicating with a Martini, or are you one of the signs who needs a glass of wine to wind down after a day at the office? This is your guide to holidays and relaxation. It could make all the difference between success and disaster when the going gets tough. A tired mind can make bad decisions, but with the right attitude there will be nothing to stop you from achieving all that your heart desires. You can even use this guide to plan a romantic trip for a loved one or a family member, to help a friend find a better path and clearer vision after a split, to recharge your batteries or just for some good old-fashioned fun!

Aries

People born under this sign are nomads at heart. Aries love exploring. They aren't afraid to go it alone and are stimulated by different cultures and people. The Ram is most likely to be found backpacking around the world, trying to cram as many countries into their itinerary as possible. A couple of weeks inter-railing around Europe and soaking up the architecture is just their cup of tea. They also have a great affection for the outdoors, so camping certainly appeals to this side of their nature. What about pitching a tent in a different place each night – the wilder and more remote the location, the better?

Although white-water rafting or rock climbing are not many people's idea of a holiday, the Ram will love the adrenalin rush. If it's not packed with excitement and stunning scenery, they just won't want to know. An athletic holiday on the ski slopes is just the thing for the Ram. A diving trip to the Great Barrier Reef would also be ideal – Aries would get high on the fact that they just might meet a shark in the depths of the ocean. Now wouldn't that be an adventure to tell the grandchildren!

Ideal destinations for an Aries: Austria, Nepal, Argentina and Spain.

Taurus

Taureans are not the sort of people to take a last-minute holiday. A trip away has to be planned as strategically as a military operation. The Bull will always do their research, poring over stacks of travel brochures before finally deciding on the appropriate destination. When they do go on holiday, they like to live the high life. Luxury is their middle name and top hotels or lavish meals are a must. Having said that, they don't need to travel far to get their fix. Taureans would appreciate the pleasures of French food, wine and cheese, not to mention the atmosphere of romantic Paris. Needless to say, their kind of holiday will do serious damage to their bank account. No camping in the great outdoors for them, thank you very much. Much more up the Bull's street is a grand tour of Europe, taking in all the beauty of Paris, followed by the architecture of Barcelona and a trip to the opera in Rome. Rest assured, after a hard day of sightseeing, they will retire to their high-class accommodation for some self-indulgence. Taureans certainly know how to travel in style and they try to avoid the cramped conditions of economy class at all costs.

Ideal destinations for a Taurean: France, Japan, the Netherlands and Thailand.

Gemini

People born under this sign are renowned for having a short attention span. The idea of a long holiday in one location would bore them senseless, as would two weeks of lazing on a tropical beach. Geminis prefer to keep on the go, travelling from place to place with no fixed route. The Twins are inquisitive people who are eager to learn as much as they can about destinations they visit. They would actually make excellent tour guides because there is nothing they like better than visiting all the sights.

Short breaks to large, vibrant cities like New York, Hong Kong and Tokyo are just up their street. They would be wide-eyed with wonder at the bustling markets and busy streets, not to mention the shopping in these huge urban jungles. The idea of a train trip through Spain, stopping at lots of towns along the way, would satisfy their desire to know a country inside and out. However, offer them a trip around the world and they are bound to politely decline – a whole year spent travelling would be pure torture for them. Remember, the grass is always greener to them and they could not bear missing out on what was happening back home. They aren't the sort of people who would enjoy the solitude of travelling alone and need someone with whom they can share the experience.

Ideal destinations for a Gemini: Spain, Greece and New York.

Cancer

Cancerians love the comfort and security of home. They lack the adventurous and pioneering spirit of the Ram and tend not to have a strong wanderlust. When the Crab does venture out, wherever they decide to go they need people around them to recreate a homely environment. They also aren't the sort of people to blow their savings on the trip of a lifetime – they'd rather watch a travel programme from the comfort of their settee.

So what kind of holiday could lure Cancerians away from their home comforts? As a water sign, the Crab would feel relaxed by a beach or a lake, where they are likely to indulge in a spot of sailing, surfing or diving. They love travelling with the family and so will visit all manner of theme and adventure parks. A rollercoaster ride is about as big a risk as they will take – the idea of rock climbing or abseiling would fill them with dread. When it comes to accommodation, the thrifty Crab will shy away from plush hotels in exclusive areas. They find all they need in a caravan and might even be persuaded into camping out for a few nights. This also gives them the opportunity to do their own cooking while on the road, and when they do have to eat out, they are bound to find the best of high-quality, good-value restaurants. Although being fair, they stay at the right places for the right price, while the rest of us are paying over the odds.

Ideal destinations for a Cancerian: Florida, Bahamas and Canada.

Leo

Leos like to sail through life with style, and the same is true when it comes to travelling. No bargain-basement, last-minute deals to the Costa del Sol for them. You'd never catch them making the most of cheap transport either – they're more likely to be found in the lap of luxury on *The Orient Express*. They are the people most likely to hire a driver to save them the inconvenience of getting from A to B. The Lion will always go to whatever country is trendy and 'the place' to visit that year, taking a multitude of friends along for the ride. Milan and Paris, with their reputation as centres of fashion, are a must, as are twenty-four-hour party cities like New York, Hong Kong and Miami. It is hard to envisage the Lion roughing it with a backpack in India and Africa. They like travelling to be a stress-free, easy experience and don't mind paying for the privilege. Leos are renowned for their love of gambling, so a trip to Monte Carlo would not go amiss, with a night at the casino followed by a stay at an exclusive hotel. If the urge to try their luck at roulette is particularly strong, a jaunt to Las Vegas will be firmly on the itinerary. The bright lights and excitement are a temptation Leos just won't be able to resist.

Ideal destinations for a Leo: Boston, New York, Singapore and Miami.

Virgo

Virgo's worst nightmare is for something to go slightly awry or not according to plan. Switzerland immediately comes to mind when thinking of ideal holiday destinations for them – they like clean streets, order and fresh air. This sign will rarely let the fact that they are on holiday affect their routine. Every day is bound to be organized down to the last detail, from where to eat to when they go to bed. Their intentions are good – they want to make the most of every minute and ensure they see everything on their list. Virgos enjoy culture and history. They will spend hours trailing around museums in their quest to learn.

They should avoid cities that are bound to cause them distress; Rio, with all its hustle and bustle, springs to mind. This does not mean that Virgos should only visit sanitized, rather dull parts of the world. They might enjoy more unusual destinations, like Scandinavia or even Tibet. Virgos are one of the most health-conscious signs in the zodiac, so a hiking holiday somewhere picturesque or perhaps a cycling holiday would give them pleasure.

Ideal destinations for a Virgo: Switzerland, Malta and Austria.

Libra

Ruled by Venus, goddess of love and all things beautiful, it is no wonder that Librans are drawn to places of luxury and beauty. Needless to say, thrift does not come into the equation when planning a Libran holiday. Plush hotels and only the best food and wine will do, but their biggest vice is souvenirs. They are liable to head straight for the most expensive shopping area in town to purchase mementoes of their travels. Shopping is an important factor when considering where to go on holiday, so New York and Hong Kong are always popular.

Librans generally do not enjoy travelling alone and have much more fun with a loved one beside them. Their desire for balance and harmony makes them great travelling partners because they will only be happy when their companion is too. Social animals that they are, Librans will be drawn to events like the Rio Carnival or New Orleans's Mardi Gras. Occasions like this will give them the chance to party and mingle in the most exotic of locations. Dressing up is important and you will rarely see Librans making a beeline for places without a dress code.

Ideal destinations for a Libran: Rome, Shanghai and Hong Kong.

Scorpio

Scorpios are the sort of people who love to try anything and everything – the more unusual, the better. They are not drawn to conventional destinations, but rather yearn to go further afield to experience as many weird and wonderful things as they can. Columbia or Algeria are appealing, as are the red-light districts of the world! People who come back from their travels having had a major personality change are most likely to be Scorpios – travel is an opportunity to get to know their inner self as well as different parts of the world. They are passionate about risky activities, from white-water rafting to bungee-jumping. When it comes to food, Scorpios are the kind of people who love to sample all the local delights, be it fried grasshoppers or snake soup. They will rarely plan where they are going to stay – half the fun is not knowing where they are going to end up. Whatever happens, they aren't bothered about luxurious restaurants and hotels. A chance encounter with one of the locals will give them much more pleasure!

Ideal destinations for a Scorpio: Angola, Egypt and Costa Rica.

Sagittarius

Think Sagittarius, think explorer. This is the sign of travel and Sagittarians belong on the road, searching for adventure and excitement. There aren't many places in the world that Sagittarians would not be willing to visit – every place is likely to stimulate them in some way.

Off-the-beaten-track locations are the best bet for a Sagittarian with itchy feet. A trip to China with a boat ride down the Yangtze would be ideal, as would an activity-packed holiday in the Himalayas. Sagittarians will get along with people they meet on their travels and are hungry to learn about the lifestyles of those from different cultures. Meeting up with street hawkers in Mozambique or praying with monks in Tibet is about as good as it gets for gregarious Sagittarians. For someone who is seeking 'the truth', issues such as accommodation or where to eat are mere trifles. In fact to the typical Sagittarian, eating is a waste of time, taking them away from more interesting activities.

Ideal destinations for a Sagittarian: Bangladesh, Lebanon and Kenya.

Capricorn

If you do manage to persuade a Capricorn to leave the office for long enough to go on holiday, rest assured it will be a very organized and carefully planned affair. Capricorns like to be comfortable when travelling, and holidays are sometimes all about social status. Cities with charm and elegance are high on the agenda, so Barcelona, Geneva and Madrid fit the bill. Like Leos, Capricorns are lured to the 'in' destinations. Luxury cruises are also a perfect choice because the Goat loves to see places but prefers not to have to walk too far. They don't shy away from travelling in a group and are happy to adopt the role of leader. They like to take their time when travelling and enjoy strolling around a museum at a leisurely pace. If you are looking for an adventurous holiday, then don't go away with this sign. Capricorns are more interested in eating and staying in the trendiest of places, though that does not extend to sampling the more exotic local delicacies.

Ideal destinations for a Capricorn: San Francisco, Australia and Spain.

Aquarius

When an Aquarian goes travelling, it is likely that they have saving the planet in mind. One of the more socially conscious signs in the zodiac, the Water-Bearer would love saving the rainforest in Brazil or rescuing endangered species in Malaysia. People born under this sign are usually surrounded by friends, so the idea of travelling in a group would appeal to them, as would taking on the role of leader. Because of their sociable natures, Aquarians feel at home in big, bustling cities, where they can hit the hotspots and party till dawn.

They are keen to collect fresh and exciting experiences, and will go anywhere, no matter how obscure and remote. They are extremely adaptable and are just as happy to sleep in a tent as in a five-star hotel, though their philosophy is usually to do as the locals do. This involves eating adventurously and trying all the local delicacies, whether shark's-fin soup or ostrich steaks.

Ideal destinations for an Aquarian: India, Mexico, Venezuela and New York.

Pisces

Pisceans are drawn to places where they feel they can do some good, for they are compassionate folk. They rarely travel without a particular purpose in mind – a trip to Guatemala will involve working with street kids and this is because they are one of the most charitable signs in the zodiac. They will make the utmost effort to get to know local people wherever they end up. Pisceans also tend to go through life in a dreamlike state. Their heads are always in the clouds and they sometimes need to be pulled back down to earth. They prefer not to be in charge of the more mundane aspects of travelling and will leave the job of booking tickets, making reservations and reading timetables to someone else.

Because of their yen for meditation and contemplation, Pisceans would feel most at home somewhere like Tibet or India, or even Lourdes, where they can continue on their spiritual journey. The Fish also have a strong artistic side to their nature and are stimulated by places rich in culture and art. A painting holiday or a trip to the opera in Italy is just the ticket for creative Pisceans.

Ideal destinations for a Piscean: Brazil, China and India.

Chapter 14

PARTIES

Are you a perfect dinner party host or a disaster waiting to happen? Do your friends secretly nickname you Porky Pete or Lady Lucy because of your table manners? Time to find out some home truths about your eating habits.

Guess who's coming to dinner

Aries

I'm afraid these people really are scoffers who would prefer to eat with a shovel rather than a knife and fork. If you see them nipping in and out of the kitchen, they are more likely to be sneaking an extra mouthful than washing dishes. They can drink quickly as well, so make sure you give them little and often if you want them to last the distance at a dinner party. They are usually pretty good cooks, so if you get an invite round to theirs, then go. They can whip up a delight in no time, as they have no fear about mixing the strangest of ingredients.

If you want to know the best dishes to serve and indeed even seduce an Aries, then make them spicy, the hotter the better; and if they down enough wine, they may even enter a chilli-eating competition. Just beware if they start mixing cocktails early on in the day, though, or you could have the hangover from hell. This is one sign who doesn't do anything by halves, but I'm sure you wouldn't have them any other way. They are both fun and unpredictable, as I'm sure you will have discovered by now if you have an Aries in your life.

Taurus

The funny thing with a Taurean is that they spend so much time talking about how they are looking forward to hosting a gathering and making sure that all of the fine details are perfect, but when it actually comes round, they are too busy in the kitchen to see the looks of joy on their guests' faces. Remember to thank them for the effort they have gone to; it's sure to have been a lot. Take them a gift if they are the host – something to eat or drink would be good. If they're coming to yours for food, then watch out, as they'll be opening the wine they've brought you as a thank-you gift quicker than you can say, 'Take your seats.' I have a brother who is a Taurean and a typical one at that. He used to stab his fork into my potato and say, 'Do you want that?' He's mellowed over the years and has taken on many traits of his Gemini girlfriend, so I no longer have to guard my plate.

The Bull will eat starters, main courses, the lot, but by far their favourite has got to be the dessert. No matter how much they've eaten, when pudding arrives they'll secretly loosen their waistband and tuck in, knowing full well they will be unable to move for an hour afterwards. They enjoy their food and like nothing better than sitting round a table drinking, eating and talking with their loved ones.

Don't give them second-rate food or drink – they're far cleverer than you can imagine and know the price of everything, so make it top quality, especially given the time and effort they are sure to have put into your gift, which they'll have already unwrapped for you!

Gemini

This is a sign who really will drive you round the bend. They say they are starving but by the time the food is put in front of them, they are busy talking and will have to be told at least a dozen times that their food is going cold. They don't mean to be rude, but they can come across that way, especially those of them who smoke and tell you that they really don't mind if you eat while they finish their fag. They are great socializers, though, and will invite all and sundry into their home, although I can't always guarantee what you are going to get. Any thank-you gifts are sure to be inventive, if they remember to bring these with them! Yours is sure to be just one of many gatherings to which the Gemini has been invited.

Their weight can go up and down over the course of the year depending on what is happening in their very active life. They may annoy you with the way they eat and talk at the same time, but don't tell them off, as I can assure you that you'll really want to hear the news they have to share with you, even if it has been embellished thanks to their very vivid imagination.

Cancer

Social gatherings round a dinner table are more important to the Crab than you can possibly imagine, as it gives them a chance to catch up with their nearest and dearest and to tell them for the hundredth time how much they love them. They have a habit of living in the past, so don't be surprised if they bake the biscuits you loved as a child. They will think they're doing good even if you grew sick of them years ago. Just smile and pretend to enjoy them.

Please be careful what you give this sign to drink, as they really do have a problem with handling alcohol. It will only take two shots of gin to have them crying into their pudding over a childhood sweetheart. They don't need a lot to get drunk; in fact for many of them, just the smell of alcohol is good enough.

As for food, Cancerians love certain foods and hate others. They put the same passion into food that they put into life. This is the character who will hate tomatoes but love tomato ketchup. The dishes they can do they will do well, so make sure you take up that invite to dinner – you're bound to find yourself having a ball.

Leo

Now this is a sign who is far more worried about what something looks like than the taste of it, so don't forget to sprinkle parsley over a dish before you serve it up to them. This fire sign goes through foods fads, and I don't think I'd be too far off the mark if I told you to look in magazines to see what the celebs are eating or what diet they are following, as Leos are sure to be hot on the heels of the latest trend.

They are very sociable souls who will go out of their way to make sure you aren't hungry and that your glass is never empty. You must praise them often, though, as omitting to mention every five minutes how fabulous the dessert was (even if it was bought and not made!) would devastate them. You will find the dinner-table conversation enchanting, as they talk about themselves and then ask you what you think of them; but you can't help but love them and the way they make you laugh and help you to forget the stresses of the day. It's all about effort with Leo, and they'll go to the ends of the earth for you, so make sure you remember to thank them. Their heart is always in the right place!

Virgo

I do love dear Virgo, but if things don't go exactly to plan, then don't we all know about it! This is a sign who will put name-cards on the table even if you have sat in exactly the same place for the last ten years. In their eyes this helps to avoid any confusion. You are sure to find all of your firm favourites on the dinner table as long as Virgos are around, which is bound to make you feel special. I don't know a sign who is more considerate of others' needs, even if it can drive you to the point of distraction sometimes – they will make you drive ten miles out of your way to buy the right ingredients for dessert. You have to know that they are doing so out of love.

If a Virgo is your dinner guest, they will have some pretty peculiar eating habits and the most unpredictable likes and dislikes when it comes to food. An evening with this sign will most certainly be unforgettable and fun!

Libra

Balance and harmony are vitally important to this air sign. They like to be able to follow their plans and their heart, which can often have some confusing results and some very late-running arrivals and departures, as they will do their famous disappearing act when they see fit. Librans are like children and expect a dinner party to be a little like a tea party with games and laughter on the agenda. You would be better to give them lots of fun foods rather than just one big meal; they want to be able to pick, to talk, to pick and then talk some more.

They like to drink, but start them off too early and they'll be the ones snoring in the corner while the rest of us are eating dessert. They also enjoy after-dinner games, but don't be put off by their childlike image: this is one sign who knows how to enjoy life, and you can be sure that if they're cooking for you, it will be a meal to remember with a setting right out of a storybook.

Scorpio

Scorpios look upon dinner parties with both excitement and dread. They love to gather round all the familiar faces, but they dread to think what past issues may be dragged up in the process. This sign has a lot of secrets and so they like to keep certain areas of their life private. You always find that one or two things come to light during any occasion that involves alcohol.

Scorpios are an extreme sign who will be either a great or a dreadful cook; there really is no in between. They give their heart and soul to everything they choose to do, so if they have decided to look into the world of cooking, they will have learnt properly and could probably cook a meal from every country in the world if asked. If the world of gastronomy has not appealed to them, then even beans on toast will be too much to expect. They either like alcohol or can't abide it, and if they do indulge, then they will throw it into their cooking too, so watch out – that fruit cocktail could well be all alcohol and no fruit. Dinner with a Scorpio is sure to prove unmissable, so get round there.

Sagittarius

The Archer will spend much time telling you with great excitement what they are going to cook when you come round, but by the time you get there they will have had a complete change of heart. They may even end up ordering a Chinese takeaway, so unpredictable are they. Fire signs make up their mind about something but don't have much patience, so a week later everything can change, although I'm sure they won't have had time to tell you. Don't believe them if they tell you it's fancy dress when they arrange a gathering: double-check if you want to avoid embarrassment.

Sagittarians like new and exciting foods, but can suffer from indigestion, so try to avoid cooking overly rich dishes for them. They will say they enjoyed the meal, but you may miss out on their very stimulating company when they spend the next hour in the bathroom. They like champagne and cocktails, and love to talk – or should I say gossip? You'll have great fun with this sign at any gathering, but with a Sagittarian you must expect the unexpected!

Capricorn

The earthy Capricorn adores having their loved ones around them, and although they are very kind souls, you may want to double-check with them if you are thinking of inviting friends to a gathering. You see, there are times in their life when they only want to be with their nearest and dearest, and they don't take too kindly to having their parade rained on without notice or without their written consent.

They can party with the best of them and don't mind donning a party hat; in fact, they probably brought them. They are children at heart and love to enjoy good food prepared by loving hands; they will even help you clean up if you get them on a good day. No dinner party is complete without a Capricorn, for they provide the party atmosphere that will bring smiles to the sternest of faces. Give them traditional food, though – they prefer their meat and two veg to anything you may have read about. If you go without pudding, then you may as well phone them a cab: some things are essential to them, and this, my friend, is one.

Aquarius

Aquarians just love the social side of dinner parties. They may promise to do something to help out, but they are usually so busy running around dishing the dirt and finding out what they can about the other faces who are attending that they forget the essentials. They can talk their way out of any problem, though, so don't even think about scolding them – they'll just laugh at you. The Aquarian will make your dinner party complete; they'll have you in stitches with laughter and will know all the latest jokes. They are not always on time, though, as they are too busy thinking about tomorrow to remember today. They make a party and can also make a great meal when they calm down and concentrate on the job at hand. They're sure to know all the latest dishes, their favourite being light bites so that they can keep going back for more in between the wine and fun but naughty stories.

Pisces

This is a sign who will go to extremes to make sure that your dinner party is all you dreamed. If they say that they will cook, then make sure you are hungry, as they are more likely to do ten courses than three or four. They want to create a dramatic impression, and they do. If you go round on a Friday, then you may not find yourself leaving until Sunday. If they like you, they love you and will have a dinner table laden with exotic and hard-to-find goods. They can drink you under the table, although that doesn't mean that they won't be completely and utterly sozzled; it just means that they refuse to give in. Drinking games are not an unusual suggestion from them either. Careful, though, as those ice cubes could well be full of gin or vodka. Those Pisceans who don't drink really don't drink, and those who do, well, they drink like a fish of course.

Treat them well and they will treat you even better. The conversation round the dinner table is sure to tantalize and surprise. This is one sign who knows how to enjoy a gathering to the full, even if there are a few casualties who will need to be attended to!

Downtime: party pooper or disco diva?

Will it be back to yours for a party, or are you aghast at the thought of anyone's dirty shoes even crossing your front door? Let's take a look at which of you signs are ready to party and which would rather turn in for an early night.

Aries

You Aries are a masculine, fiery lot! Needless to say, your life is a series of competitions and you play every game to win. This makes for a stressful life and there is no better way of forgetting about the pressures and strains of everyday life than having a party. You are the sort of person who is full of combustible energy begging to be burnt off. There should be no half-measures when it comes to planning your ideal party. You are very home-loving and probably would not be able to relax enough to enjoy a party at your place. Hiring out a hot nightclub for the evening is more up your street – you won't need to worry about people dropping food on the floor and wine stains on the sofa. Many of you Aries have excellent singing voices and are good dancers, so maybe a spot of karaoke wouldn't go amiss. Let's not forget party food, Aries! Variety is definitely the spice of life for you, so lots of appetizers are in order. Cheese and pineapple or sausages on sticks must be banned from your party – you hate bland things and like it hot and spicy. Salsa, chilli dips and samosas should be on the menu. When it comes to music, to say you are cutting edge does not do you justice. Only the most up-to-date, loudest tunes will have you hitting the dance floor, and once there, you are bound to party till dawn.

Taurus

Your sign is one of the most conventional and practical in the zodiac – as an earth sign, your feet are planted firmly on the ground. Of course, this does not mean to say you don't know how to let your hair down. You are extremely sociable creatures and there is nothing you like better than being surrounded by friends and family. A nightclub is no good for you – frenetic dancing and loud music just leave you exhausted, not exhilarated, and besides, how can you hear yourself think? In order to relax, you need to be creative. Planning an elaborate dinner party is nothing but stress to many people, but not you. You relish the opportunity to nurture the ones you love in a comfortable and relaxed environment.

Slow and steady is how you like your music. Thrash metal is out of the question, as is anything harsh and grating; you prefer music to be in the background, setting the mood of the party, be it classical or country. If you do decide to hold your party outside the home, a posh location with a great menu is essential. You like to be in beautiful surroundings and eat sumptuous food – anything remotely resembling a fast-food joint is not even an option!

Gemini

Organizing a fantastic party is always a difficult task for you Geminis. You get bored at the drop of a hat and are liable to switch off unless there's enough variety in your life. You thrive on doing ten things at once and are only happy when surrounded by stimuli. As the festive season draws closer, Geminis are in a prime party position. Your best bet would be to go to as many different parties as possible. This is because you are sociable creatures with a genuine interest in other people. Your idea of bliss is a huge room full of people to mingle with, talk to and find out their life stories. Sometimes you are given an undeserved reputation as a flirt (how dare they!), but this is only because you are in your element chatting to different people – if they happen to be gorgeous, then all the better!

Your music tastes are eclectic to say the least, and your CD collection is bound to span a good few decades. When it comes to party food, you aren't too fussy – fast food is sometimes your thing, though you aren't afraid to be adventurous and sample something new. A night spent flitting between people and parties should give you enough of the variety you desire.

Cancer

Homebodies that you Cancerians are, a house party is your best bet. You love being close to friends and family, though tend not to venture out of your social circle very much as you are extremely suspicious of outsiders. Sending out invites will eliminate the problem of gatecrashers! As you are highly unlikely to be a glutton or a heavy drinker yourself, any party of yours is bound to be extremely civilized.

Because of your interest in the past and all things historical, a theme party would be right up your street. Pick a decade and let your imagination run riot creating costumes and decorations to match. An Eighties party could also feature some typical Eighties food – chicken in a basket and prawn cocktail, anyone? However, with your delicate tummy, steer away from anything too spicy and exotic.

Your music taste reflects your passion for the past; sentimental music from the good old days will make your party go with a swing. James Brown, Otis Redding and Frank Sinatra should feature in your CD collection. You'll have trouble hiring a DJ to play the kind of things you want to hear, so maybe your dad or uncle will do the job just as well.

Leo

You are about as masculine and as fiery as it gets! You do everything to the best of your ability, and that includes throwing a party. No small, intimate soirées with simple food and wine for you; loud and proud is how you like things to be. You are renowned for your generosity and, rest assured, you won't skimp or take any short cuts with any party you throw.

You love food and good wine, and this has to be of the best quality. Spicy food from warm places should be on the menu, though you may well decide to hire a caterer to take some of the inconvenience out of planning the event.

Lions adore drama and action, so colourful personalities will be a welcome addition to one of your parties, though you can't abide wallflowers who don't contribute to the vibe.

You love listening to music and may well play an instrument yourself, though only the biggest and best of musical genres will do. Your extravagant streak will easily stretch to hiring a hot DJ or a band for the night. Yours are the sort of parties that everyone will talk about for weeks afterwards – lots of decadent goings-on are bound to be on the agenda, and the neighbours will almost certainly complain!

Virgo

Cool as a cucumber, with the ability to keep everything under control, is the hallmark of your sign. Your parties will rarely turn into the sort of chaos that leaves your garden destroyed and your carpets awash with wine, beer and whisky. A wild party is probably your idea of a nightmare – you are more suited to a small gathering in a pub or a club. And woe betide anyone mucking up your home! You hate to play the part of the host with the most, as you are happier in the background than the foreground. Some people misinterpret you as being unfriendly, though you are simply quite shy. When people get to know you, they will discover that you have a wicked sense of humour and that you can liven up any social gathering.

You will want a proper meal at one of your parties – this has to take the form of three courses, as you cannot abide finger food and buffets. You don't have strong musical tastes and probably won't notice what the background music is, so long as it doesn't distract too much. Easy listening music is best suited to any party of yours, so dig out those classic Andy Williams CDs and don't forget the jazz singer himself, Neil Diamond.

Libra

You Librans just hate making decisions, don't you? If you are planning a party, please do so at least eight weeks in advance, otherwise you will rush about madly organizing things. There's nothing you hate more than doing things at the last minute – it makes you irritable and sends you into a panic. However, you are excellent people to have at any party, as you are great conversationalists and very friendly.

Choosing the music is an integral part of your party: you love music and don't want anything you play to offend your guests. You are dying to strut your stuff, so make sure you have cleared a space for the dance floor, or choose to go to a club where you can boogie with style.

When it comes to food, you love ginger, mint and vanilla, so try to incorporate these flavours into the party buffet. Alternatively, stock up on some flavoured vodkas. Plan, plan, plan and your party is bound to go off with a bang!

Scorpio

Any party of yours will not be a low-key event. You have a high energy level and love to live life to the full. If you are holding a party, everyone will know about it and it's bound to be an event to remember.

Your sign is all about intensity and this should be reflected in the type of music you choose to play. Only sounds that get you dancing frenetically will do – you like the latest music with the loudest base line, and the louder and faster the music is, the better. As for the food, simple and bland should not feature. You love spices and concentrated flavours, so dips rich in herbs and garlic are ideal, though to be honest, there are many other things you would rather be doing at a party than eating. There are people to meet and flirting to be done!

You will definitely dress up at the drop of a hat in order to attract some attention – the more extreme the outfit, the more attention you will get. Extreme fashion that only you can carry off ought to achieve the desired result. Your party will be packed full of interesting and colourful personalities (not to mention yourself), and there's bound to be lots of gossip circulating the morning after!

Sagittarius

You are fiery and happy-go-lucky creatures who are always ready for a party. You enjoy keeping up with new trends, and this includes going to or holding fashionable parties. With your wanderlust, a party with a theme would be ideal. A Spanish-themed party would give you a chance to indulge the wilder, more sizzling side of your nature. Hot and spicy salsa with mounds of seafood paella are just the ticket, as are jugs of fruity sangria. You will love researching and getting your costume to look as authentic as possible, whether you choose to be a flamenco dancer or a matador.

You are passionate about world music and your own collection is bound to contain everything from reggae to calypso. Maybe you will have picked up some foreign dances on your travels and are ready to show off what you know. As for the location of your party, the more exotic, the better. If you have no choice but to hold your party at home, you'll probably decorate the place well to fit in with your theme. This will get everyone into the party spirit and dancing till dawn!

Capricorn

It is notoriously difficult to organize a party for people born under your sign. This is because Capricorns are such a varied bunch! Some are far too serious for their own good, whereas others know how to let their hair down and party the night away. Some of you are painfully shy and retiring, whereas others are outgoing to say the least and love a riotous time! Generally speaking, you are extremely cautious about spending money, but the thought of a party sends you into spendthrift mode!

An ideal event for you would involve going to a club – you love music and have a natural sense of rhythm – and let's not forget about the food! As a rule, you like simple foods that fill you up. You aren't a fan of garlic or spices, so delicate flavours like parsley and nutmeg are best for you. A trip to a restaurant followed by a club could be on your agenda. Pick the club carefully because you like listening to the music you were brought up on, so anything too up to date won't be your cup of tea. This doesn't mean to say that the only option open to you is ballroom dancing on Blackpool Pier – there are plenty of Seventies or Eighties nights on at discos around the country. Retro is your best bet!

Aquarius

Trying to categorize or pigeon-hole you Aquarians is a futile task. You are one of the most individual signs in the zodiac and each of you has your own way of going about things. Needless to say, any party you hold is bound to be out of the ordinary – no greatest-hits party album for you! The best thing for you would be to choose an unusual location for your get-together; hiring a barge or holding your party in a local swimming pool would be ideal. Your party does not have to be huge to be successful, as you will have a good time anywhere, provided you are surrounded by close friends. Food won't be the focal point of your party, as you would rather snack or get a takeaway than sit down for a traditional three-course meal. However, you do like bold flavours, such as garlic and basil, so maybe some Italian nibbles would go down well. When it comes to music, you are particularly fond of singalong classics, so long as they aren't too painful to listen to. Rest assured, with a bit of planning your party will be one of the most original to be held for a long time!

Pisces

You are the hopeless romantics and dreamers of the zodiac and let your hair down in a relaxing way. The atmosphere of an underground blues club would be perfect to transport you away from the drudgery of daily life. Jazz music will soothe your spirit and appeal to your artistic side – how could you possibly think creative thoughts with techno music pounding and strobe lights blinding you? If Miles Davis isn't your thing, then a night of salsa dancing will appeal to your saucy side.

Many people mistakenly think that you don't have the stamina to party along with the best of them. This is pure myth, though you need to be especially wary when it comes to alcohol. You don't handle booze very well and should remember to alternate your drinks with water if you are planning a big night out. A meal before the club is also important and, as a water sign, seafood is your best bet, be that smoked salmon or prawn piri piri. Invite lots of your friends and family along, but keep it fairly intimate – too many people you don't know very well can leave you retreating into a corner and your deep contemplations.

Chapter 15

THE PLAN

So here it is: the plan that will help you cope with whatever situations life throws your way. So far in *Life Signs* we've considered how your sign faces the challenges of relationships, health, finances and career. Hopefully you've come to know yourself better and worked out where you've been going wrong and how you can get on the right path.

Just remember that life will never be predictable. If it was, we would all be very bored (yes, even you Virgos and Librans!). By being armed with the right information, however, you can ensure that your journey through life is a fun one. It's all too easy to lean on our loved ones and to blame them when things go wrong. Think how good it would feel to know that you are the one in the driving seat and that you are responsible for the successes the future is going to bring.

A client whose husband had died came in to see me. She no longer knew how to go on with her life, having never paid a bill, used a credit card or even ordered anything for herself. She felt useless and, as she admitted, suicidal. Linda, as I shall call her now, didn't know how to take that first step. She was an Aquarian, so a bright spark, but enjoyed listening to other people speak. She had never had the chance to draw on her own strengths and I could see just by spending ten minutes with her that she was a flower waiting to bloom. I sat down with Linda and explained the basics of paying money in and out of an account, then sent her to the bank to open up her very own first account. She returned the following week, but this time with a spring in her step. I noticed there was a big change in her already and she proudly opened her purse to reveal a cheque book. She was like a kid in a sweetshop. She tried to pay me immediately, but I wanted to wait until I had asked her what else she'd been doing. Well, in seven days she'd bought a travel magazine and had been reading up on the destinations she'd often wondered about as a child. She was still a little scared, though, as she didn't have a passport and had never travelled outside England, let alone gone abroad on her own. I sent her away not with any advice, as she didn't need any, but with the instruction to go to the post office to obtain a passport form and have her photograph taken.

The story runs away with itself just as Linda ran away with her dreams. I often got postcards from her from the most obscure places. All I did was inform a very scared little bird that the cage door was not closed but open. If only she'd come to see me years ago, I could have told her that there was no lock on the door; she had chosen, as many clients do, to wait until some greater power took charge of her life.

The sad part to this story is that Linda's travels only lasted a year. She died very suddenly from cancer. At least she had a year to realize dreams, though she could have had more if she had been true to herself earlier on in life. Her husband would probably have happily travelled with her had he ever known her dreams, but she'd never uttered a word about them to him.

My point is, don't be another Linda. Don't bury your own needs. If you are content, others will be happy for you. As long as you are not purposely hurting anyone else, then what is stopping you? All of Linda's children had grown and left home, and when I met them at her funeral they told me that they wished she had lived her dreams. They had known something wasn't right but they hadn't dared question what their mother was doing when she had lived that way for so long. They even said they thought their father had never travelled because she had never asked.

Live the following plan every day and enjoy life to the full. Life is for living, remember, and as long as you help others as you go on your way, then who can blame you for doing what you enjoy? The most selfish act is to neglect yourself, as if you don't put yourself first, then why should anyone else?

The Five-Step Plan

Step one: time out

Take five minutes out of your day to recharge and concentrate on your body, breathing in through your nose and out through your mouth. Take in your surroundings, then focus on one thing that brings you pleasure, still breathing in through your nose and out through your mouth. Don't say that you can't see anything beautiful. There are a zillion things the minute you open your eyes and your mind. It could be the colour of the sky, the frost on the window pane, the softness of your sheets, cool water on your skin or the first mouthful of a delicious meal. Notice colours, let them come to you and wash over your mind. We often go through life without noticing the richness of colours. They were put there to give happiness, inspiration and pleasure. What we are doing here is making sure that we train our brains to focus on the positive, not the negative.

Step two: count your blessings

Think of five things that you are looking forward to. The first one could be a cup of tea or a morning orange juice. After all, remember that others won't ever have the pleasure of experiencing what we take for granted. Further things may range from a friend we are looking forward to seeing for lunch to a new project at work or even seeing the smile on our baby's face.

Step three: a lesson learnt

Think of what you have learnt from yesterday's experiences and appreciate whatever richness that has brought to your life. You may have had to return something to a shop, and in doing so you know not to buy from there again, or it could be that you've discovered you possess an untapped skill. Every day life's rich tapestry offers us a million lessons and I want you to pick out one of them. The braver you get, the more honest you can be with yourself. You may know you were short with a partner yesterday, but by acknowledging this fact you can use today to right that wrong. I promise that by saying you are sorry and acknowledging to your partner that you take responsibility, you will feel a million times better.

Step four: giving brings joy

Spread a little happiness. Do something positive for someone today, whether it's helping an old lady cross the road or giving a sad face your best smile. I want you to be able to end today with the knowledge that you've helped someone else. The sooner you do it, the happier you will feel. Spreading happiness will attract luck and love into your life like never before.

Step five: acknowledge yourself

You are who you are. Some may not like it but you have to live with it. You know you are going to make some mistakes, but you also know you are not a bad person. In fact sometimes you even quite like yourself. Let's pick one of your attributes, perhaps one you wouldn't normally talk about, and allow that thought to wash over you. Visualize your attribute moving through your body, starting in your toes and travelling up through your legs to your knees. Let it tingle. You may even get goose bumps as it moves to your bottom and pelvis and into your tummy, then up through your spine and into your hands and arms like an electric current. Eventually it reaches the top of your head. *You are a good person and you deserve a good life.* Today Step Five may feel different from other days, something more minor or more major, but you are going to carry this attribute with you all day. It is your golden ticket and will ensure that something good comes to you.

Key words for each sign

Don't give up on yourself or the ones you love. Look to your many attributes and remember that the glass is always half full, *never* half empty. Every problem brings opportunity, and every wrong turn shows you a new right way to go. Experience is what makes us wise. You must never regret what you've done, only what you haven't.

Use the following words to help each sign gain in confidence. These words encapsulate the heart of each person and will help them to become the best that they can be.

Aries

Personality. Help the Ram to have faith in who they are. Help them to accept themselves, faults and all. Teach them that any dents in their character add colour and definition. These are the lessons they need to build a better future.

Taurus

Finances. The Bull is a sign who is always worried about money and often leaves it too late to face financial dilemmas. However, their strength is that they are the most able sign in the zodiac when it comes to making money. Teach them to trust in the decisions they make with finances.

Gemini

Communication. This sign knows what it wants to say but often spends too much time talking about everyone else's problems before addressing their own. Keep bringing the focus back on to them and help them realize they deserve to put themselves first for once.

Cancer

Home and mother. Cancerians often have issues with their mother. They place great importance on the past and where they come from. Help them deal with this in a constructive way, even if it means seeing a counsellor. Their base is important, so help them make it secure.

Leo

Creativity. Teach the Lion to trust in their flair for knowing the right things to do in life. They are all too often held back by less inspirational signs and they need to be encouraged to break the mould and dare to be different. Great things will occur if they do.

Virgo

Work and health. The Virgo can really make their mark professionally, but their health often lets them down. A healthy mind leads to a healthy body, so Virgos need to address their emotional state. Get them into a routine; they'll love it and then the sky will be the limit.

Libra

Relationships. Let the Libran know that they are loved and that they have the faith and trust they need to build a really secure base. If they don't have someone to love them, they wilt like a flower without water. Support them and nourish them and they will bloom. They also need to learn to love themselves.

Scorpio

Interests and issues. Scorpios must do what they enjoy in life. To force them to pursue something their heart is not in can only lead to disaster. No matter how crazy an idea it may seem, support them. This is one sign who will surprise us all with the success they can achieve when focused.

Sagittarius

Spirituality. The Archer finds it hard to get in touch with their inner self. They spend so long trying to make money and find success in the rat race that they rarely pay attention to their spiritual and emotional needs. Encourage them to do so and then they can achieve anything.

Capricorn

Career and achievement. Allow the Capricorn to put their work first and you will see the other areas of their life just fall into place naturally. Support them and help them to put their dreams first and success will follow at lightning speed.

Aquarius

Aspirations and friendships. Allow them to dream and one day they will surprise you by turning their dreams into reality, not to mention a very large cheque. Believe in the impossible with them and you'll be in for a treat.

Pisces

Seclusion and the inner self. Give Pisceans the time out that they need to take stock of what is going on. Force their hand and they'll make bad and very dramatic decisions. Guide them gently and they will love you until the end of time.

Coping with stress

Stress is a word many of us know all too well. There are countless different areas of our life that can give us stress. It could be staying with a partner who is making us unhappy. It could be family problems, work problems or health problems. Whatever the issue there is always something you can do about it. You are not alone and you don't have to cope alone either.

No matter what our star sign, we will all face times of stress, but your sign will influence how you handle this stress and what triggers it for you.

Fire signs, which are Aries, Leo and Sagittarius, tend to let their problems run away with them and allow things to build up. They are rather like a pressure cooker whose lid is just about to blow. You can ask them if they are all right and they will say, 'Yes, I'm fine,' but you will know that's not true. Then one day things will unexpectedly come to a head. Think Sagittarian Britney Spears when she cracked under the pressure of fame! No one expected it; they just witnessed what appeared to be a crazed celebrity. Little did they know it had been building for a long time. Unfortunately fire signs often find it hard to talk when they should and so situations have a tendency to spiral out of control. If you have an Aries, Leo or Sagittarian in your life, then sit them down and talk to them. A regular check can uncover things that if left to fester, become impossible to address. Sometimes these signs have got something very small out of all proportion. More often than not the problem is money.

Taureans, Virgos and Capricorns are not usually the most stressed signs in the zodiac. They like to have their friends and family around them twenty-four seven. It is usually when their loved ones get problems that they start to get upset. They do tend to live part of their life through their family, which is not good, but is part of their make-up. It is something that those who know them well just have to come to understand. They must learn to take responsibility for their own lives, but not to feel as if they have to heal the whole world. If a child does something that is not right, it is not their fault. They are learning. Often an earth sign takes others' problems more to heart than those who are actually experiencing the difficulties.

Air signs, Libra, Gemini and Aquarius, talk their way into stress. They make promises they cannot keep and they want to make everyone happy. They often share problems with the wrong people. To get rid of stress, the key is not to stop talking but to learn who they can safely confide in. When you talk to a neighbour about your marriage problems and she comments on them to another neighbour, you will soon find the whole street is talking. Address the core of the problem and stress will slowly but surely start to drift away.

Cancerians, Scorpios and Pisceans need to learn not to jump head first into their problems. To say that they take things too much to heart would be an understatement. It is only by addressing a worry one stage at a time that they can ever find a viable solution. They give their heart and soul to whatever they are doing and would go to the ends of the earth to help out a friend or a family member. That involves digging into their own pocket. Problems can often arise when they take a stand for people who are not really their responsibility. They need to learn to save themselves and maybe one person at a time instead of the whole world.

If you want to know how best to handle the stress you are under, then you **fire signs** should simply talk about things as they happen and not ten years down the line. Aries, you are a leader and passionate about what you do, so choose a new path and soon your problems will be in the past. Leo, you are proud and generous, and impress others far more easily than you think, so just knock on the door you really want and see how quickly it will open for you. Sagittarius, you are honest and expansive, so take your seed of a dream and watch it grow as you take those first new and important steps.

If you want to know how best to handle the stress you are under, then you **earth signs** should live your own life and not keep sticking up for people who wouldn't do the same for you. Taurus, you are stubborn and loyal, so use these traits to create a new base. Before you know it, you will have a brighter and better future. Virgo, you are practical and intelligent, so do something you've always wanted to do but never dared try. You may just surprise yourself. Capricorn, you are ambitious and disciplined, so go back to your original dream and push aside the dead wood that's been holding you back.

If you want to know how best to handle the stress you are under, then you **air signs** should talk about the issues at hand instead of everything but. Gemini, you are generous and adaptable, so find some fresh faces to share in the many ideas you have and you will find new solutions. Libra, you are sociable and artistic, so don't pretend otherwise. Meet the people you have been admiring from afar. Aquarius, you are intelligent and funny, so use your charm and brains to look for new horizons and make new resolutions. Start from the top, where you belong.

If you want to know how best to handle the stress you are under, then you **water signs** should deal with a problem as it stands and not always imagine the worse-case scenario. Cancer, you are loving and caring so find something that will thrive on what you have to offer. This will give you the satisfaction you truly crave. Scorpio, you are determined and clever, so choose a goal and don't look back. Pisces, you are imaginative, talented and strong, so stop pretending to be weak to keep those around you happy. Show your true colours. The world is waiting.

Shining stars

I would like to leave you with a list of famous people of your star sign, so that you can see your true potential. Look up your star sign and you will see that these are people with the same qualities as you, the same foibles. They did it, and so can you.

Aries

Leonardo Da Vinci *painter*
Tennessee Williams *playwright*
Thomas Jefferson *politician*
Tom Clancy *writer*
John Major *Prime Minister*
Sarah Jessica Parker *actress*
Sir Alan Sugar *businessman*
Victoria 'Posh Spice' Beckham
 singer

Warren Beatty *actor*
Russell Crowe *actor*
Elton John *singer and songwriter*
Eddie Murphy *actor*
Quentin Tarantino *director and
 actor*
Mariah Carey *singer*

Taurus

Elizabeth II *Queen*
Charlotte Brontë *writer*
Catherine the Great *Russian royalty*
Irving Berlin *composer*
Michelle Pfeiffer *actress*
Naomi Campbell *supermodel*

Uma Thurman *actress*
Cher *singer and actress*
Janet Jackson *singer*
Craig David *singer*
George Clooney *actor*
Jack Nicholson *actor*
David Beckham *footballer*

Gemini

Lenny Kravitz *singer*
Paul Weller *singer*
Eric Cantona *footballer turned actor*
Denise Van Outen *presenter*
Liz Hurley *model and actress*
Elisabeth Shue *actress*
Kylie Minogue *singer*
Brooke Shields *actress and model*

Johnny Depp *actor*
Mel B. *singer*
Paul McCartney *singer and songwriter*
Courtney Cox *actress*
Bob Dylan *singer*
John F. Kennedy *President*
Angelina Jolie *actress*

Cancer

Princess Diana
His Holiness the Dalai Lama XIV
Meryl Streep *actress*
The Duke of Windsor
Nelson Mandela
George Bush *President*
Tom Cruise *actor*
Jamie Redknapp *footballer*

Chris O'Donnell *actor*
Pamela Anderson *actress*
Chris Isaak *singer*
Liv Tyler *actress*
George Michael *singer and songwriter*
Tom Hanks *actor*
Harrison Ford *actor*
Ernest Hemingway *writer*

Leo

The Queen Mother
Mick Jagger *singer*
Andy Warhol *artist*
Karl G. Jung *psychiatrist*
Dean Cain *actor*
Matt LeBlanc *actor*
Sandra Bullock *actress*
Matthew Perry *actor*

Gillian Anderson *actress*
Ulrika Jonsson *presenter*
Madonna *singer*
Geri Halliwell *singer*
Robert De Niro *actor*
Coco Chanel *designer*
T. E. Lawrence *adventurer*
Danielle Steel *novelist*

Virgo

Queen Elizabeth I
Shania Twain *singer*
Harry Connick Junior *singer*
Cameron Diaz *actress*
Sir Sean Connery *actor*
Hugh Grant *actor*

Michael Jackson *singer*
H. G. Wells *writer*
Prince Harry
Ray Charles *musician*
Sophia Loren *actress*

Libra

T. S. Eliot *poet*
Julie Andrews *actress*
John Lennon *Beatle*
Oscar Wilde *writer*
Luciano Pavarotti *opera singer*
Michael Douglas *actor*
Will Smith *actor and singer*

Keith Duffy *Boyzone member*
Jodie Kidd *model*
Bryan Ferry *singer*
Sting *singer*
Toni Braxton *singer*
Gwyneth Paltrow *actress*

Scorpio

Indira Gandhi *politician*
Martin Luther King *political leader*
Prince Charles
Pablo Picasso *artist*
Microsoft's Bill Gates
Winona Ryder *actress*
Julia Roberts *actress*

David Schwimmer *actor*
Bryan Adams *singer*
Meg Ryan *actress*
Ian Wright *footballer*
Louise *singer*
Demi Moore *actress*
Ralph Macchio *actor*
Davinia Murphy *actress*

Sagittarius

Charles de Gaulle *President and statesman*
George Eliot *writer*
Brad Pitt *actor*
Britney Spears *singer*
Denzel Washington *actor*
Teri Hatcher *actress*
Kim Basinger *actress*

Ray Liotta *actor*
Daryl Hannah *actress*
Sammy Davis Junior *singer and actor*
Mahara Ji *guru*
Ludwig van Beethoven *composer*
Jane Austin *writer*
Steven Spielberg *producer*

Capricorn

Louis Pasteur *scientist*
Henri Matisse *artist*
J. R. R. Tolkien *writer*
Joan of Arc *Saint*
Nostradamus *astrologer*
Nicholas Cage *actor*
Vinnie Jones *footballer turned actor*
Jim Carrey *actor*

Mel C. *singer*
Sade *singer*
Jude Law *actor*
Janis Joplin *singer*
Mel Gibson *actor*
Kate Moss *model*
Carol Vorderman *presenter*
Christy Turlington *model*

Aquarius

Edwin Aldrin *astronaut*
Christian Dior *designer*
Plácido Domingo *singer*
Lord Byron *poet*
Humphrey Bogart *actor*
Virginia Woolf *writer*
Paul Newman *actor*
Lewis Carroll *writer*
Franklin D. Roosevelt *President*
Vanessa Redgrave *actress*
Ronald Reagan *President*
Babe Ruth *sportsman*
Charles Dickens *writer*
Emma Bunton *singer*
Jennifer Aniston *actress*
Robbie Williams *singer*
John Travolta *actor*
Matt Dillon *actor*
David Ginola *footballer*
Natalie Imbruglia *singer and actress*
Bridget Fonda *actress*
Chris Rock *actor*
Sheryl Crow *singer*

Pisces

Prince Edward
Sydney Poitier *actor*
George Harrison *Beatle*
Elizabeth Taylor *actress*
Rex Harrison *actor*
Neville Chamberlain *Prime Minister*
Rudolf Nureyev *dancer*
Albert Einstein *scientist*
Michael Caine *actor*
Jack Kerouac *writer*
Dr Seuss *writer*
Bruce Willis *actor*
Rob Lowe *actor*
Drew Barrymore *actress*
Patsy Kensit *actress*
Cindy Crawford *model*
Melinda Messenger *model and presenter*
Billy Zane *actor*
Jon Bon Jovi *singer*
Niki Taylor *model*
Juliette Binoche *actress*
Sharon Stone *actress*

Never regret what you've done, only what you haven't done.